11. 25

THE FOUNDATION OF THE GERMAN EMPIRE

Select Documents

THE FOUNDATION
OF THE
GERMAN EMPIRE

Select Documents

EDITED BY
HELMUT BÖHME

TRANSLATED BY
AGATHA RAMM

OXFORD UNIVERSITY PRESS

1971

Oxford University Press, Ely House, London W. 1

GLASGOW NEW YORK TORONTO MELBOURNE WELLINGTON
CAPE TOWN SALISBURY IBADAN NAIROBI DAR ES SALAAM LUSAKA ADDIS ABABA
BOMBAY CALCUTTA MADRAS KARACHI LAHORE DACCA
KUALA LUMPUR SINGAPORE HONG KONG TOKYO

PRINTED IN GREAT BRITAIN
BY WILLIAM CLOWES AND SONS LIMITED
LONDON, COLCHESTER AND BECCLES

FOR
GEORG RAUCHINGER

TRANSLATOR'S NOTE

My reason for making this translation is the wish to introduce to the English-speaking reader Dr. Böhme's research and the conclusions he has drawn from it. Dr. Böhme's own selection of documents and his comments upon them, in the introductions to his four chapters, seemed the most convenient way of doing this. But I should wish the reader to bear in mind that it is not a selection made to meet his special needs; nor one in any sense representative of all the work being done by German-speaking scholars. If it leads the reader to Dr. Böhme's larger work, *Deutschlands Weg zur Grossmacht*, my translation will have been justified.

I have tried to keep faithfully to Dr. Böhme's book. I have, however, deliberately departed from it in the following respects. I have replaced Dr. Böhme's long bibliography, mainly of German works, by a shorter list of my own suggestions for further reading, which I hope may be of more use to the readers of a translated text. I have not hesitated to include books on aspects of the subject not covered by Dr. Böhme. On the other hand, I have preserved Dr. Böhme's long bibliographical notes to his preface and first chapter; since they constitute a review of what has already been written about the foundation of the German Empire. I have thought this review, besides being valuable in itself, necessary to support his argument. Dr. Böhme's book had a list of documents, together with a note of the sources from which they were taken, printed at the end. I have transferred the list to a Table of Contents, printed at the beginning, and have noted the source of each document immediately under its title in the text. Where, however, a document was published for the first time in Dr. Böhme's book, I have given a brief indication of the source (e.g. Austrian State Archives) in the Table of Contents. Finally, I have not always translated Dr. Böhme's titles to the documents. I have adopted, instead, a standard form with the aim of enabling the reader to see at a glance the date, the author, and the kind of each document (e.g. article, diary, letter, or memorandum). I have, however, retained Dr. Böhme's practice of sometimes printing two documents under one title of a more literary sort, and then I have translated this title in addition to using my standard form for each of the documents so printed. Some of Dr. Böhme's documents are translations into German of speeches, despatches, or telegrams originally in English or French. I have printed the original English and translated directly from the original French. Of the Peace Preliminaries of Nikolsburg there is a well-established English version, which I have printed from E. Hertslet, *Map of Europe by Treaty*. I have added a few explanatory footnotes, which I have marked 'translator' or 'T'. The figures in the text refer to notes at the end of the book.

I owe a debt of gratitude to colleagues, the staff of the Clarendon Press and others who have saved me from many errors.

A.R.

PREFACE

THE development of the German question in the nineteenth century and the genesis of the Empire of 1871 have much occupied Germany's historians. Because of the intensity of the historians' effort to expound and clarify this subject, any selection of documents on it runs the risk of offering a simplification, unsatisfactory from a scholarly point of view. Nevertheless it seems useful to introduce to the public those who were interested as historians in the problems of the period of the German Empire's foundation and at the same time to publish a selection of documents illustrating the central parts of the problems concerned. To give documentation for a set of problems which much preoccupy historical scholars, but are not yet solved by them, seems to be justified on three further grounds.

First, it is now possible to consider the German movement for unification from a greater distance of time. Particularly in a subject which has for so long been directly related to contemporary politics, it is an advantage, in seeking as objective an historical verdict as possible, that investigation should no longer be burdened with a legacy of obligation to the Prusso-German national state. At a distance, longer or shorter according to one's generation, from national-patriotic ideas—whether of Conservative or Liberal origin—it has become possible to avoid seeing the development, which in the nineteenth century led to the Empire, as only part of the national achievement of a single man, Bismarck, and to look to right and left of the hero figure; to turn one's attention, that is, to the *conditions* in which his individual policy was conducted.

A second justification for a new set of documents relates to historical method. Modernization of method now rules out attempts to illustrate the trends of the period of the Empire's foundation by concentrating exclusively upon the diplomatic and political documents relating to Great Power politics. To a far greater extent than has been traditionally so, problems going beyond questions of biographical analysis must be involved. This will mean a different emphasis in historical presentation. This in turn means that the history of the Empire's foundation can no longer be written as a part of the biography of Otto von Bismarck. Documents from beyond the diplomatic and political fields, documents which up to now have lain outside the historians' range of vision, must be made accessible. A second consideration in relation to method derives from the mutual interdependence of a nation's historical writing and its political development. After 1870 it became more and more usual to consider the history of the period of the Empire's foundation from the Prussian standpoint. At the same time the policy of Austria and of the south, central, and small German states moved out of the range of even fair and critical historical discussion. The Empire's development is not, however, to be described only from a knowledge of its 'Prussian taproot'. Thus it is necessary, as has not been customary up to now, to illustrate the ideas, the hopes, and the possibilities on the non-Prussian side as things of importance in their own right.

Finally, and in the third place, there is yet another ground on which to justify this set of documents. The sources for Prussian and Austrian policy in the period of the Empire's foundation have been published in distinguished critical works. Although notable gaps have to be bridged with the help of memoirs and contemporary publications, the *diplomatic* history of Prussia and, in part, of Austria is well documented by this work, if it is taken in conjunction with the French and Italian publication of documents and especially with the great collection of material in *Die Gesammelten Werke* of Bismarck. Most of the new versions of the history are based on these sources; for no new, essential, and extensive collection of sources has appeared since the thirties. The documents of the non-Prussian states have, therefore, lain outside the purview of the new versions. This material lies in the archives, mostly undisturbed, especially in so far as economic and social questions are concerned. This book, therefore, publishes a whole series of documents for the first time; since any improvement in method must languish if work in the archives does not follow. Yet given this framework of documentation, it can only be a matter of reproducing a selection of the documents which I hope to see put together in a comprehensive collection edited by myself.

It will already have become clear that the foundation of the Empire is not approached in this set of documents from the narrow viewpoint of the candidacy to the Spanish Throne, the Franco-Prussian war, the negotiations with the German states in the autumn and winter of 1870–1 and the final proclamation of the German Emperor on 18 January 1871. A further complex of problems has been taken into view. An analysis of the German imperial constitution is particularly important in indicating the wider circle of problems within which the period of the Empire's foundation must be seen. This shows that the Empire was Prussia's counter-stroke to the plans for the creation of a great political and economic dominion comprising the Austrian Empire and Germany. German unity is essentially the product of the Great Power policy of Austria and Prussia. Each state attempted to make use of the National-Liberal supporters of a German unitary state. From this standpoint it will be clearly seen that neither the year 1859 nor the year 1864 can be regarded as the beginning of the movement for unity. These years mark no more than stages on the way. The essential economic factors were already more or less firmly fixed by 1864. From 1865 onwards German unity was only a question of time.

The actual ascendancy of Prussia was decided when Berlin and Vienna settled scores with each other during the years from 1849 to 1864. In these years Prussia succeeded in manoeuvring Austria out of the German area in economic matters. This period provided the foundation for the Prussian-*kleindeutsch* (Germany-without-Austria) solution of 1870–1.

The next step was the 'Europeanizing of the German question'. This was begun by the Prussian Foreign Minister, Count Bernstorff, and systematically continued by Bismarck. In this he was less concerned with Germany than with Prussia—with the enlargement of Prussia through Germany. Prussia's German policy was above all a piece of power politics—not only within the Germanic Confederation but also in Europe. Bismarck always understood how to couple his policy over the solution of European problems with an increase of Prussian power in the German sphere. Thus possibly after 1863, and definitely after 1865, any hope of a *grossdeutsch* (Germany-with-Austria) development was illusory. The successes of Prussian policy meant at the same time a marked strengthening within Prussia of the traditional power of crown, nobility, and civil service. National enthusiasm was indeed used, but not one iota of power was given up.

The movement for unity came to a standstill after 1866. The southern states accepted the economic unity of Germany, but declined to dissolve their own identities in an enlarged Prussia. Prussia waited for her chance to be able to link the future of the nation with her own. It was thus that she came to accept the Spanish offer to the Catholic branch of the Hohenzollern House of the throne of Spain that had become vacant.[1]

Conceived within this outline, this collection of documents will have four parts. In the first, public opinion before 1870–1 and the historical verdict on the foundation of the Empire will be sketched; in the second, the years 1849–64; in the third, the years 1864–8; in the fourth, the time to 18 January 1871. All the documents have been selected with four ends in view: first, to make clear the diplomatic and political development; second, to make intelligible the significance of the military decisions; third, to indicate the relevance of the economic factors and to facilitate their recognition; and finally to enable the intellectual currents and political parties to be understood. It is self-evident that given the wealth of what has come down to us and the desirability of securing a wide circle of readers, only a small selection can be published. The documents—especially those from the archives—are in an old-fashioned style of writing. The flavour of the past must be retained along with a modern approach to the problem. It should also act as a warning that sometimes the striking language of the documents presupposes a different interpretation. The same word used today may only mean approximately what it meant a hundred years ago. The footnotes have been reduced to a minimum. A thorough correlation of the documents with the literature of the period has been deliberately foregone. The scholarly discussion is conducted elsewhere.[2]

Hamburg, May 1966   HELMUT BÖHME

CONTENTS

II. PRUSSIAN-*KLEINDEUTSCH* OR AUSTRIAN-*MITTELEUROPÄISCH*. THE ALTERNATIVES OF THE YEARS 1848 TO 1865

I · CONTEMPORARY AND HISTORICAL VERDICTS

IT is now nearly a hundred years ago that, on 18 January 1871, the German princes and the heads of the German corps of Generals assembled in the Hall of Mirrors in the royal palace of Versailles—on French soil, that is—with the recent victory over France fresh in their minds, for the proclamation of the King of Prussia as German Emperor. Germany, it seemed, had measured out to its end the long road to unity. By reviving memories of the old Holy Roman Empire a new German Emperor was to be the means of restoring power and reputation to the Germans (Doc. 1). He was to reassure sceptics, Democrats, Ultramontanes, south Germans, all the forces, in short, opposed to Prussia and to the National Liberals and to pledge them to a higher aim and a more important task [than any they had so far dreamt of].

Even on the morning of the celebrations, there was uncertainty about the title of the new *primus inter pares* of the German federal princes and free cities which were represented in the *Bundesrat*,* as the joint bearer of their sovereignty. King William insisted obstinately on his wish to be proclaimed Emperor of Germany. Bismarck, according to his own account, had struggled in vain to persuade him to abandon this claim. The title of Emperor, as King William claimed it, would in the Chancellor's opinion have offended and alienated the German princes and would at once have subjected the structure of the Empire to a severe test of its strength—the Empire that he had carefully built up on federal lines so as to take account of the old state traditions. Even the Crown Prince's proposal, 'Emperor of the Germans', was on these grounds unacceptable to Bismarck.

* In the constitution of the North German Confederation (1867) there was an elected Parliament, a Federal Council (*Bundesrat*) made up of nominees of the princes, and a Federal Chancellor. (Translator's note, T. hereafter.)

This was at a time when, although the south had gone hand in hand with the Prussian north against France, it was still by no means certain how public opinion there would receive the new state treaties* which were to establish the unity of Germany,[1] or whether the south-German Parliaments would even ratify them.[2] The supporters of German unity had greeted and celebrated the war with France (Doc. 2), and the great New Year of 1871 with glowing enthusiasm as the end of an epoch. Unity was there for the grasping and national self-awareness had risen to the point of *hubris*. Yet the scorned particularists (that is, the supporters of a distinctive south-German statehood and political tradition), the Ultramontanes or Catholics, and the Democrats of Hesse, Baden, Württemberg, and Bavaria were far from silent (Doc. 3). On the contrary, they strongly opposed the 'unedifying process of unification through blood and iron' and condemned the 'royal Prussian work of amalgamation'.[3] Even the Prussian Old Conservatives only grudgingly submitted to Bismarck's imperial policy which, in their opinion, would mean 'a liberal infection' in their Prussian kingdom. Bismarck's policy, therefore, did not rest upon a harmonious alliance between north-German Conservatives and the National Liberal party.

The southern traditionalists said that the general expectation of further and more gruesome wars should be a warning to the National Liberals in their conviction that 'general peace' and 'a real European balance of power' would be attained only when Germany had been united as a national state, and in their rejoicing over the military successes of the Prusso-German armies. They asserted that, with the established, albeit complicated, constitution of Germany (the Germanic Confederation of 1815) the existence of the 'conservative elements' as well as the 'basis of an international system of right' had been preserved (Doc. 4). All this would now be at an end. Now an *imperium Germanicum* would indeed be attained; and a *beata tranquillitas*, imposed 'by means of soldiers', would determine the future.[4]

The Liberals were confident of the further development of the Empire according to their views. Their enemies on the left, especially the 'petty bourgeois Democrats', were convinced that

---

* Signed by the King of Prussia for the North German Confederation, with Baden and Hesse, 15 November 1870; with Bavaria, 23 November 1870; with Württemberg, 25 November, 1870. T.

the war had laid the foundation for a reaction—a reaction of Prussian origin (Doc. 5).

They answered the Prussian and National Liberal doctrine that war had been forced upon Germany with the assertion that Bismarck had unleashed war (Doc. 6)—a war which had developed into a war of conquest, a very war of races. After such a war, they thought, any peace would only constitute a pause. Prussia, they said, would still mean to the south censorship, taxation, and military service (Doc. 7). While the supporters of the new Empire grew excited over the restitution of the 'German imperial title' (Doc. 8), their enemies remained 'cold at heart' (Doc. 9).

At the beginning of 1871—especially in the Ultramontane camp—a certain weariness and resignation, in the face of the quick and brilliant Prusso-German victories, showed itself. On the other hand, the spokesmen of the south-German traditionalists—particularly Dr. Jörg* in Bavaria and M. Mohl** in Württemberg—unwearyingly affirmed the dangers of a great Prussian kingdom, the *capitis diminutio* of subjection to one dominating state (Doc. 10). Since Bismarck would not let the new Empire, the new unity, appear as a fulfilment of the Liberals' wishes, but would have it believed that it had been founded by the old forces of throne, altar, and army, he had had to use every available diplomatic weapon to avoid a head-on clash between the ruling houses of north and south. William's obstinacy in the matter of the imperial title seemed to him, therefore, a catastrophe. The Chancellor of the North German Confederation did not deceive himself: Prussian sabres were still the best guarantee that the new Empire, as he hoped to constitute it, would hold together. His provident diplomacy was essential, because, as he was aware, the south-German princes and governments had only bowed to circumstances. They had only reluctantly given their consent to the imperial constitution proposed by the Chancellor, although he was crowned with success, feared, and already even reverenced.

Above all, time pressed. Bismarck feared the intervention of the European Powers in France's favour (Paris had still not fallen); differences of opinion with the Generals crippled his

---

* Joseph Edmund Jörg, journalist and Member of Parliament. T.
** Moritz von Mohl, member of the Frankfurt National Assembly, 1848–9. T.

power to act. The new treaties gained *full* agreement neither in the south nor in the north: they were too liberal and too centralist for the Conservatives; for the Liberals they were too particularist and conservative. Nor had men fully come to terms with *Kleindeutschland*, that is, the idea of unity without Austria. Because of this a certain disenchantment showed itself on the democratic wing of the Liberal party. Bismarck could not do without the almost primitive enthusiasm of the National Liberals, who at first forgot to ask, now that unity was at last established, what form it would take. He had to use the German imperial title as a symbol binding on their loyalty.

There was, as we have said, disagreement in Versailles about the title. The possibilities were: Emperor of Germany, Emperor of the Germans, German Emperor. The Chancellor, it was known, had not been able to convince his monarch. It had remained uncertain whether the Grand Duke of Baden, who was to raise the first *vivat* for the new Emperor, had succeeded during the morning of 18 January in bringing King William to Bismarck's point of view. The Grand Duke took people by surprise and released the tension when he found a way out by crying 'Long live the Emperor William': not 'the German Emperor' nor 'the Emperor of Germany'. Thus the proclamation was rescued. 'His Majesty', reported Bismarck, 'bore me such ill-will for its wording that, when all the princes left the raised platform in front of the space where I was standing alone, he ignored me and went past me to offer his hand to the Generals standing behind me.'[5] Was this a symbolic action or transitory ill-humour? (Doc. 11.)

Despite the disagreements which preceded the proclamation of the Emperor, the acclamation was experienced as a charisma. It was preserved for the future by a solemn painting which, distributed through countless reproductions, afforded expression (as many a learned book testified) to the self-consciousness of the new Prusso-German nation and to the mark Bismarck had put upon it. It helped, moreover, to found a new historical tradition and attitude. This was Anton von Werner's 'The Proclamation of the Emperor at Versailles'. The painting, with its honouring of the soldier Chancellor—the iron Chancellor—as a prince of victory presented theatrically in coat of arms and high boots, was inspired by the impression made by the war and a brilliant victory. In 1877, when it was given to the new *Kaiserhaus* [imperial gallery] and to the German public, intellectual Germany—to use Jacob Burckhardt's phrase—found itself in the middle of 'changing its skin'.

The passionate struggle between non-Prussian and Prussian political ideas and interpretations of the past had been decided in favour of the north-German Great Power. The south-German opposition was overcome with surprising speed. In 1870, the south-German, conservative, and pro-Habsburg approach to the historical development of the German area, and the south-German verdict upon it had found sharp expression in public polemics[6] (Doc. 12) against Prussian partisans such as Sybel, Ranke, Waitz, and Treitschke. After the final victory of the Great Prussia party over France and the capitulation of Paris (Doc. 13), such polemics were no longer possible. The elections to the new *Reichstag* completely destroyed the basis of the south-German opposition. Its members resigned themselves to the inevitable. The attitude of the *Preussischen Jahrbücher* in 1872—and it met with no notable criticism—was that 'Prussianism was a thoroughbred kind of Germanism in which Germany's most essential characteristics—industry, method, responsibility, energy—were developed after they had been disembarrassed of the casual licence with which the south-German people, even today, so readily identify freedom'. By the seventy-fifth birthday of the Emperor William (22 March 1871) the German imperial state was thought of with enthusiasm even in the south. Continuity of succession, loyalty, power and dominion, the great traditions of the Ottos and the Hohenstaufen were ascribed to the new Empire (Doc. 14). Historical writing centred on Prussia and in the year 1870–1 the new attitude began to overlay older traditions and standpoints[7] (Doc. 15).

The description of the *renovatio* of the German *imperium*, 'the greatest achievement of mankind' (Ranke), from now on became more and more the central concern of historians of the new Empire. Jacob Burckhardt was to be right with his witty comment that the great majority of German historians began to draft world history afresh, painting it from Adam onwards in the colours of victorious Germany. Yet in the seventies there was still opposition to this enthusiasm for a national German state without Austria. Prussian Old Conservatives and Left Liberals viewed the new creation with a jaundiced eye and held aloof from efforts to readjust the history of the German area to a climax in 1871. In the opinion of the Conservatives 'the individual states and the particularist forms of political life' (W. Bussmann) were too little safeguarded and, according to their conviction, too little of the Prussian tradition was preserved in the new Empire. Moreover, Bismarck by his alliance with the Liberals, they considered, had lowered 'all the barriers which had resisted the pressure of the propertyless masses'. To them the chief evil of Bismarck's policy was the concession of universal suffrage.* The Conservatives considered that, because thenceforward men would not vote in classes, with votes of unequal value, and elections would not be indirect and public, but voting would be equal, direct and secret, religion would be destroyed and all social bonds, as they called them, would be threatened with dissolution. The way would open for concessions such as the right of association, of free movement, of local self-government and civil marriage which would destroy the existing order.[8]

Yet at first their views were of no more political importance than those of the Liberals who had sought an Empire 'in alliance with democracy and freedom'. Bismarck had taken them by surprise in 1870. They had fallen in with the universal rejoicing over victory and offered opposition only when they were disenchanted with the very conservative imperial constitution. But their idealist conviction of the individual's right to self-determination no longer evoked an echo. Bismarck had found a middle way, as liberal as need be, as conservative as could be. Opposition was forced to be silent, so brilliant was the power which streamed out from the new alliance contrived by Bismarck between the Empire, the Kingdom of Prussia, the nobility, the army, the civil service, the Protestant established churches, the universities, the schools, and, not least important, economic interests. Bismarck had been able to bind the upper bourgeoisie —the standard-bearers of the idea of unity—to the conservative, dynastic, and territorial forces in the splendour of the new Empire.

* First in the election of the North German Parliament and, in 1871, of the German Parliament, or *Reichstag*. T.

Its constitution was based upon the German people; for on this Bismarck had reached a compromise, by diplomacy, with the south. The Germans had gratefully received their state from the hands of the German princes (Doc. 16). Bismarck had unhesitatingly given universal suffrage, as a marriage gift* to the Liberals; for to him the problem of the Empire lay in overcoming the dangers that threatened the Prusso-German state from the dynasties and from the varieties within the German stock. He had no fear of the mass movements which might be fostered by the new suffrage. He believed that both Conservatives and Liberals considered mass movements (Th. Schieder) as alien, unteachable, not to be controlled by reason and, therefore, to be feared by rational people.[9] But he, Bismarck, judged mass movements only constructively, and in relation to his own policy. He believed he could rely upon the conservative outlook of the average man of the countryside who would always vote conservative. On that account, he at first discounted the dangers of universal suffrage. He considered the agreement, that had already been established with the National Liberal front, more important. This 'unity' first and foremost must remain unbroken. And although the Crown Prince himself—sympathetic, full of good intentions, even if somewhat sceptical—might write in his diary (23 February and 7 March 1871) that he saw the coming task of German policy 'in the free internal consolidation of the Empire according to contemporary ideals' and that he understood the solution of the social question to be the most urgent task of all (Doc. 17), it was just the social question which remained untackled, unsolved, and was then to shake Bismarck's Empire most severely. There was and there remained 'no place for the fourth estate' in Bismarck's Empire (P. Rassow).

The political threads now ran together in Bismarck's hands; for he was Imperial Chancellor and Minister President in Prussia, the most powerful state of the Confederation. He stood at the centre of all political combinations; he had—as the Liberal, H. Baumgarten, resignedly acknowledged—now 'made the Empire' once for all, 'and we must bear his mark' (Doc. 18).

* The German word means a gift by the bridegroom to the bride on the morning after marriage, and the allusion is to Bismarck's co-operation with the Liberals after 1870. T.

By 1872 all those forces, which had sought to offer opposition, whether to Great Prussia, to Bismarck, or to the new imperial constitution, were obliged to conform. The Conservatives in increasing numbers came to terms with the new situation: the three-class franchise* guaranteed their future political influence in the Lower House of the Prussian Parliament; the structure of its feudal Upper House was equally unimpaired, and the power and reputation of the Prussian Crown and its army was more splendid than ever. The Democrats were silent. To them remained only the hope that 'the Empire, because of the development of its technical and economic power, would be victorious as a democratic factor over the anachronism of the Prusso-German state structure' (W. Bussmann).

For the time being, however, the Empire under Bismarck's leadership appeared to be a guarantee of economic expansion and international peace and any oversetting of the established order seemed out of the question. While neighbouring Powers viewed with mistrust the new Power, bristling with arms in the centre of Europe, and the struggle for the European balance of power was begun on a new scale (Doc. 19), in the Empire itself the process of turning the iron Chancellor into a public monument began with vigour.

The Liberals realized only one of the aims for which they had striven. Germany—although without Austria—was united. The bourgeois opposition to the Brandenburg player of power politics was checked; the liberal fire of the Wars of Liberation was long since burnt out.

'Whence at my age shall I take new substance into my life?' With this well-known question the historian Heinrich von Sybel characterized the temper of the leaders of the National Liberal party in a letter to H. Baumgarten, written on 27 January 1871, that is, a few days after the proclamation of the Empire. 'How have I earned so much of God's favour as to be

---

* This system of voting existed in Prussia. It grouped all male taxpayers over twenty-four in three classes for the purpose of electing in each constituency electors or *Wahlmänner*. One *Wahlman* was elected by each group in each division of the constituency. Thus the large number paying a small amount of tax had the same representation as the smaller number paying more taxes and as the still smaller number of heavily taxed persons. The *Wahlmänner* elected the members of the Lower House. T.

allowed to live through such great and mighty experiences? And how shall I go on living? What has for twenty years been the substance of every wish and every aspiration is now realized in such an infinitely magnificent way!'

As early as the seventies there arose out of this feeling of gratitude and fulfilment the first full-scale exposition of *The Foundation of the German Empire by William I*,[10] as Heinrich von Sybel entitled his version written chiefly from the Prussian state documents. Heinrich von Treitschke's *German History in the Nineteenth Century*,[11] written with a fiery enthusiasm, influenced the historical awareness of the rising generation in Germany more than Sybel's dry interpretation, written from the documents and supervised by Bismarck. Here for the first time German history was uncompromisingly conceived as Prussian history and the Protestant state and the 'true German way of life' seen as 'politically embodied' in Prussia—as Ranke had already expressed it (W. Mommsen). The Conservative Ranke, however, fully acknowledged the duality, under Austria and Prussia, of the organization of power in central Europe. 'Both German Great Powers exist', he asserted, 'each in its own way: and may it remain so.'[12] Treitschke, coming from the National Liberal camp, rejected duality. For him the arrangement of historical events so as to lead up to the climax of 1871 was the only principle of critical historical work valid for the adequate understanding of German history. Whereas Ranke considered Bismarck's conduct to be contrary to Prussian tendencies, Treitschke saw in his policy for the foundation of the Empire the realization of Prussia's destiny.

Treitschke sought to present its historical growth to the young nation as a development geared to Prussia and its destiny. Treitschke's views were enthusiastically adopted. Thenceforward it became one of the main tasks of German historians to view the picture of Germany's past almost exclusively from the perspective of Prussian development. There came into being a theory—still to be found to some extent, for example, in school textbooks—of a Prussian line of imperial succession going from the Margrave of Brandenburg, by way of the Great Elector and Frederick the Great, to William the Great (William I). Prussian policy became German policy. Thenceforward German policy was assessed by its contribution to the development of the German Empire. Thenceforward for many German historians Bismarck was the model for every political action in Germany.[13] The movement for unity and political personalities and groupings in the nineteenth century were chiefly judged from the national standpoint attained by the foundation of the Empire.[14] The historians' field of vision necessarily, therefore, remained narrow.

Because historians concentrated on the description of the wars of 1864, 1866, and 1870–1 and on Bismarck's national achievement, the foundation of the Empire, any exposition of the 'comprehensiveness of modern development' (K. Lamprecht) was beyond their range. Their efforts were, rather, directed to bringing home to the German people their destined development from Prussian roots, with a very strong emphasis upon personality and a like stress upon diplomacy. Their effort to throw light upon the life and thought of Bismarck, in every ramification of his being, overshadowed any attempt to inquire into the conditions under which he had acted.

It has been said that 'the very uniform in which the national fantasy had grown accustomed to see the Chancellor had precluded any look at the reality of his personality'.[15] But what is much more important, even 'looking at the reality of his personality' in turn contributed to weakening the impulse to investigate economic and social forces, the conditions in which Bismarck's conduct must be understood. German historical writing directed itself in the years before 1918 to political, constitutional, legal, intellectual, and diplomatic problems. It continued to do so in the years after 1918.[16] After Germany's defeat in 1945 and the outbreak of heated discussion on the subject of war guilt, criticism of the period of the Empire's foundation— and accordingly of the later Bismarckian period, with its policy of adjustment to Germany's situation as a sated state— became once again the central concern of historical effort. Once again the past was judged from the standpoint of contemporary problems and Bismarck's achievements moved afresh into a blaze of intense admiration. The more German policy after Bismarck was considered to have been negative, the greater the emphasis upon the model character of Bismarck's political proceedings during the period of unification and afterwards. Studies of Bismarck from the period before and during the war were re-published and now ran through several editions. Weimar was confronted with Friedrichsruhe.

At the same time the publication of documents prepared during the war, on the age of Bismarck and William I, was pushed forward and the basis created for a new preoccupation with Bismarck's political genius. The editors (H. von Petersdorff, Fr. Thimme, W. Frauendienst, W. Andreas, W. Schüssler, W. Windelband, G. Ritter, and R. Stadelmann) of the vast publication of sources in the *Collected Works (Gesammelte Werke)* of Bismarck have succeeded in a comprehensive way in bringing alive the personality of the founder of the Empire. No less comprehensive was the work of the Historical Imperial Commission (under the guidance of E. Brandenburg, O. Hoetzsch, H. Oncken, and W. Hoppe) which prepared the diplomatic documents on the *Foreign Policy of Prussia (Die Auswärtige Politik Preussens)* from 1858 to 1871.[17] The latter documents began to appear in 1932, *Die Gesammelten Werke* in 1924. Yet despite this publication of documents—it has been completed from Austrian sources[18]—the questions asked have remained the old ones; the theoretical premises, on which the German view of the history of the Empire's foundation was based, have remained, without any new precision. As before, the intellectual and diplomatic interpretation has prevailed. Despite many contradictions the historical categories, which were used to clarify the century of the movement towards national unity in its political polarization, have still remained Liberal and Conservative, *grossdeutsch* and *kleindeutsch*, 'World Citizenship and National State'.[19]

In 1925, after living through the Empire and the war of 1914–18 J. Ziekursch spiritedly asked whether the foundation of the Empire was against the trend of the times.[20] F. Hartung had already asked whether the political unity of the Germans as Bismarck shaped it, expressed the realities of the German political world and the life of German society.[21] But these beginnings were not followed up. At the end of the twenties there was every reason for a new version of the historical account, governed by political considerations, placing the great personality at the centre of historical analysis and emphasizing the model character of autocratic conduct. The description of the rise of Prussia to imperial power and greatness, with Bismarck as the central figure, became again the task which the new German historians set themselves as the object of their research.[22] There was a controversy between the Prussians, E. Brandenburg[23] and F. Hartung,[24] and the Austrian, H. Ritter von Srbik,[25] who in his attempt to produce a history of the whole of Germany gave expression to the Austrian aspect of its development.[26] It was a pity that these first attempts at a history of 'the whole of Germany' were too quickly expanded into works on Greater Germany and became lost in arguments with the political propagandists of the thirties and forties of the twentieth century.

Efforts to set Bismarck's policy more thoroughly into relationship with the labour question or with economic and social development met the same fate. Nor did the more conservative approach—of inquiry according to the specifications of the Prussian tradition—bring the progress expected and hoped for from the point of view of method. Too many questions had to be left unanswered[27] in the perpetual concern with Bismarck and the idealized presentation of Prussia's political identity. 'It was widely conceded', in Wilhelm Mommsen's judgement, 'that Treitschke's *Germany History*, which assessed all the political forces of the first half of the century in the light of Bismarck's work, was bound to be one-sided. But yet when a fresh attempt was made the evaluation was always the same, though perhaps less crass, and so the picture as a whole suffered from over-simplification.'[28]

This sublimation of method, though unaccompanied by any widening of the field of vision, was characteristic of historical writing on the period of the Empire's foundation even after 1945. The impulses which led in 1945 to a reappraisal, and were even then being questioned,[29] did not persist.[30]

The concern with Bismarck's personality and his political influence has continued to dominate research on the nineteenth century. The age of national unification—looked at from the German side—still bears Bismarck's name.[31] Nowadays this does not express a simple identification, but a complicated view of Bismarck's relationship to the state. Nevertheless, seen from the standpoint of *method* the light thrown on the subject remains almost the same as it was nearly fifty years ago (Doc. 20). This holds good too—though with limitations—for the careful and well-considered investigations into the history of parties, economics, and society. These disciplines stand unfortunately, at present as in the past, in far-reaching association with each other.[32] Even in investigations which have cut loose from tradition the consequences of the method of inquiry into intellectual and diplomatic history continue to govern the historical picture of that time. Recently the diplomatic and political appraisal of the period of the Empire's foundation has met with stronger criticism and increasing prominence is given to a method of approach which places more emphasis upon the economic and social coherence of the period. Starting from an essentially theoretical statement of the problem of how to construct an historical account, historians, researching into the period of the foundation of the Empire, aim at so writing history as to paint a fully comprehensive picture.[33]

In *contrast* to this one-sidedness of the German tradition, international research, increasingly since the twenties, has seen a widening of method. But even here, right up to the most recent publications, certain national clichés and patterns following preconceived methods can be recognized and the history of the foundation of the Empire is still seen under their influence.[34] But in this subject, more than in any other, national clichés and patterns following preconceived methods preclude any unemotional or objective appraisal of the past. The danger inherent in the trend to pragmatic evaluation in historical learning is shown with great cogency in the history of historical writing on the foundation of the Empire.[35]

Document 1 Extract from Gregorovius'* speech at the celebration of peace by the Germans in Rome
(*Wochenschrift der Fortschrittspartei in Bayern*, 1871, p. 154)

Our first German Empire was called the Holy Roman Empire of the German Nation. Voltaire mockingly said of it: 'Everything in this pompous title is untrue; it is neither Holy, nor Roman, nor German, nor an Empire.' Much in this satirical remark was correct, especially during its last powerless years. For centuries a noble institution of universal citizenship, it was dissolved by the very

* Ferdinand Gregorovius, historian. T.

freedom which it itself had implanted in the nations. Its last remnant was extinguished in the year 1806. See it now after an interregnum of sixty-five years, revived in a new form as the second Empire (*Reich*). Today it is more modestly and happily styled the German *Reich*. No Voltaire shall dare to mock this true title.

There is nothing Roman about it except the great memory or myth of its descent from the Rome that ruled the world. There is nothing Holy about it, if a connection with the Roman priesthood is meant: but Holy we hope it is in its origin in the moral force of the people and its mission for the peace of the world. Everything about it is German: its head, its members, and all its beautiful land from Kant's city* in East Prussia to beyond the Rhine, to Strassburg Minster over which the German flag is flying again at last . . .

Documents 2a and 2b   The equilibrium of the future: a million soldiers

2a Extract from Der neue Deutscher Bund. Ein Beitrag zum Verständnis und zur Geschichte seiner Verfassung, *by* einem Süddeutschen (Stuttgart, 1870, p. 4)

. . . Nothing could have regained for Prussia the sympathies not only of the south Germans but of Europe more quickly and surely than this wanton attack by the Caesar of the Seine with his mamelukes and praetorians. At first, indeed, after the declaration of war an anxious and gloomy mood lay upon south Germany. The first concern was what would the south-German states decide. Would they, men asked, allow themselves to be forced by the democratic and *gross-deutsch* majority into neutrality? This was a dangerous threat. But the cabinets, loyal to their treaties** and guided by national insight, took a firm stand by the side of Prussia, and the south-German population, striding forward beyond their democratic and *grossdeutsch* leaders with youthful enthusiasm joyfully applauded. In Stuttgart and Munich those, who a few days before had been eager for the neutrality of the southern states in the duel between Prussia and France, were publicly scoffed at and obliged to beat a retreat as quickly as possible. A sharp wind of national enthusiasm blew from the North Sea and the Baltic to the Bavarian Alps, through the Black Forest and the Swabian Alb to the Lake of Constance. The

* Königsberg, where the philosopher Immanuel Kant (1742–1804) taught at the University after 1755. T.
** The military alliances signed in August 1866 with Württemberg, Baden, and Bavaria and in April 1867 with Hesse-Darmstadt, see below, p. 23. T.

ill-will of south Germany against Prussia was forgotten. The feeling of unity again irradiated the German nation . . .

In order to establish a proper picture of these days, it must, above all, be emphasized that the note of simple religious emotion, struck in the official bulletins, found an echo in countless hearts. Everybody streamed to the appointed thanksgiving services and I saw men weeping tears of grateful joy. I had every reason to believe that they were the first tears of joy they had wept in their lives.

With equal force the German feeling for unity found vent in mass demonstrations . . . Everywhere men wished to make sacrifices so that the successes won for unity through the blood of the dead and wounded of Hagenau and Wörth, of Gravelotte and Marslatour, of Sedan and Strassburg, through the victories gained by common exertion on the battlefield, might be made secure on the political field. No voice ventured to deny that this was only possible on the basis of the constitution of the North German Confederation. In Stuttgart the colours of the North German Confederation flew for the first time from the state buildings, side by side with the colours of Württemberg, for the celebration of the capitulation of Sedan. Every late arrival of a piece of victory news brought a quiet crowd to the front of king's castles, war ministeries, foreign offices, and not seldom the apartments of Prussian representatives, to express their loyal and patriotic enthusiasm. These are the facts which one must remember in order to give this period its proper due . . .

2b   *Wimpffen (Berlin) to Beust,* 13 August 1870*
(Vienna, Haus- Hof- und Staatsarchiv, PA III, no. 102, Bl. 168–70r)

The Prussian victories and their consequences exceed all—even the boldest—expectations and annihilate logic and policy; since they have created a situation which I can only describe as caused by the strain of the most arrogant consciousness of victory. On a terrain where self-conceit has always been more evident and perceptible than elsewhere—indeed, it is a national characteristic—it is to be found today in such a high degree that an observer can hardly conceive the idea of its possible increase, let alone tolerate it.

Of course, it is thought that in the next few days the French must be offered another great battle; but it would be criminal to doubt for a moment the victory which is to open to Prussia the way to Paris,

---

* Friedrich Ferdinand, Count von Beust, Saxon Foreign Minister, 1849–66, Austrian Foreign Minister, 1866–71. T.

or rather *into* Paris, for nobody believes any longer in a genuine resistance. There is no concern over the next steps, or the form of government which will follow the approaching end of the Emperor Napoleon, or over the rest of Europe and the future peace. Somebody told me that the other day when he ventured to allude, in a Prussian gathering, to concern about the European balance of power, he was at once answered: 'We ourselves with a million soldiers are the equilibrium of the future.' Such are the expressions of general opinion, to describe which is my sole purpose in writing these lines; for it would be a quite impossible task to talk of any particular policy so long as there is no turn in the situation, or before at least some clarification of it comes.

I learn from a well-informed source that there is a firm intention to demand from France two milliards in war indemnity. At the same time, with the growth of conviction that Alsace should never be given up again, Prussia's south-German allies, who today are being flattered in every way, appear to have yielded to the hope, among other illusions, that this booty will fall to them; that is, that as a reward for their co-operation, it will come to be divided between Bavaria, Württemberg, and Baden.

Out of the present situation I gain only this one conviction that an intervention to produce peace, which might come from one or other of the Great Powers, would now meet with nothing but the most decisive rejection from Prussia and that such an offer would have a chance of being heard and received with respect only if it came from all the Powers at once and derived from the affirmed union of them all.

Document 3 Extract from 'Das grosse Neujahr'* by J. E. Jörg, 1871
(*Historisch-politische Blätter für das katholische Deutschland*, vol. lxvii, 1871, p. 1)

The age-old presentiment of serious minds has come true: *novus nascitur saeculorum ordo*. We have, of course, only come to the breakthrough and the beginning of the new order of things and no one, apart from the German Liberals, is quite sure in his heart whether or not men are to be congratulated on the first steps. But this much is sure: that we are rid of the old situation, thoroughly rid of it, and this is in itself much to be thankful for.

* The Great New Year; Joseph Edmund Jörg was a journalist and Member of Parliament. T.

The restoration of the German *Reich*! Whose soul has that word ever failed to rouse? But is it and will it be in truth a German *Reich*? We distinguish—and rightly so—between the concept of a *Reich* and the existence of a centralized and militarized national state. A German *Reich*, in the last sense, has never existed. On the contrary, it was the Empire of the Bonapartes which exemplified such a *Reich*. 'Great agglomerations' on the principle of nationality took a prominent place among the ideas of the last Bonaparte [i.e. Napoleon III] for the reorganization of Europe. Had he only succeeded in agreeing with Count Bismarck over the inclusion of Belgium in the French 'agglomeration', that which is now about to be attained after bloodshed (of course with the exception of Alsace Lorraine) could have been attained almost without *any* blood being shed. My views of law and freedom have not yet let me entertain the conviction that this will be a true German *Reich* and not merely a Prussia, enlarged with many important provinces . . .

The new German *Reich* begins by adopting the Russian principle that all treaties may be destroyed as soon as they become inconvenient to one of the contracting parties and it has the power to shake off the burdensome fetter. In this way the end of the Treaty of Prague* has been procured.

The sequel cannot be a peaceful shaping of the near future. Rather should one say: the more surely we have an Emperor, the more surely we shall have war. On our side, we have always kept in mind a simple test to distinguish the true from the false unification of Germany: whether or not it diminished or increased the military burden. But who may expect from the new German *Reich* even the thought of disarmament?

A twofold tendency was always innate in the Empire of Bonaparte: political tradition and political nationalism worked side by side. He had no use for the old European system. Yet he sought for a new system and sought its foundation, moreover, by the European Concert in a congress. The new German *Reich* proceeds quite differently. Having emerged from the dreadful struggle with its western neighbour, it can from the outset permit no intervention or mediation. Furthermore, since it arises as a pure, though still incomplete, national state, it cannot, by its very nature, allow frontiers to be drawn for it by binding treaties. On the contrary, it must reserve the right, at the next favourable opportunity, to draw within its framework those areas of German nationality still remaining

---

* Treaty of Peace between Austria and Prussia, 23 August 1866. The allusion in the previous sentence is to the Russian repudiation in 1871 of the Black Sea clauses of the Treaty of Paris (1856).

outside. It was no exaggeration, but a correct prognosis when some months ago it was announced from Berlin that the new German *Reich* must be a world empire strong enough, without alliance or treaty, to be a match for any single Power and also for a coalition of all the foreign Powers.

. . . How could or should one rationally conceive of Germany and France living together side by side with the abyss of irreconcilable hate that has opened between them? How are the two nations ever again to exist side by side in peace, if the entire French nation bequeaths to its children and children's children a fierce desire for revenge?

The answer is easy from the military standpoint but, alas, there is little comfort in it. From this standpoint one can soar to the colossal idea that France must be held on the bridle henceforward as a vassal state or feudal domain of the new German *Reich*. There is no need for concern about the other Powers, whose initial sympathy has now turned into ill-humour and mistrust; for whoever does not like it will, according to the new law of Europe, be beaten down!

In any event this much is certain: a political war between Prussia and France could have been concluded without essential alterations in the general situation of Europe. But a war between nations or races, such as was kindled between Germany and France, creates a new situation, turns all relationships upside down, and gives rise to the fear that the humanity and civilization of the nineteenth century will be turned during the last third of that century into a new iron age.

. . . What may happen in France after the peace, it is true, eludes all calculation . . .

This French republic, whether blue or red, will make propaganda, according to its nature. In the Latin countries, where internal causes have everywhere led to the abdication of the monarchy, it will have an easy task. With its seductive way of speaking it will find other means of access and, in necessary reaction, provoke sharper repression. The doctrine of the solidarity of peoples will appear as an intolerable provocation especially to the new German *Kaiserreich*. Thus Europe will have cause more than ever to think of the famous prophecy of Napoleon I: 'Half republican, half Cossack'.

Document 4   Extract from 'Die neue Lage, und zwar erstens die grossen Machtstellung',* Anon.
(*Historisch-politische Blätter*, vol. lxvii, 1871, pp. 389–96)

. . . The most striking aspect of the great crisis is that it has brought an extraordinary simplification of the European power constellation. As long as there existed a European system of right, the power constellation was, by contrast, of a very complicated nature, since its complexity was inherent in the very conception of an existing and established system of right. The existence and the strength of the conservative elements depended upon this complicated relationship [between states] linked by a thousand threads. These threads have been torn asunder at a single stroke. All is now as dull and sterile as in religious nationalism. Everywhere a few 'great agglomerations' of power—also a Napoleonic invention which has exploded against its originators—and their relationship to each other determine events. The multiplicity of personal rights has disappeared and with it any interest in the maintenance of the *status quo*. Soon men will no longer know what it means to be conservative.

On looking more closely, we may further observe that it was precisely the small and the medium-sized states which were the very basis of the [old] international system of right. They chiefly constituted its purpose and *raison d'être*. The general law of the sanctity of treaties arose for their protection. Out of the protection by right of the weak arose the ordering of rights among the strong. This is so true that with the final extinction of the majority of the small and medium-sized states—those that continue to vegetate lack any future and must sooner or later be drawn into the great agglomerations—with the extinction of this structure of states the idea of an international system of right has very nearly lost its purpose. In contrast, of course, the idea of the higher right of force has a wholly intelligible content. By another name it is called the 'world dominion' of one or other nation.

It is no secret that Count Bismarck at least gives himself the appearance of striving for the formation of a new Holy Alliance. Initiated politicians, moreover, in the so-called *rapprochement* of the imperial German cabinet to the imperial Austrian cabinet, have not failed to welcome the first step taken by Count Bismarck towards the formation of a new Holy Alliance. But surprisingly even this new alliance is basically different from the old Holy Alliance. Whatever fault one may find with it otherwise, the old Alliance laid the foundations for a period in the life of the European states in which

---

* The new Position: in the first place, in the Great Power constellation.¦T.

governments were inspired by 'regard for the individualities of the small states, a feeling for the solidarity of all thrones against the efforts of the Carbonari* and cosmopolitan parties of disturbance, and for the sanctity of treaties'. Can these purposes be the purposes of the new Holy Alliance? Obviously not . . .

What aims and purposes can Prussia pursue by the renovation of the Holy Alliance? Obviously not general principles! And therewith all is said. To Prussia a new alliance of the northern Powers can only mean a coalition against France; so that the new German *Reich* may consolidate itself in peace and Prussia be able to assimilate her new annexations in tranquillity—the older ones of 1866 as well as the newly incorporated territories in south Germany. Naturally this would not be the case so long as the prospect remained open to the French, at the first European complication that comes along, of winning Russia or Austria as an ally for her war of revenge against Prussia. The task of the new Holy Alliance at this point becomes quite clear: to serve as nightwatchman for the treasures mined from the goldfield of recent Prussian policy. The alliance must provide at one and the same time the form and the cloak for the 'Germanic world dominion' of the new German *Reich* . . .

We said months ago that the final result of the localized war between the two Great Powers would be that it would find in Russia its mocking heir. No Austrian statesman worthy of the name can conceal this from himself. In fact not one of them mistakes the true position of things. 'France will have no other choice than to sue for the alliance of Russia at any price. She would in no way forsake her tradition if she entered an alliance with Russia. The efforts of Prussian, or as they will be called in future, German diplomats will be directed to preventing such an alliance. As a result the Russian Court will fall into the happy position of permitting the beginning of a competition for her friendship with the object of bestowing it upon the highest bidder.

. . . The nominal victor in the struggle is the Emperor William, but the actual one to triumph is the Emperor Alexander. On the battlefields of France the German people lost its right of self-determination and was delivered over to the power of a family of masters from which it will not be able to wrench itself away. On the same battlefields Russia's star has risen in a blaze of light. The last bulwark has fallen, which could prevent her from bringing the testament of Peter the Great to fulfilment.'

The satisfaction of Russia, however, means the sacrifice of Turkey.

---

* An Italian political secret society which, originating during the Napoleonic occupation, aimed at the political independence of Italy and its organization as a free state. The high-water-marks of its activity were 1820–1 and 1848.

Russia's victory in the Near East would mean the decline of Austria . . .

Thus the tense situation of Europe, the feverish waiting for things to come, will not end with the impending conclusion of peace. Permanent readiness for war will not give place to a new feeling of tranquillity. Nor can we disregard the opinion that the new outbreak will follow before the dragon's teeth sown in 1866 have had time to spring up.

The last political war will be the one which will definitively decide the future of Austria and Turkey. A localization of this war is a complete impossibility from the outset. It will probably not even be limited to Europe but will draw the North American Union too into its whirlpool . . .

Documents 5a and 5b   Is reaction beginning?

5a   Extract from 'Die neue Lage, zweitens die Rückwirkung auf das innere Staatsleben',* *Anon.*
(*Historisch-politische Blätter*, vol. lxvii, 1871, p. 397)

Will the prospective peace relax the tension among the Great Powers? Will it not rather bring only that transitory external peace, which is bought at the high price of colossal armaments, and will it not keep the world in continual anxiety and excitement? If so, then a serious improvement in the domestic life of the nations cannot be expected to begin immediately. The nations cannot take thought for themselves so long as they are compelled by circumstances to submit to government by the military spirit and to imprisonment in military barracks. A new era in the domestic political life of Europe cannot begin until the last political war has ended. It is for this reason that we are of opinion that politics as a whole depend more than ever upon international complications.

The first result of the fearful conflict of the two nations of central Europe will apparently, so far as *Prussia* is concerned, be that a strong reactionary current will set in. Apart from the increasingly imperious military spirit, the politics of reaction will recommend themselves on account of the annexed territories. The consolidation of the German Empire demands the repression of extreme liberalism as much as it demands that a sharp watch be kept upon the refractory elements of south-German self-regard. Moreover, parliamentary government may well retain its dignity as the plaything of grown children. But freedom as the vehicle for a moral policy of conquest must be foregone in the German Empire; for it is bondage, the opposite of popular

* The new Position: in the second place, its domestic effect. T.

self-determination, that has brought about the foundation of this Empire.

5b   *Jacob Burckhardt* to Friedrich von Preen** Basle, 27 September 1870*
(Jacob Burckhardt, *Briefe*, edited Max Burckhardt, Basle, Stuttgart, 1963, vol. v, p. 111)

... Since the receipt of your letter I have been waiting and waiting for a pause, an armistice, which would allow me time to bring the causes and consequences into some sort of sense. But things just go on and on. France is to drink her cup of wretchedness and ruin to the very dregs before she is allowed a word at all. Dear Friend, where will it end? Does no one fear that the pestilence from which the conquered suffer may also attack the victors? This fearful completeness of revenge would have some justification (relatively speaking) if Germany were really such a completely innocent party, so much the injured party, as she is made out to be. Is it intended that the German army should advance even to Bordeaux and Bayonne? If so, logically, Germany with her million men must occupy the whole of France, perhaps for many years ...

This constitutes a new element in politics, a depth of humiliation, of which former victors have known nothing or at least have made no conscious use. The Germans are seeking to humiliate the conquered so deeply in their own eyes that they shall never again believe themselves capable of doing anything right. Maybe Germany will attain this aim; whether she will be the better or happier for doing so is another question.

Oh! What a mistake the poor German nation will make, if she puts the gun in the corner of the room and applies herself to the arts and pleasures of peace! Then they will say, let us drill, let us drill! And after a time no one will be able to say what is the purpose of living at all. For now a Russo-German war is appearing in the middle distance and gradually it will come into the foreground of the picture ...

The world must get used to a wonderful sight: the Protestant House of Hohenzollern as the one effective protecting Power for the Pope when he shall become the subject of an Italian empire.

Now I have talked enough politics! Heaven grant that we may see each other again in some tolerably quiet interval ... And now

---

* The Swiss historian, 1818–97. T.

** 1823–94, a close friend of Burckhardt, he served in the judicial branch of the civil service, ending his career as *Oberregieurungsrat* in Baden. T.

my warmest good wishes. We shall have to readjust ourselves intellectually in more ways than one. A Europe without France, amusing, decorative as she is! . . Ugh!

Document 6 Extract from 'Der Krieg zwischen Preussen und Frankreich',* Anon.
(*Historisch-politische Blätter*, vol. lxvi, 1870, p. 240)

. . . In order to trace the historical roots of the misfortune which has come upon the peaceful peoples of Europe, you must go back at least to the year 1859. It never occurred to anyone in the so-called *kleindeutsch* party at that time to recognize a national cause in the French Emperor's bold attack** upon the first German Power [Austria], Prussia herself, contemplated this outrage against German national interests, calm and undismayed, until too late . . . The French Emperor had a secret understanding with Prussia right up to Sadowa, but he was cheated of his reward for acquiescing in the aggressive policy of Prussia and Italy, because Austria succumbed to Prussian arms completely and with unexpected speed. Prussia had not needed the actual help of France, and so paid nothing for it. On the contrary, she turned her victory to advantage by annexations, or semi-annexations, prepared in advance, with a rapacity no reasonable man in Europe would have thought possible . . .

Peace used to follow war; but what followed the war of 1866 deserves far less the name of peace than even the treacherous period of 1859 to 1865. France now did what she had so far neglected to do. She organized her army, armed afresh and equipped herself, taking advantage of Prussia's experiences. Prussia had contrived a considerable addition to the strength of her army by the treaties of alliance*** imposed upon the south-German states. In all the states of the North German Confederation contingents for its army were organized after the Prussian model . . .

It is no secret that both Powers, one on this side and one on the other side of the Rhine, had put themselves permanently in a position where each was always ready to spring to arms against the other. This was especially true of Prussia because she was aware that, although she had garnered the fruits of her policy of 1866 as against Austria, she had not done so as against France. Indeed, her

* The War between Prussia and France. T.
** The reference is to the war of 1859 in northern Italy. T.
*** Military alliances signed in August 1866 with Württemberg, Baden and Bavaria and in April 1867 with Hesse-Darmstadt. They obliged these states so to organize their armies that they could be incorporated in the Prussian army in time of war, see below pp. 140, 144, 179. T.

quarrel with France had only been interrupted and not allayed. It was clear to her that the debts France owed her must be paid at last, or else wiped out by French blood. Knowing this, she drove up the level of military taxation to dizzy heights . . .

We shall not go into the circumstances which made any peaceful settlement between the two Powers impossible. But one official fact is too characteristic to be omitted. The Prussian ambassador in Paris had sent to Berlin a detailed report of his conversation on 12 July with the duc de Gramont. He wrote: 'The Duke asserted that what chiefly mattered was that a seed of lasting ill-will between the two Powers should not be left behind. He began, therefore, from the premiss that we had not observed a friendly course in our behaviour towards France as, to his knowledge, was recognized by all the Great Powers. He could honestly say that he wished for no war with Prussia but for friendly and good relations, and he knew that I aimed at the same goal. We must, therefore, consider together whether there was not some means of exercizing a calming influence and he put it to me, whether a letter of the King to the Emperor was not the right way out. He appealed to the chivalrous heart of Your Royal Majesty which would surely give . . . the right inspiration . . .'

. . . What did Count Bismarck do on receipt of this report and what did he reply? In the sitting of the *Reichstag* of 20 July the Federal Chancellor gave the following information on the report of Freiherr von Werther* who, we hear, fell into immediate disfavour: 'I vouchsafed no official reply to the ambassador except that I said I was convinced that he had misunderstood the verbal overtures of the French minister; overtures of this kind appeared to me absolutely impossible, and in any event I declined, in my capacity as responsible minister, to lay this report before His Majesty for official treatment.' For my part I must say that a cold shudder ran through me at this speech of the Federal Chancellor.

Document 7 Extract from a contemporary article
(*Wochenschrift der Fortschrittspartei in Bayern*, 1870, p. 415)

. . . Among the Ultramontane papers the *Volksbote* expresses itself very unfavourably. This is to be excused by its great disappointment. It writes:

The treaty was ours and our ministers were back from Versailles with success, so they thought, but we regret that we have to offer due thanks; since they also brought with them in the ministerial bag the further agreements reached in collusion with Prussia which,

* Prussian ambassador in Paris, 1869–70. T.

if they ever come into force, will be the death of the independence of the Bavarian Crown and country. These agreements can be summed up in the following three points: (1) Bavaria capitulates (2) Prussia commands (3) the Bavarian people must pay, pay, and pay again. German unity there is—in that Prussia alone rules; there is also freedom, but only freedom to pay. Otherwise everything is as it was. Obedient servants!

Document 8   Extract from a contemporary article
(*Ibid.*, p. 426)

This new star that has risen in the German sky is the German Emperor. The most noble and idealistic German prince, King Ludwig II of Bavaria, has annointed him; Germania will set the German imperial crown upon his head; the German people will lay the victor's laurels at his feet; and the German army will surround him with the iron radiance of a million bayonets to protect him and the whole of Germany against every enemy let him come from whence he will. The hereditary enemies of Germany are now destroyed! France's star—her Emperor—has now set! Let the new star arise—the German Emperor!

Document 9   Extract from a contemporary article
(Ibid., p. 434)

. . . As far as this *German Emperor* is concerned we are cold at heart.* Now that Caesar's crown has, to the satisfaction of all honourable people, been snatched from the head of the man of Sedan, we cannot bring ourselves to rejoice that it should be placed on the more precious head of another. A Prussian is a Prussian whether he is given the title of King or Emperor. Let us imagine how the glorious Roman Emperor would consider himself side by side with this successor—if he were not long since dead. We cannot possibly take this granting of the imperial title serious, however seriously we take the consequences which, according to all appearances, Prussia wishes to derive from it. Moreover, we consider, indeed we are certain, that this Prusso-German *Kaiserreich* will not last long.

* The German phrase, 'kühl bis ans Herz hinan' (lit. cool to the very heart) is a well known line from Goethe's poem, *Der Fischer*, *Werke*, Hamburger Ausgabe, 1949, vol. i, p. 53.

Document 10   A further contemporary view
(M. Mohl, *Für die Erhaltung der Süddeutschen Staaten*, Stuttgart, 1870, p. 4)

What the so-called German question has now become might have been foreseen at the outbreak of war by anyone who had followed the course of things since the year 1866 with keen observation or was acquainted with the efforts of the party that has adopted this question as its own . . .

One may be of opinion that it would be better if Germany were one single state. We do not share this opinion. On the contrary, we think that the total amount of culture, morality, and prosperity, the mass of civilizing and humanizing institutions (such as universities, art and professional schools), the closely woven net of communications and so many other advantages which Germany has over France and over other great empires, have their origin in the number of centres from which they may take their beginning and in the mutual competition of the individual German states. It is precisely south Germany and Saxony that are very significant evidence of this. No right-thinking person will deny that intellectual and political freedom would have had a better home in a many-membered Germany than it has ever found in a unitary monarchy.

Who would dare to answer the question whether the Reformation, for example, would have happened in Germany had it been a unitary state or say whether it would not rather have been extirpated by Dragonades as in France? The variety of its political, constitutional, and administrative arrangements has safeguarded Germany from the onesidedness of the whole cultural and educational system, which characterizes France, and from its petrifaction, which characterizes England. This variety has made the Germans the best educated people in the world. This is the most noble blossoming of a nation's history. We grant that political unity has its advantages for a great nation, and we are not so prejudiced as to be hostile to those who consider this standpoint conclusive and honourably speak in its favour. But he who knows from experience the waste and neglect of so many important economic interests in the provinces of great empires and compares that with the more concentrated vitality and the quicker pulse of life in our south-German states will not, for very love of our fine and happy principalities, counsel us to prefer a unitary state in Germany.

The situation with which we are confronted is to be rejected absolutely. It is that of lands subject to one great state, the *capitis diminutio* of submitting to a ruling people. *This is* the character which would be imprinted on our states, if they entered the North

German Confederation. It will be no different and no better for the fact that the varied and noble north-German states will have preceded us into this situation by their submission after the events of 1866.

The North German Confederation is only a federation in name. In its real life it is an empire in which a number of vassal states have subjected themselves to the King, the government, and the representative assembly of one great state [Prussia]. The vassal states receive the law from the master state. Their position is all the worse because their people have to bear tax burdens imposed both by the ruling state [Prussia] and by the subject governments, without enjoying any substantial influence over the former nor being at home masters in their own house. Nothing would be changed in all this by the entry of the south-German states into the North German Confederation as can easily be mathematically proved and as their unfavourable position in the Customs Parliament* already adequately shows.

The supremacy of the ruling state would have this result, even if (but the direct opposite is true in the North German Confederation) constitutional limits were set to the exploitation of its supremacy; for, as is well known, even in the Germanic Confederation of 1815 Prussia, conscious of her power, refused to allow herself to be governed by the majority even when majority decisions had been constitutionally taken . . .

In everyday life we say in Swabia: it is not good to eat cherries with the great. The relatively small state which lets itself be linked with a great one in a league, in which the latter through its power or its voting rights calls the tune, may make whatever stipulations it likes, it will not succeed in much restraining the greater. It will still be the subject of the greater and play second fiddle. Moreover south Germany is such a dear and well-loved land to us that we do not wish for this situation for its princes and its peoples. The history of Bavaria and Swabia for a thousand years and up to this very day is so honourable that they should not end this way, at least not voluntarily. With the exclusion of Austria, whose participation was required for the balance of power in Germany, there is no longer any possibility of agreement with Prussia on a federal constitution to suit the south-German states.

* Set up in 1868 to comprise representatives of all states, the south-German included, who were members of the Zollverein. T.

Document 11   Extract from the diary of the Crown Prince
(H. O. Meisner, editor, *Kaiser Friedrich III. Das Kriegstagebuch von 1870–1*, Berlin, Leipzig, 1926, p. 342)

. . . After the *Te Deum* had been sung, the King, followed by us all, betook himself to the platform, that had been built in front of the *Salon de la Guerre*, and upon which the junior officers were already stationed with the flags and standards. He summoned the standard-bearers, with the war-torn flags of the first battalion of the First Regiment of Footguards and the three from his Grenadier Regiment, one of whom also bore a flag that had been shot to pieces, so that they came straight to him and stood directly behind him, side by side with me. To the right and left of this middle group—surely an unusual one—the German reigning Princes and Hereditary Princes took their place and behind them flags and standards came to rest.

After His Majesty had read a short address to the German sovereigns in his usual rough tones, Count Bismarck stepped forward. He looked quite furiously out of humour as he read the address 'to the German nation'. He read tonelessly, using an official manner and without any trace of festive mood. At the words 'Extender of the *Reich*' I noticed a convulsive movement through the whole assembly, which otherwise remained without a sound.

Now the Grand Duke of Baden, with the natural, quiet dignity that was so characteristic of him, stepped forward and cried aloud with his right hand raised: 'Long live His Imperial Majesty, the Emperor William!' A thundering cheer, repeated at least six times, thrilled through the room, while the flags and standards waved over the head of the new Emperor of Germany and 'Hail Thou in the Victor's Crown' resounded. This moment was powerfully striking, indeed overpowering so, and made a wonderful sight. I bent my knee before the Emperor and kissed his hand; he raised me up and embraced me with deep emotion. I cannot describe my feelings but everybody understood. I even saw unmistakable emotion among the standard-bearers.

Now the Princes, one after the other, offered their congratulations, which the Emperor received with a friendly shake of the hand, whereupon a sort of file past took place, but on account of the unavoidable press of people it lacked any proper formality. The Emperor next walked along the line of flags and their bearers, stepped from the platform towards those standing in the front and, as he walked through the hall, addressed a few words in passing to the officers and men standing on both sides. I had commanded the band to play the Hohenfriedberg March as soon as the Emperor prepared to leave the hall, so that His Majesty left the assembly to these magnificent sounds, and so, greeted by the cheers of the Headquarters Guard, he left the palace.

Document 12   Extract from a contemporary article
(E. Trautwein von Belle, *Deutsche Vierteljahresschrift*, no. xxxiii, 1870, p. 1)

. . . He who would nowadays undertake a discussion of the choice between Hohenzollern and Habsburg, must direct his immediate attention to Prussia. She is the ambitious neighbour, who has driven Austria, that earlier possessed the imperial crown and later the dominating influence, from the position she occupied and, by the Peace of Prague, has severed her from further co-operation in the re-organization of Germany. Since 1866 Austria has no longer been *ex officio* a member of the German body of states; and therefore, so far as the consideration of the German position is concerned, she has been dismissed to the *second* place. The initiative lies (if political documents can assign it) with the power of Prussia alone. But for that reason the principal *responsibility* also rests upon Prussia's shoulders. The maintenance, the defence from all sides of the existence, the greatness, the right, and the power of the German nation has become the task of Prussia. Prussia, as a result of Count Bismarck's policy, has assumed aims which are not only equal to those of the Hohen-staufen but go far beyond them.

. . . For all the arguments that a true and candid friend of Prussia can adduce against the system of alienating Austria, or, in brief, the *kleindeutsch* system, those who wish to encourage Prussia in her gigantic work, have in readiness a weapon of universal application: it is 'Prussia's German Mission'. Wherein lies this mission? In the restoration of Germany—the restoration of a Prussian Germany. It consists in this: that Prussia should absorb the other German states, in order to incorporate them into the exclusive German state. Thus the struggle with Austria, who out of envy will not suffer this, is spontaneously provoked. Prussia has understood her 'German mission' from the *kleindeutsch* historical outlook, or rather on the authority of her own history. She is the Protestant state *par excellence*, the state of tolerance, of modern progress. It is fitting that her Princes should have supremacy in Germany, because she has always stood at the head of German, as of human, ideas; because she alone has given flesh and bone to a genuine German policy during the last century; because she alone has loved the welfare of her subjects. This is a series of exaggerated claims, and, if one applies the most favourable standard, it is still truth mixed with falsehood. According to the *kleindeutsch* doctrine which the followers of Häusser, Sybel, and

Droysen have made so convincing to the German nation, 'historic Prussia' has the power to venture everything *for* Germany and therefore the well-founded right to win everything *in* Germany. From this standpoint, any true German community disappears as soon as one withdraws from the sphere of the Prussian state or the circumscription of Prussian power. The German and the Prussian communities coincide, yet so that the latter determines the former and not contrariwise . . .

The *kleindeutsch* community is only an idea. The 'German mission' of Prussia is an idea too, with abstract defenders, but here we should like, also, to observe that the 'free self-determination of the German nation' too belongs to the sphere of ideas, even if for the present it has been pushed back into the realm of pious hopes. Battles in the field can decide the fate of a nation, but not the rightness of an event or of a point of view. Whether Prussia has any right to swallow up Germany, the battle of Königgrätz cannot decide, just as little as any victory of Germans over Germans can decide whether this party's or that party's way of looking at history is the true one, or whether one or other of the two confessions, in which the Christian community of Germany is split, can provide the nation with the ideal norm for its standard of justice and morality. The Prussia of the Gotha Party* is the Prussia of their ideas and not the *historic Prussia* at all . . .

The idea of Prussia which is put forward by the supporters of the *kleindeutsch* hegemony of the historic Prussia, is, according to the view of these exaggerators of the true rights of the north-German Great Power, superior not only to Austria, but also to all other Germans in respect of its *national* character. Since the national character of Prussia is constantly brought before us, we have arrived at a wonderful expression, heard more and more during these last years: '*Prussia, the only pure German state* among the great states of the German race'! One hardly believes one's eyes when one reads this confident expression. But it is constantly uttered, with touchingly innocent emphasis, by the foremost publicists of the Gotha Party. As if every one who has advanced beyond the first steps in ethnography did not know that Prussia possesses several millions of non-German subjects and shows precisely herein a great similarity to Austria! Four and a half million Prussian citizens are Slavs, almost half a million are Lithuanians, and, beyond that, in Schleswig there are 200,000 Danes. Half of all the West Prussians, a fifth of the East Prussians, five-eighths of the people of Posen, a quarter of the Silesians

---

* National-Liberals, who had been members of the Frankfurt National Assembly and in a conference at Gotha in June 1849 attempted to rescue something from the national movement of 1848. They were the same men who signed the declaration of 21 May (Doc. 23 below).

are Poles. One meets a fair number of Wends in Upper and Lower Lusatia, Cassubans in Further Pomerania, Walloons and French in the Frontier Circles of the Rhine Province. Such is the 'only pure German Great Power of German race' . . .

Prussia is neither the 'pure Protestant' nor the 'pure German' state. Nor has a national policy been the constant rule of conduct of her most distinguished rulers. The two princes to whom the Brandenburg–Prussian state owes most worked quite frankly for the *particularist interests of their country*, without any ferocious hypocrisy, yet with outstanding success. Frederick William, the Great Elector, and Frederick II, who was called 'the One and Only' as well as 'the Great', *exactly in accordance with the ideas of their times* and no differently from their fellow German princes, considered the well-being of their own state as the cardinal standing ground of their political conduct. They did so more powerfully and with greater insight and decision, but no less unmistakably, than their neighbours. Neither the one nor the other deserves special blame from the standpoint of those times which almost wholly lacked the concept of a common German patriotism, nor praise from the standpoint of today's national consciousness. That the policy of the Hohenzollerns, who unerringly and with tireless energy encouraged the expansion of their own state, has met with such harsh criticism during the last four generations arises, for the greater part, from the fact that the most distinguished pro-Prussian historians have presented this strong particularism of their princes and of the Prussian stock as incomparable 'Germanism' and have set it in circulation as the 'national policy of the Hohenzollern House'. So unwarranted authority has been ascribed to the simplest facts in order to give them the colouring of *patriotism to the Reich* or at least of *patriotism to the nation* . . .

The real Prussian state, in its development through history, shows no trace of the fantasies attributed to it by the National Liberals. According to Frederick's intentions Prussia was to be a *European Great Power* and not the ideal focal point of Germanism. The Great Fritz meant to rely on his Prussia alone. Neither plans for universal happiness nor ideas of German reform originated from his practical acumen. He considered the situation of the Holy Roman Empire much too dubious for it to have occurred to him to anchor the Prussian ship of state by that sea-shore . . .

Documents 13a and 13b   The Capitulation of Paris

13a   Extract from a contemporary article
  (*Wochenschrift der Fortschrittspartei in Bayern*, no. 5, 1871, p. 1)

Paris has capitulated. The proud capital of the enemy, the city 'that could not be taken', sacred Paris, must open its gates to the German victor. This is the final decision of the war which France, jealous of our growing unity and power, unjustly forced upon us. An honourable peace will soon follow this glorious event. Thus Germany stands, before the eyes of the world, united internally, powerful externally, crowned with glorious victories, and we, the sons of the Fatherland, give grateful praise that we have been found worthy to live through such a noble and magnificent time. Each man pledges himself to the task of doing honour to the great Fatherland, and of helping it to remain on the heights it has attained. God grant that it may!

13b   Extract from a contemporary article
  (Ibid., no. 5, 1871, p. 57)

. . . Hurrah Germania! The *Reich* is complete, the Ultramontanes and their adherents are defeated, the black night of spiritual brutalization is beginning to disperse and the dawn of German unity and freedom begins to gleam on the horizon of the Fatherland . . .

Document 14   Speech by W. Maurenbrecher, given on behalf of the Albertus University of Königsberg, 22 March 1871
  (*Grenzboten*, vol. xxx, 1871, p. 77)

In joyful, exalted mood we celebrate today the seventy-fifth birthday of our noble monarch, William I, the seventh King of Prussia, the first Emperor of Germany. And if the hearts of our nation always beat warmly for their princes on such festive days, today a quite exceptionally vivid feeling of gratitude, reverence, and devotion fills us all. If the year of his life that has just passed has been incomparably magnificent for our King, how much more so has it been for all his people!

During this year great things have happened through the agency of our King and our people. The seventy-fourth year of the life of King William has been filled with events of universal historical import. The history of Germany and of Europe has today reached a turning-point. A new development has begun. We shall not live to see its course, but its mighty beginning has filled all the world with astonishment and admiration.

. . . The achievements of this time of war have been magnificent. Even a German patriot, with the most glowing imagination on last year's celebration of this day, would not have believed it possible to attain within one year what has been attained. Leaving aside the great moral blessings and the spiritual influence of this great time upon our own and the next generation, I shall name two priceless tangible benefits that have come to us.

The frontier province in the west [Alsace-Lorraine] has been won back for the national community. The estranged and lost sons of our common German mother have come home. . . Simultaneously with the regaining of the old lands of the *Reich* [i.e. of the Holy Roman Empire] the old German *Reich* has been restored to life. We have again a German *Reich*, a German Emperor! . . .

The reawakening of the Emperor Barbarossa* has been a dream in the imagination of one people and a theme of the songs of our poets. And lo! dreams and fantasies, songs and sayings, hopes and aspirations have suddenly found fulfilment in a wholly unexpected way . . .

With the new German Empire we have renewed our contact with memories of Germany's past. We hear of the *restoration* of the German *Reich* and of the *renewal* of the German Empire. It sounds as though the Germany that has now arisen should be thought of as a resurrection of dead institutions. It sounds as though the ancestors of our Emperor William in the *Reich* should be those medieval hero figures who first wore the imperial crown in Germany. Is this really serious? Is the new Empire of the Hohenzollerns to be the continuation of that of the Ottos, the Salians, and the Hohenstaufen? Did the 'Holy Roman Empire of the German Nation' really celebrate its resurrection on 18 January 1871? . . .

An historian of the tenth century, the Saxon monk Widukind of Corvey, tells how, after the great victory of King Otto I over the Hungarians in 955, which laid the foundation for the security of Germany, the victorious army greeted the triumphant King with the cry of 'Emperor'. From this point onwards our chronicler gives Otto that title . . . The Empire originated in Otto's military services to Germany. The defenders of the land of Germany went so far as to honour him with the dignity of an Emperor.

The Empire of our victorious King owes its origin to the same kind of event . . .

Otto I won the imperial crown on the battlefield against the Hungarians: William I on the battlefield against the French.

---

* An allusion to the legend of the Emperor Frederick Barbarossa who did not die but fell asleep in an unknown cave. T.

Occasion and origin in the tenth and nineteenth centuries alike exhibit related and congruent characteristics . . .

The history of the German medieval imperial period has latterly been much studied, investigated, and expounded . . . Let us recall the facts. The first of the medieval Emperors was Charlemagne. He was undoubtedly the model for Otto I and his German successors. Now this Charles, King of the Franks, with his far-seeing, carefully calculated methods, pressing forward step by step, was finally—in the year 800—able to obtain the imperial crown for himself; nevertheless . . . in the Investiture Controversy . . . all the bad humours in the body of Germany found opportunity for rank self-assertion. The princes with self-seeking greed and the states with their particularism allied themselves with the revolutionary papacy. These hostile forces, allied together, became in fact masters of the Empire. . .

There came a time when an attempt was made to restore the old Empire. The powerful personalities of the Hohenstaufen Emperors worked with persistent pressure, with cleverness and versatility for a restoration of the earlier power of the Emperors. Once again the Emperors regained their influence over the election of bishops; once again they rested their power upon an alliance with these ecclesiastical princes . . . But this attempt too, though for a time favoured by fortune, ended after a struggle lasting eighty years, with new defeats at each and every turn that shook the structure to its roots.

In the end the universal Christian empire of the German Empire was reduced to a theory . . . The unity of the nation was lost. The fragmentation of the *Reich* had become a fact.

Such are the fruits of our imperial period . . .

The memory of that time lasted longer in the nation than the effects of the catastrophe to the *Reich* in the thirteenth century. We thought back with sentimental longing to the ruined power of Germany, the lost dignity of the Kingship, the decline of the unity of the *Reich*. Yet the splendour and glory surrounding the figures of the Emperors grew more and more. It was natural that popular imagination should cease to distinguish between the two powers, so closely linked, of Emperor and King. In men's minds the position with the greater external splendour and the higher dignity took pride of place. They now thought of the Emperor as the representative of German unity. As soon as this longing for greater unity became strong in the German nation, the call for a return of Emperor and *Reich* was raised . . .

In all periods of deep national emotion in Germany this thought has forced its way through . . .

The phrase 'Emperor and *Reich*' even up to our own day exercises its magic in all classes of the nation . . .

The government of our illustrious King has fulfilled the hopes and aspirations of German patriots. A German *Reich* has come into being, with the free agreement of all the German princes and all the German states. Prussia's hero King wears the crown of Emperor of the German *Reich*—symbol of German unity. With lively confidence we link all our hopes to this newly risen *Reich*. We believe that we can graft the new *Reich* on to the heritage of the national German Kingdom without going astray in romantic memories, without being misled by the imperial sound of the name. We know that it is in the concentration of national strength, not in unsatisfied lust for conquest, that we should maintain the new Empire's power to stand and endure. By the cool, objective separation of questions of Church and State the spirit of modern life shall imbue all relationships. With self-awareness, serious work, and the whole nation's loyal participation the new German *Reich* will avoid the wrong road of the Roman *imperium*, the medieval universal empire, and French Caesarism.

On the foundations that have been laid, in association with that firm kernel of Germany, the Prussian state of the Hohenzollerns, the new *Reich* shall grow to be the permanent blessing of our German nation. May it be granted to the founder of the *Reich* to see the rich flourishing of the seed that he has sown! May it be granted to the *Reich* to live long under the protective care of its first founder!

God maintain, God protect, God bless our Emperor!

Document 15 Jacob Burckhardt to Friedrich von Preen, 31 December 1872
(Jacob Burckhardt, *Briefe*, edited Max Burckhardt, Basle, Stuttgart, 1963, vol. v, p. 182)

. . . Certainly everything is apparently quiet in politics. But our Berlin masters are, I believe, full of anxiety, not on account of foreign countries but on account of their basically false position in face of the nation. The external apparatus of so-called freedom has been allowed to come into existence, but they are secretly resolved to act for all time according to their own will—not that I would deem absolute government an especial misfortune as compared with the consequences of universal suffrage. I have become extremely cool about such things. But I fear a new war as the only diversion from internal complexities . . .

Why *filius** was not conscripted is a mystery to me; but still I congratulate father and son on this release, which is a truly great

* i.e. Paul von Preen. T.

benefit for higher education. Works on modern history (by which you chiefly mean our own worthy century?) I do not read and do not know. Since Gervinus* I have a distaste for such books and so far as the theme itself, that is the said century, is concerned, I have my one-sided spectacles through which to look at it. Moreover, in your place I would take the best short book covering the facts in some kind of superficial pattern; for modern exposition is in the middle of 'changing its skin' and we shall have to wait a few years with our purchases and then the whole of world history from Adam onwards will be painted in the colours of victorious Germany and oriented towards 1870–1. We shall certainly win the next war too, provided the National Liberal way of looking at things has meanwhile suffered some considerable questioning.

May the year 1873 bring to you, my honoured friend, and to me a sense of calm, tranquillity, submission to our fate, and a clear head with which to look at the world!

So I wish you a happy New Year.

Document 16   A modern view
(P. Kluke in *Deutsche Geschichte im Überblick. Ein Handbuch*, edited P. Rassow, Stuttgart, 1960, p. 521)

. . . The final act of the foundation of the *Reich* was the personal achievement and performance of one great statesman. He was sustained by the deep longing of the nation, he exploited the general aspiration, but allowed the final scenes to appear as the achievement of the sovereigns and their governments . . . The people's representatives remained supernumeraries. This was so even on the occasion of the assumption of the imperial crown, when a deputation of the *Reichstag*, under the leadership of the same Eduard Simson,** who in 1849 had been the spokesman of the Frankfurt offer to the Prussian King, voiced in Versailles the plea of the *Reichstag* that he should accept the offer made by the princes; for the princes had adhered after all to the Bavarian offer. In the symbolism of these two incidents was contained the meaning of German development after 1862—the extraordinary increase of the power of all governing authorities, as against the power of the representative assembly. Bismarck's conduct of affairs had that brought about.

---

* G. G. Gervinus (1805–71), *Geschichte des neunzehnten Jahrhunderts* (1855–66). But Gervinus was as disappointed as Burckhardt with developments in Germany after 1870. T.

** Eduard von Simson (1810–99) Prussian Liberal, third President of the Frankfurt National Assembly, President of the *Reichstag*, 1871–4. T.

Document 17   Extract from the diary of the Crown Prince
(H. O. Meisner, editor, *Kaiser Friedrich III. Das Kriegstagebuch von 1870–1*, Berlin, Leipzig, 1926, p. 394)

. . . Our next mission after the peace is the solution of the social question at home. To this noble purpose all the treasures of German education and German intellect must be devoted. France cannot do it, from want of intellectual principles, nor England, on account of the excessive distinction between rich and poor that prevails there. Germany, however, in which no such colossal fortunes exist, offers a productive field for a thorough solution of this question. The principles prevailing here at the moment will, indeed, afford no help for this, for the innate prejudice to be found in influential circles leads to blindness or to an incorrect understanding of the requisite means for the solution. Let us hope that the failure of the republican outbreak in France may act as a wholesome warning to our countrymen. For my part, when I return home I shall find a thorough investigation of that social question an attractive and instructive occupation.

Document 18   Jacob Burckhardt to Friedrich von Preen, 26 April 1872
(Jacob Burckhardt, *Briefe*, edited Max Burckhardt, Basle, Stuttgart, 1963, vol. v, p. 160)

. . . As far as military affairs are concerned: I have no doubt that I shall see you gradually and cautiously circling round until you steer towards my view of the origin of the last war. In the meantime does it not sound as if it had been deliberately intended and willed? . . .

I am not unreasonable. Bismarck has only taken into his own hands what would have happened anyhow with the passage of time, but without his aid and against his interests. He saw that the growing democratic-socialist wave would somehow provoke a state of absolute power, whether through the Democrats themselves or through the governments. So he spoke: *'ipse faciam'*—and waged the three wars of 1864, 1866, and 1870.

We are, however, only at the beginning. Is it not true that all our action so far is advised because it is agreeable, dilettante, and fanciful in an increasingly laughable contrast to the high purposefulness, thought out in all its detail, of the military system? This must now set the pattern for all existence. For you, honoured friend, it is now most interesting to observe how the political and administrative machine is reorganized on military lines; for me, how the school and educational system etc., is treated. The workers will fare in the most surprising way. I have an inkling, which at present looks like complete folly and yet it will not entirely leave me, that the military state must become a great manufacturer. Those agglomerations of people in the great workshops cannot remain eternally the victims of their need and their greed. A fixed and superintended mass of misery, graded and in uniform, which begins and ends every day at the beat of the drum, that is what logically must come about . . .

Document 19   Disraeli in the House of Commons, 9 February 1871
(Hansard, *Parliamentary Debates*, third series, vol. cciv, 81–2)

. . . This war represents the German Revolution, a greater political event than the French Revolution of last century—I don't say a greater, or even as great, a social event . . . You have a new world, new influences at work; new and unknown objects and dangers with which to cope, at present involved in that obscurity incident to novelty in such affairs . . . But what has really come to pass in Europe? The balance of power has been entirely destroyed . . .

Document 20   A modern verdict on Bismarck's achievement
(H. Rothfels, *Bismarck und der Staat. Ausgewählte Dokumente*, Stuttgart, 1953, Introduction, p. xxxvii)

First as far as *foreign policy* before 1870 is concerned, was it mistaken for Bismarck himself to adopt national unification as his one compelling objective when the Liberals in north and south were pressing with increasing resolution for it and the Customs Parliament was preparing the way for it? Was it mistaken for him to bring about the war with France as a necessary means, deliberately adopted, towards his end? When Bismarck in 1871 was addressed by General Superintendent Büchsel with the remark: 'How wonderfully everything has succeeded', he answered: 'I wished for things to be *so* and they turned out quite differently. I will tell you something: I am glad, when I notice in which direction God is working, if I can hobble along afterwards' . . .

Without going into details, we shall be right to say that Bismarck in fact did not deliberately bring about the war of 1870. He manoeuvred Napoleon into a position that threatened his prestige, but it became an inescapable position only because French policy was caught up in an emotional nationalism which Bismarck himself was determined to keep within bounds.

If one looks at the *domestic policy* supporting the foundation of the *Reich*, the association of parallel ideas as its basis will be clear. Bismarck was no nationalist, nor was he a centralist. Neither in the one sense nor in the other was the nation, one and indivisible, his inflexible ideal. 'Unification by measures of force', he asserted in the *Reichstag* in 1869, 'would leave behind wounds which "would bleed internally", even if these measures were taken to accord with the constitution. In the German states one should not ask: "What can we have in common, how far can the wide mouth of the common-wealth bite into the apple?" But one should ask "What absolutely must we have in common?".' Thus the new *Reich* would be united only so far as it seemed absolutely necessary: militarily, diplomatic-ally, in the modern branches of the economy—and even there with graded exceptions and reservations. Culture and the greater part of domestic administration would remain matters for the individual states. Even in the detailed characteristics of its institutions Bismarck took a middle way between the loose, federal constitution of 1815, which had been integrated into Europe, and the national state constitution of 1849...

In this very sphere there was a mixture of fundamentals: Bismarck sought to assure a leadership which was not centralized, but concerned with fastening itself upon living historical [federalist] ten-dencies. He sought to integrate the rights of individuals (*iura singulo-rum*), to achieve things from contradictions, one could say, to respond to challenge. His was more than an opportunist's recipe and there was something more than mere personal will to power which caused him to withstand the Liberal proponents of the unitary state. He sought to knead together the manifold elements of a notion of order which he had thought out in a wider context than that of Germany alone...

Bismarck thought in political and historical patterns, not in ethnic, according-to-nature patterns, and he saw in Pangermanism a danger no less than in Panslavism...

II · PRUSSIAN-*KLEINDEUTSCH* OR AUSTRIAN-*MITTELEUROPÄISCH*. THE ALTERNATIVES OF THE YEARS 1848 TO 1865

WHEN King Frederick William IV of Prussia at the end of April 1849 finally refused the German imperial crown,* offered to him by the Frankfurt National Assembly, and rejected the constitution (Doc. 21) whose adoption it had advised, the work of this 'Assembly of Professors' failed. What did it matter that twenty-eight governments had recognized the new imperial constitution? The two German Great Powers, Austria and Prussia, rejected what they considered to be revolutionary institutions and thereby sealed the fate of the Frankfurt Assembly.

The traditional forces in Prussia and Austria were able to re-establish themselves by military power (Doc. 22). They imposed constitutions and deprived the Frankfurt National Assembly of the power to determine action. Whereas the Paulskirche** Assembly was swept into the vortex of the struggle between the radical Democrats and the conservative-constitutional groupings and so increasingly lost power and standing in Vienna and Berlin crown, army and civil service succeeded both in re-assuming their old posture and in drawing over to their side those representative elements of economic life that had originally been the protagonists of liberal reforms and German unity. So the stormy, and at times revolutionary, outbreak of the German bourgeoisie in the spring of 1848 spent itself surprisingly quickly. The idea that it was possible to unite

---

* He called it a 'diadem moulded out of the dirt and dregs of revolution, disloyalty and treason'.

** The Church of St. Paul was the meeting-place of the Frankfurt National Assembly (May 1848) whose meeting had been organized by the governments of the German states on the basis of an electoral law decided on by the *Vorparlament* —a self-invited assembly of German Liberals sitting from March to April 1848. T.

Germany by a movement of the people had proved an illusion.

The members of the Frankfurt Assembly resentfully resigned themselves to defeat; the majority simply left the Assembly (Doc. 23). Only the radicals continued to remain in the Parliament. They were, however, forced to migrate to Stuttgart. The Württemberg army chased even this Rump Parliament away. The republican and national revolutionary risings in Baden, Saxony, and the Palatinate in May 1849 were just as quickly quelled. Prussian troops under William, 'the Cartridge Prince', (the future German Emperor) restored peace and order everywhere. The social-revolutionaries, nationalists, and radical-republicans of the opposition, which had united for one last show of resistance in 1849, were hounded out of the country.

Prussia, so is seemed, now broached with her own power the task bequeathed to her by the Frankfurt Assembly: to unify Germany without Austria. The odds seemed favourable. Austria was still busy subduing the Hungarians, the central and southern states of Germany were still dependent on Prussian military assistance and lacked outside support. Baron Joseph von Radowitz* exploited this situation. He had been a right-wing member of the Frankfurt Assembly as well as a minister of Frederick William IV and by his plan of a German Union sought to attain unification without Austria on Conservative legitimist lines. This plan provided for a German *Reich* as well as a German 'Union'. Whereas in the 'Union' Austria would be loosely linked with Germany, for the *Reich* the Frankfurt draft constitution, deprived of its Liberal provisions, would be the constitutional basis—with Austria excluded (Doc. 24). Prussia would thus have been able to dominate the *Reich* without antagonizing the Austrian Emperor. In pursuit of this policy Prussia succeeded in concluding an alliance with Saxony and Hanover. This 'Three Kings' Alliance' of 26 May 1849 remained a torso (Th. Schieder). Bavaria and Württemberg feared Prussia's hegemony and held aloof from her. Austria,

---

* 1797–1853; General in the Prussian army; after 1836 he acted for Prussia in reforming and strengthening the federal army, advised Frederick William IV on federal reform and acted for him in negotiations with Metternich on this subject in 1847–8. T.

free once again in the mid-summer of 1849, raised objections to Prussia's intentions, demanded the restitution of the old Federal Diet under Austria's presidency in Frankfurt, and gained for these plans the support of Russia, who had observed with mistrust the possible formation of a German national state on her western frontier. Prussia had to submit.

The old policy of Metternich's time seemed again to become the hallmark of Germany's development. As after the Congress of Vienna in 1815, an apparent equality of rights between Austria and Prussia was to guarantee peace and order in the Confederation and at the same time ensure a halt in Germany's development towards unity. The old policy of moral pressure seemed the only one open to Prussia: it was 1814 all over again.

This was, however, mere appearance. 1848 had not passed without leaving a legacy. The feeling of nationality, which flared up in the revolution, was to have its influence on future development just as much as the German bourgeoisie's resigned acceptance of the failure of the revolution—especially in the Rhineland—and its final co-operation with Prussia.

It was, however, at first Vienna, and not Berlin, which determined the new policy. Here the new Minister President, Prince Felix zu Schwarzenberg,* hoped to overcome the national movement by developing a policy of asserting Austria's power. He hoped to be able to bind together under German-Austrian leadership, the separate parts of the monarchy, which were striving to break apart. For that reason he had fought all the *grossdeutsch* plans of the Frankfurt Assembly and for that reason too he turned sternly and with the utmost effort against Prussia's Union plan. He had a vision of the renewed consolidation of the monarchical system to be attained if the whole Austrian Empire should establish itself as 'the leading Power of a *Mitteleuropa* controlled by Austria and Germany' (Srbik). First, he had to deprive Prussia of all power. Guided by this aim, he directed his policy after 1849 broadly speaking to three objectives:

(1) to revive the Federal Diet under Austrian presidency and politically to bind closely the medium-sized states to

---

* 1800–52, Austrian Minister President, 1848–52. T.

Austria. This last could only be done hand in hand with Prussia. Therefore his second objective was

(2) to effect a *rapprochement* with Russia and thereby to isolate Prussia. An isolated Prussia would have to come to Austria. This policy was an indirect way of opposing Prussia. At the same time, by political means, Schwarzenberg, supported by his Minister of Trade, Baron von Bruck, sought as his third objective

(3) to render Prussia impotent and to reduce her to a second-class state. In particular he strove both by force and eloquent persuasion to create a Customs Union with the Zollverein that had been led by Prussia since 1834 (Doc. 25). In this project Schwarzenberg saw his most important instrument for the foundation of a lasting dominance of Austria in Germany and therefore on the Continent (Doc. 26). The relationship between the two Great Powers was thenceforward one of political, military and economic antagonism such as had not been known throughout all their conflicts in the eighteenth and early nineteenth centuries.

The political and military conflict did not come to the surface in the fifties, for Prussia felt still too weak for an open confrontation. The economic duel was, however, being fought as early as the fifties with virulence, bitterness, and ruthlessness. The economic question determined Germany's development in these years to a much greater degree than any question of federal reform or any diplomatic or military crisis. Indeed it can be asserted that the *kleindeutsch* national state (whatever its form) became possible, not least, because Prussia successfully foiled all attempts at a single economic system in the German area, conceived in an Austrian or central European (*mitteleuropäisch*) sense.

The superior brain which was the first on the Prussian side to recognize this link between economic policy and power politics, and to oppose Austrian aims at every opportunity, and unerringly to pursue its object of an independent Prussian and Zollverein policy was not that of the Prussian Minister President and later Foreign Minister, von Manteuffel, nor that of the

Minister for Trade, von der Heydt, nor of the Foreign Minister, von Schleinitz; it was that of the under-secretary in the Ministry of Trade: Rudolph von Delbrück.

Delbrück's prescription for thwarting Austrian activity was simple. Austria wished for a Customs Union with protective tariffs. She needed these for her industry. This would, however, have altered the Prussian economy to suit Austria's interests and brought the agrarian importers of industrial products east of the Elbe into direct competition with the Hungarians and would have limited German trade to the Continent. Apart from German industrialists, nobody in the Zollverein needed protective tariffs. Delbrück, therefore, pleaded for a free trade policy; for free trade would represent the interests of the Prussian exporters of agricultural products and meet the similar economic interests of merchant bankers and even of the manufacturers themselves (Doc. 27). Austria could not afford free trade. Any lowering of tariffs provoked an outcry among Austrian industrialists, who, owing to their early connection with the nobility, had a much more important influence in shaping public opinion in the Danube monarchy than the Prussian industrialists had in Prussia. Bruck hoped for support from Prussian heavy industry and from the textile industry of the central and southern states which were both demanding tariffs. He believed he would be able to satisfy all parties in Austria and Germany with a moderate, protective tariff. He was to be disappointed. He overrated the influence of the industrialists in Prussia.

It became clear that every step taken by Prussia towards free trade obliged the other German states to go with her. Prussia's economic path dictated their political position. Even if the greater German states—Saxony, Bavaria, and Württemberg—believed that they could take up an independent political position in relation to Austria and Prussia, they could not ignore the economic power of Prussia. During these years Prussia's foreign policy was like a ball in a game, thrown hither and thither between Russian, British and Austrian interests, and her domestic policy was governed by stifling reaction; and yet her economic policy showed, if one may use the word, 'progressive' traits. The economic legislation of 1848-9, allowing freedom of movement, was in essentials unaltered.

Political reaction was not taken to the point where it would run counter to economic interests.

It was clear early on in Prussia that the bourgeoisie and the landed, feudal, ruling class shared common economic interests. These classes strove for two objectives: free trade and the maintenance of peace and order. Even if the bourgeoisie sank to the position in this alliance of a mere chorus supporting the political decisions of the old ruling class, the coalition had advantages for both partners. Economic development could continue its course to the end without political disturbances; political decisions could be carried through so as to run Liberal ideas into certain specific political channels. Prussian economic policy rested on this basis.

Prussia, knew, moreover, that Germany depended upon her in economic matters. She could afford to wait. But she must ward off Austria's plans for a Customs Union. This she did by alterations of reserve and cynical frankness according to the demands of her relationship with the southern states or according to the reaction of public opinion in Germany to Prussian policy. For however loudly the Habsburg party was praised in the south, no government would or could do without Prussia in budgetary or financial matters (Doc. 28). Prussia, therefore, despite political defeats recorded successes, in the long run.

This was shown even in the first confrontation over the German question at the end of the year 1849. It was then that Schwarzenberg and Bruck opened their offensive for the Customs Union (Doc. 29). To the Viennese success seemed assured. They succeeded in gaining a modest measure of agreement from the medium-sized states to their plans for the Customs Union (Doc. 30). Prussia, however, was evasive, agreed to all plans *in principle* and rejected each *in particular* (Doc. 31).

A few months later, in May–June 1850, the game was repeated. Bruck published a memorandum (Doc. 32). During a meeting of the Zollverein at Cassel, and for the occasion of it, Austria drew attention again to her overtures (Doc. 33) and pointed out that they were still open. Prussia again out-manoeuvred the Austrians. Everything remained as it was (Doc. 34).

Then, however, Prussia overplayed her hand. She sent out invitations both to the Parliament of the German Union at Erfurt and to the Tariff Conference in Cassel and she sharpened the conflict in Hesse-Cassel: all at the same time. Radowtiz wished to assure the military roads between Prussia and the Rhineland* and placed himself without reserve on the side of the Parliament of Hesse-Cassel, which, in contrast to the Elector had given its agreement to the German Union, and stood by this decision. Prussia had gone too far. The Parliament of the Union stood 'in a vacuum' (Th. Schieder); the south German states did not put in an appearance. Radowitz next sought to bring about a military confrontation in Hesse. Austria supported the Elector; Prussia supported the Parliament. But the military clash between Austria and the Confederation, on one side, and Prussia, on the other, did not and could not happen; for Russia, on the side of Austria, had mobilized the Prussian Conservatives. Anxiety to avoid a trial of strength with the Austrian Empire was the prevailing emotion in Berlin. Radowitz had to go and Prussia had to suffer the humiliation of Olmütz (as it was later called in countless speeches). Prussia for the time being accepted her position as junior partner in *Mitteleuropa* but in doing so she deprived Austria of the very opportunity to create *Mitteleuropa* at once by military force. Thus Prussia's withdrawal at Olmütz and Dresden, so often criticized, became an advantage for her.

At the Conference of Dresden, convened a few months later at the beginning of 1851, to consider the German question, Prussia in fact re-entered the Confederation and gave Austria renewed assurances that she recognized her as the leading Power in it (Doc. 35). But on the economic-political field Prussia stiffened her resistance. Austria, after Olmütz, had hoped that she would be able to impose the Customs Union upon Prussia (Doc. 36). But when the Austrian negotiator, Baron von Hock, left Dresden he had not seen even a gleam of hope on the horizon for the Customs Union. The outcome was what Austrian diplomatists, who criticized Schwarzenberg's policy, feared, even before the Conference met, it would be (Doc. 37). After the Conference and the snub administered

* These passed through Hesse-Cassel. T.

by Austria the medium-sized states drew near again to Prussia, despite her defeat. They were true to their policy and to their conviction that Prussia could do nothing without Germany, but that Austria also needed Germany's support in order to safeguard her position in the European constellation of power.

So it came about that after Olmütz Prussia conducted herself as a Great Power and continued to 'weigh the tariff and trade question on the scales of Prussia's rise to power'.[1] This division of power distinguished political history thenceforward. Prussia could continue to build up her economic position in north Germany by trade and by political agreements. The Austrians, on the other hand, could only continue their fruitless economic-political opposition to north-German supremacy in the Zollverein. Its futility was shown with the utmost bluntness when, in 1852, Prussia suddenly gave notice of the dissolution of the Zollverein. Bavaria, Württemberg, Saxony, the two Hessen, and Hanover saw themselves face to face with the decision for or against Prussia. The envoys of the medium-sized states in their first fright went off to Vienna and conferred with Austria, without consulting Prussia: at this point they wished to go hand in hand with the Austrians. They next conferred in Bamberg and Darmstadt, without consulting Prussia or Austria; for their second hope was that they would be able to take an independent position In the end, however, they conferred in Berlin with Prussia, but without Austria and here, despite warnings from Vienna, they reluctantly accepted Prussia's terms for a renewal of the Zollverein (Doc. 38).

Berlin could afford to let it come to a division between north and south Germany—the Prussian Conservatives strove for that very object—for the southern and medium-sized states felt drawn to Prussia, however highly they prized independence. Political factors may have favoured Austria (Doc. 39) but economic factors (Doc. 40) favoured Prussia. That was the drift underlying all developments, however politically exciting they might be (Doc. 41).

After these defeats Austria was at first resigned. The industrialists' opposition to a Customs Union did not cease. Schwarzenberg had died, Bruck was no longer in office.

Their successors, Baron von Buol-Schauenstein* and Ritter von Baumgartner, wished to see the wretched Customs Union affair buried; for them Schwarzenberg's principles of policy were no longer prescriptive. Above all, the new Foreign Minister, Buol, believed that he must put a brake on Russia's policy over the Bosphorus and Dardanelles by means of an active Austrian policy in south-east Europe. He hoped thereby to gain indirectly a strengthening of Austria's position in the Germanic Confederation. He, therefore, reached an understanding with Berlin. The Emperor Francis Joseph opened the negotiations with a visit to Berlin in December 1852 and Bruck, as special envoy, brought them to a conclusion.

The treaty, which finally came into being, was a mere truce, though doubtless a very important one.** Twelve years were to elapse before the conclusion of peace in economic questions. For Austria the treaty opened the way. Buol hoped to turn from the affairs of south-east Europe back to those of the Confederation with his hand strengthened. Then the Customs Union, the Austrians believed, would meet no further resistance. For Prussia the treaty postponed decision. Her freedom of action was unimpaired. She had maintained her position as the leading Power in the Zollverein. Her further policy would be directed to preventing any basis at all for negotiating an Austrian Customs Union. This, then, was Delbrück's chief task: to procrastinate and to wait on events.

The same maxims governed Manteuffel's foreign policy. In the events preceding the Crimean War Austria relied on the alliance of 1854 with Prussia and the medium-sized states. Buol, however, saw himself cheated. The medium-sized states and Prussia acted together and decided to observe armed neutrality. Vienna was told that 'it is all one to us whether Russia or England is master at Constantinople'. Like 'a phalanx under Prussian command' (Kalchberg) the third Germany turned against Austria's policy of expansion in south-east Europe. Prussia recorded a great success. Her independence and her position as a Great Power were emphasized anew (Doc. 42).

* Karl Ferdinand, Count von, 1797–1865, Austrian Minister President and Foreign Minister, 1852–9. T.
** The reference is to the Austro-Prussian treaty of alliance of 20 April 1854. T.

Austria, on the contrary, reaped no advantage from her eastern policy or from her co-operation with the western Powers against Russia. After 1854 Austria's trade stagnated owing to military and economic taxation. The monarchy was derided as the refuge of an adverse rate of exchange, a desolate economy, and a corrupt officialdom.

In every respect Prussia afforded a brilliant contrast: her rate of exchange was steady, her economy developing madly, her officials obsessed with duty. Moreover, Prussia had become the leader of industrial development on the Continent. One hundred and nineteen joint stock companies had been founded between 1851 and 1857. Banks provided the credit—although at first in a small way—for the centres of trade in commodities and for industrial production. Capital streamed into Prussia and into the Zollverein from Britain, Belgium, and France. As Prussia's mining industry developed, Berlin began its career as a stock exchange. The railway network was doubled, new trade routes were opened and the Zollverein was integrated into the world market.

The Crimean War 'conducted far away from civilized Europe' (as the banker Hansemann considered) stimulated economic growth still more. The value of the Zollverein's exports rose rapidly from 356·9 million *taler* in 1853 to 456·1 million *taler* in 1856. Austria's by contrast fell from 184·3 million *taler* to 150·3 million *taler*. Whereas in the Zollverein the relationship between raw material, finished goods, and distribution was regulated in a new way, Austria adhered to traditional economic methods that were long out of date. Above all Vienna did not succeed in knitting together a comprehensive network of her own for raising capital. Only Prussia understood how to share to the full in the speeding up of the distribution of goods, in the cheapening of the costs of production, in new industries and new positions and, after 1857, how to exploit them politically.

At the end of the Crimean War and after the collapse of overspeculation in North America, an economic crisis rocked the European states, but the full extent of the economic depression did not make itself felt in Prussia until 1859. Austria, however, had no reserves with which to meet the crisis. Its effect there was already devastating by 1857 and the call for a protective tariff accordingly became louder. Prussia, however, believed that she could still afford free trade (Doc. 43) and the wishes of the industrialists for future tariffs were overridden. Such was the economic situation of the two rival Great Powers. With regard to the German question Prussia was the winner.

Procrastination had also paid dividends politically. Through her neutrality in the Crimean War Prussia won a profitable position in relation to Russia. Austria came out of it with empty hands. The western Powers did not forgive Buol's vacillating attitude during the war. Napoleon III paid the fee he owed to Vienna for its policy, by supporting Cavour— even during the peace negotiations in Paris. The Italian movement for unification and Austria's multi-national policy were mutually exclusive. A cleft was driven between Germany's neighbours [France and Austria], but as the Prussian envoy in Frankfurt, Otto von Bismarck, affirmed, entirely to Prussia's advantage. Bismarck recommended that this favourable hour should be used to keep the relationship with France open (Doc. 44) and thenceforward took it upon himself to conduct his policy exclusively according to Prussia's interests: Prussia should no longer pay any attention to Austria nor to the states of the Confederation (Doc. 45).

The 'old' cabinet of Frederick William IV had so far done well with its policy of waiting, groping, shilly-shallying, and non-commitment. This policy, therefore, was still maintained. In her customary way Prussia strangled any Austrian initiative in the Confederation, but initiatives of her own, such as Bismarck demanded, were refused by her Ministers. All attempts of Buol and Bruck, after the fiasco of the Crimean War, at least to gain harbour for the Customs Union ran aground. The time when the German question was essentially summed up in the Customs Union project had now passed. Thenceforward the rivalry between the two German Great Powers was more and more played out on the European field. But thenceforward it was Prussia, not Austria, who was on the offensive.

At the end of the year 1858 Prince William took over the regency from his brother who had fallen ill. In 1848 he had passed for an obstinate reactionary, but during the fifties

he had developed into an enlightened Conservative and now in
1858 he replaced the old Conservative cabinet by one Liberally
inclined. In his first address to the new Ministry of State
he emphasized that Prussia must make moral conquests by
her domestic legislation, by promoting all morally good
elements and by exploiting all the elements of unity. These
were rays of hope for the German bourgeoisie. The newly
elected Prussian Parliament (*Landtag*) was overwhelmingly
Liberal. A new era seemed to have begun. Prussia showed
herself ready to co-operate with Austria in the hope of gaining
advantages for herself in Germany. The opponents of this
policy—Bismarck in particular—were cold-shouldered. Prussia
was more and more considered as the standard-bearer of
National and Liberal ideas. The name of the Prussian Foreign
Minister, Schleinitz, became a German programme in itself.

This programme, however, could not be easily executed.
The limits irrevocably set by 'Kingship by divine right',
'adherence to the law and the constitution', 'national loyalty'
and 'the strengthening of the victorious army', 'faith and fear of
God'—all of which figured in the Prince Regent's programme
—took too little account of the national revolutionary unrest.
The authorities wanted to make use of contemporary pheno-
mena but not to be governed by them. This was apparent
in the summer of 1859 when Austria, trusting to British and
German aid, declared war on Piedmont-Sardinia, Napoleon's
ally. In the south and in the north Catholics, Democrats,
Liberals, and Conservatives passionately took up the cause of
Austria. Warning voices died away (Doc. 46). Anxiety lest
there should be a new Napoleonic mastery of Europe silenced
the sympathies of Democrats and Liberals for the Italian
national movement. Germany stood on the eve of a war with
France. Yet Prussia was paralysed. Vienna offered no compensation in the German affair as reward to Prussia for her
intervention. Russia went in with France, and Britain remained
neutral. So Prussia and, with her, the Confederation remained
with 'arms at the ready' (Doc. 47).

While Austria now buried her plans for a Customs Union,
her German policy and her economic policy, on the battlefields
of northern Italy, Prussia was able to make further improvements in her position. After Austria's defeat the supporters of

German unity saw that Prussia alone had the power to unite Germany. These supporters of German unity *über alles* now organized themselves on the Italian example into a National Society (*Nationalverein*). Liberals and Democrats united for the purpose of the unification and free development of the German Fatherland. As in 1848, they again set their hopes on Prussia (Doc. 48) and this time Prussia took her chance (Doc. 49). For not only did the *Nationalverein* set its hopes on Prussia, but the countless sports clubs, song and cultural societies did so too. Historians such as Ranke, Sybel, Droysen, and Gervinus and, above all, the supporters of free trade, who were now organized in the Congress of German Political Economists, drew the conclusion from Austria's wretchedness that they should support Prussia. From the industrial middle class to the capitalist magnates every man desired unity, that is, unity of economic organization. They were tired of principles: 'The German nation', so Julius Fröbel wrote in 1859, 'has had enough of principle and doctrines, literary greatness and theoretic existence. What it wants is power—power, and yet more power. To him who gives it power, it will pay honour, more honour than he could ever imagine.' The supporters of the *kleindeutsch* Prussian solution took their decision. Yet their adoption of the cause was not to be easy.

After the Peace of Villafranca, which ended the Austro-French quarrel about Italy, Prussia's policy took a new turn. She was still at heart on Austria's side, but was disillusioned with her (Doc. 50). William and his advisers were not sure whether they should play the Austrian or the French game. Schleinitz, the Foreign Minister, backed Austria. By going hand in hand with Austria and by exploiting her needs, he sought to gain successes for Prussia in the German question. The Prince Regent and his colleagues in the ministry shared this hope, only they did not wish to stand unreservedly by Austria; for since January 1860, they had taken soundings in France about a commercial treaty.

Prussia thus had two irons in the fire. On one side, she pretended to co-operate with Austria, negotiating at Teplitz*
in the summer of 1860 for a defensive alliance, and showing

* Prince William and the Emperor Francis Joseph met at Teplitz on 6 July 1860. T.

herself not disinclined to the plan of an eventual Customs Union. On the other side, the Prince Regent William had conferred with Napoleon III at Baden-Baden and had speeded up the negotiations for a Franco-Prussian commercial treaty without regard for Austria. The acceptance of this commercial treaty would bring about a complete orientation of the Zollverein towards the west.

Austria had acquired a new Foreign Minister: the specialist in Federal Diet affairs, Count Rechberg von Rothenlöwen. His name was also identified with a German programme; for Vienna hoped to be able to exploit the resentment in south Germany at Prussia's holding back in 1859 and so to be able to force Prussia into a close alliance, a mutual guarantee of the entire dominions of each and a resumption of discussions on the Customs Union.[2] Accordingly the Austrians entered into negotiations with Prussia. Teplitz was to bring about the commitment of Prussia's military power to Austria's policy. Rechberg gave no thought to any 'countervailing gifts' such as Prussia hoped for. On the contrary, he hoped to be able to isolate Prussia and to outplay her.

Finally the *German Federal States* strove, after the Austrian débacle of 1859, to outdo each other with a multiplicity of proposals for reform of the Confederation. The Bavarian, von der Pfordten, strove for a firmer organization of the third Germany. He sought to create the idea of the Triad in preparation for the cohesion of these states, when the antagonism of the two Great Powers should cause the Confederation to fall apart (Doc. 51). The Saxon, Beust, followed him in these efforts and hoped for a closing of the ranks in Germany without Austria and without Prussia. A peripatetic and modified Federal Diet, meeting in the north under Prussian, and in the south, under Austrian presidency, together with a *Direktorium* of three and a Parliament of delegates from the states, should compose the institutions of a united Germany (Doc. 52). Finally, the Badenese, Franz von Roggenbach, since 1859 Foreign Minister in Baden, drafted a programme for a United States of Germany. This United States should come into being by means of free agreement; Austria was not to be a member; Prussia was to have the Central Executive Power but it should be controlled by a Parliament elected by universal suffrage (Doc. 53). These projects and negotiations of the years 1859–60 were accompanied by an ever growing partisanship on the part of the public. By taking sides for Prussia or Austria, for a Prussian *kleindeutsch* or an Austrian-*mitteleuropäisch* solution of the German question, they more and more tore apart and split the whole of German life in all its range (Doc. 54).

There was now a complete breakdown. How would events develop? Did Teplitz bring a chance for an Austrian settlement of the German question? Would the projects for reform put forward by the medium-sized states find supporters? They found none, nor did Teplitz offer any basis for a project of understanding *à deux*. Vienna overestimated her position and misjudged in her evaluation of Franco-Prussian antagonism. The third Germany fared no better. Prussia alone had the power to make a choice and, in contrast to the fifties, she again became active.

When, after the negotiations at Teplitz, Vienna made no arrangements to give Prussia equality in the Confederation (Doc. 55), Prussia sought to combine with the west. She now spared no effort to intensify the negotiations for the commercial treaty with Napoleon III, sought links with western Europe, and confronted the southern and medium-sized states afresh with the possibility of a breach of the Zollverein, if its members did not conform. The negotiations for a defensive alliance with Austria slumbered. The Prince Regent William relaxed his reserve towards Napoleon. Schleinitz, the protagonist of the policy of agreement with the Austrian Empire, was dismissed. [In October 1861] Count Bernstorff,* the determined battler for a strictly Prussian policy of self-interest, was named Foreign Minister. The cleft between Austria and Prussia had again become the governing factor in the German situation.

'Prussia', said Rechberg, acknowledging his failure, 'does not want a league of states, she wants complete hegemony in a federal state; it is not possible to come to terms with Berlin.'[3] In fact Prussia no longer wanted even this. Her German policy was replaced by a definitely Prussian one.

---

* Albrecht, Count von Bernstorff (1809–73), since 1854 Prussian ambassador in London. T.

Bernstorff at once took the first opportunity offered to him to push aside all projects for the reform of the Confederation (Doc. 56). Radowitz's Union policy of 1849 was revived. Prussia let it come to a duel with Austria and the medium-sized states.

This change in Prussia's policy is *the* great and decisive landmark in her German policy. After 1862, Bismarck pursued Bernstorff's idea, but with more consistency and greater impetus, so that Prussia's game of power politics set the scene for Germany's development from now on. After the snub administered by Prussia, the states of the Confederation again bound themselves closely to Austria; they even signed secret treaties with her in which they engaged themselves to support no project for the reform of the Confederation which would force her out of it. In identic notes Austria and the other German states warned Berlin not to take the game too far (Doc. 57). It was all in vain. Prussia was not at all disturbed. She said that she was 'pained' (Doc. 58) but knew herself—this was the deciding factor—to be supported by France and Russia in representing 'the German idea' (Doc. 59). The commercial treaty between France and Prussia was initialled in March 1862. German resistance had only hastened the negotiations to a conclusion.

Yet Rechberg did not give up the struggle. He hoped for support from the southern states and paid no attention to his ambassadors' warnings that Prussia was master in the Zollverein and that the Franco-Prussian treaty was built upon her strength there. He paid no heed to the opinion that Württemberg, Bavaria, Hesse-Cassel, in fact all the states, were still hesitating in this sphere (Doc. 60). To him the time seemed favourable for an offensive; since the Prussian government had engaged itself in a duel with the Liberals. At the very time that Bernstorff pressed on with determination in foreign and commercial policy, the Crown resolutely directed domestic affairs again on to a reactionary path and demanded a far-reaching reform of the military situation. The Liberals were thus deprived of their hope for a 'democratization' of the country. The Liberal tinge of the new era, that had grown paler and paler during 1860–1, now finally disappeared. Could the realization of the national wish for unity check the drive for liberty? The answer seemed uncertain. At the time when it became clear that the Prussian Upper House would reject all bills with a Liberal tendency, the Liberals had already organized themselves and founded the German *Fortschrittspartei*, the 'executive of the *Nationalverein*' in Prussia. Its programme was primarily directed to unity in a *kleindeutsch* sense. It was a nationalist programme, but loyal to the King although it contained Liberal demands (e.g. for the reform of the Upper House and ministerial responsibility). Yet however loyal the new party professed to be—it accepted the doctrine, though reluctantly, that William was crowned King by the Grace of God—it maintained a firm opposition to the new King on the question of military reform (Doc. 61).

Prussia's new army reform is the second factor, after the commercial treaty with France, which clearly influenced Germany's development. Whereas, however, the commercial treaty directly furthered the construction of unity on a *kleindeutsch* basis, the army reform played an indirect part. The commercial treaty became a political lever to prepare economic unity. The authoritarian state, which between 1862 and 1866 won a victory over the Prussian Parliament in the matter of military reform, then set its mark on the constitution of the new united Germany which, in turn, owed its coming into being essentially to the new, well-drilled Prussian army. The year 1859 was the point of departure for army reform as it was for general and commercial policy. The 'unpleasant experiences' the Prussian government had had to undergo in the mobilization of 1859, when it found its militiamen mostly elderly fathers of families, caused the Prince Regent William to press for a reform of the army which should increase the annual intake to about 63,000 men and—most important—reduce its age by uniting the militia with the reserve. The older men, occupied in civilian occupations and therefore more independent, commanded by civilian officers, were thus excluded from the army in the field. The active army was to become an army of the masses, 'such as the times demanded.' But it must strengthen the Crown, not Democracy. As long as the distinctive Prussian state remained as it had existed of old, with its soldier King, the bourgeoisie could play at parliaments without doing too much harm.[4] By the foundation of the 'Prussian *Volksverein*' the government also gained support from the ranks of the Conservatives (Doc. 62).

Parliament did not reject the increased annual intake of recruits—its majority was Nationalist, loyal to the King and ready for military service—but it insisted upon two essential conditions: first it demanded that the two-year term of service should be re-introduced and secondly it rejected the forcing of the militia out of the field army. The Regent, however, obstinately stood by the three-year term of service, and the eradication of the militia spirit from the royal army. He found in his War Minister, Albrecht von Roon, a devoted high Conservative, and a resolute ally, who did not shrink from a conflict with the new 'constitutional swindle'.

The struggle for power between Crown and Parliament flared up. When the *Landtag* refused the increased grant for the royal army reforms, the King* changed his ministry (Doc. 63) and dissolved Parliament. As was foreseen, new elections resulted in a catastrophic defeat for the Conservatives and a renewed absolute majority for the Opposition. The Prussian authoritarian state seemed to have come to an end.

Austria took heart. On 26 April 1862 Rechberg outlined the steps to be taken. The press was told what to say and the states of the Confederation were put on the alert (Doc. 64). Then Rechberg demanded from Prussia that she drop the French commercial treaty. Bernstorff refused and had his policy confirmed by the hastily summoned, Liberal *Landtag*. However firm the opposition of the Liberals over the military question, on the commercial question they agreed unreservedly with the government's free-trade policy.

Despite this setback, Rechberg pursued his object undeflected. At the beginning of July he again submitted to Berlin the old plan for a Customs Union and the '70 million Reich'. Austria accepted the Zollverein tariff that she had so far refused, hoping to torpedo the Franco-Prussian commercial treaty. At the same time Rechberg revived all the Austrian projects for reform of the Confederation and—most important— he courted Bavaria.

It was now, as Bernstorff affirmed, a matter of life and death. The Prussian Foreign Minister was ready to tread the path of dualism, but he made the continuation of the Zollverein

---

* The Prince Regent had become King eighteen months before when his brother died in 1860. T.

dependent upon its adoption of the French commercial treaty. The opposition in the south and in Vienna thus knew where it stood. Prussia soon received support: Baden and Saxony accepted the treaty unconditionally.

Yet Austria too scored a victory; for Württemberg and Bavaria saw the only chance of making sure of their independent position, against Prussia, in a provisional rejection of the treaty. Of course their reservations were cautiously formulated and were by no means tantamount to agreement with the [Austrian] Customs Union.

Bernstorff and Delbrück could afford to remain cool despite all the *grossdeutsch* agitation. The crisis over army reform did not disturb their policy in the long run. Bernstorff cynically let Rechberg know that he should cherish no illusions about the Liberal opposition (Doc. 66). He estimated the value of Austria's allies as small. Whether Catholics, citizens of the small south-German towns or south-German peasants, noblemen, Democrats, supporters of German Austria, historians, or journalists, they represented only so many whims and prejudices, so many dreams and hopes. On the other hand, he knew that commercial interests and the most active section of the academic world were behind himself and his policy. Supported by the community of economic interests between Liberals and Conservatives—both German and Prussian— Bernstorff had played the game of power politics and consistently conducted an anti-Austrian policy.

As the struggle over army reform burned ever fiercer, von der Heydt and the Finance Minister, Bodelschwingh, resigned; the King, isolated, wished to abdicate; and Bernstorff then too resigned. He had no wish to govern against the will of the representative Parliament. A situation arose in which Otto von Bismarck alone declared himself willing, even against the will of the King, to rule without the budget's being sanctioned, and against the will of Parliament. The final and fiercest shot of the reactionary Divine Right Party was fired—as the *Nationalverein* jeered—with his [Bismarck's] call to power (Doc. 67).

Out of the conflict over the army a constitutional conflict arose. For four years Otto von Bismarck conducted the government without a constitutionally sanctioned budget (Doc. 67c).

He waged two wars without any grant of money from the representative assembly. He fought without scruple against all opposition and handled Parliament with hostile condescension. Press control, penal dismissals, lawsuits against Liberal officials, and the influencing of elections were the means he used for this policy. It made Prussia hated throughout Germany and threw the supporters of a National Liberal Prussia and of unity on a *kleindeutsch* basis into angry despair. The opposition went, however, no further than words. The people obeyed. There was no tradition of revolutionary spirit to lend wings to the opposition (Doc. 68). The old and new Liberals, though resentful, endured the authoritarianism of the new era; for they had no support from the peasants, brought up in Lutheran obedience and unshaken in their royalism. The government had the means of power. Its policy was followed through to its logical consequences.

The new man in the post of First Minister had fulfilled all expectations, good as well as bad. With 'blood and iron' he wished to solve 'the questions of the day' (Doc. 69). These words, from his first speech in the Budget Commission of the Lower House of the *Landtag*, have become famous. Yet his first challenge to Austria in foreign policy ended in a complete failure (Doc. 70). Britain, Russia, and France had no wish to allow Prussia to venture upon a war against Austria. Prussia should remain as she was: a thorn in the side of the Great Power, Austria. Bismarck understood this quite quickly. He then tried to solve 'the questions of the day' with 'coal and iron'. This policy too had been thought of as early as 1861.[5]

Now, at the end of December 1862, Bismarck went back to his reflections of 1861 and prepared further steps for proceeding by peaceful means: for a new organization of Germany by way of the Zollverein and by 'economic dominion' (Doc. 71). He was more successful with this policy. The German Customs Parliament, in 1861 still pro-Austrian, was on his side by October 1862. The Political Economists also hastened to the Prussian flag. Bismarck won supporters from the Liberal camp—if not from its journalist and lawyer members, at least from its commercial section. But for him this was decisive.

Thenceforward two interlocking motives governed Bismarck's

conduct: at home, a settlement of economic questions, abroad, an increase of power by a skilful juggling with every chance that offered, so as to allow Prussia to gain an equal voice in the concert of Great Powers. It was evident by the end of the year that this course would bring progress. Despite the danger of war and internal crisis, a lively trade in foreign exchange and bills on a big scale began and very favourable results were recorded on the stock exchange which indicated economic expansion and confidence in Bismarck.

The change of ministry in Prussia had no influence upon the policy of Austria and the medium-sized states. Their policy was firmly fixed. Economically bound to Prussia, in political affairs these states sought Austria's support in order to gain for themselves an independent and mediating position between the two Great Powers. The dualism of the two Great Powers was their guarantee of the *status quo*. When the conservative governments, especially in Bavaria and Württemberg, believed that Prussia was about to increase her power—when Bismarck for instance co-operated with Russia at the beginning of 1863 against the insurrectionary Poles—they drew nearer to Austria and were ready to go with Vienna through thick and thin. But if Austria's situation appeared to become too strong, they then emphasized their separate position and drew aloof from all Vienna's wishes. This policy suited their interests, but not Austria's. Indeed Rechberg wanted an indissoluble alliance. He wanted to isolate Prussia, and by means of the Customs Union to force her to give way in the question of reforming the Confederation.

These were the elements of the situation in which Bismarck inaugurated his policy. It added up to this: if he succeeded in opening direct talks with Austria, in convincing her that the Customs Union could be most quickly concluded by direct negotiations with Berlin, and if he succeeded in creating an alliance between the two Great Powers, then the medium-sized states would be isolated; they would inevitably consider themselves betrayed by Austria; the economic supremacy of Prussia would turn the scale in the political field and, in short, the Prussian-*kleindeutsch* solution for German unity would have been attained. But how, and by what means, could he tempt Austria? Where was the leverage for this policy? Bismarck found it in the Polish question (the crushing of the Polish revolt), in the Schleswig-Holstein question (that is, the annexation of the former Danish duchies by 'Germany'), and in the revolutionary foreign policy of Napoleon III. Everywhere opportunities were offered to Bismarck to use Rechberg's constant fear of revolution in order to attempt a *rapprochement* with Austria. Moreover, he showed himself not entirely unyielding in the Customs Union question. He took the line that political considerations, which united Prussia and Austria, should not be encroached upon by the economic considerations, which divided them (Doc. 72).

At the beginning, then, of the year 1863 Bismarck made much of 'the situation threatening the power structure of Europe ... a situation brought about by the solidarity of all the revolutionary elements of Europe' and he vigorously proposed a *rapprochement* between Berlin and Vienna (Doc. 73). Vienna, however, continued to hold back, for she could still find support from the economic opposition of south Germany to Prussia. For this reason Rechberg continued along the path of political dualism. He believed that Bismarck had isolated himself even on the European plane by the escapade of the Alvensleben Convention. In the summer of 1863, therefore, the Emperor Francis Joseph issued invitations to a Congress of Princes at Frankfurt. William accepted; Bismarck declined (Doc. 74). He had an intense horror of such reforms as would assure the supremacy of the alliance between Austria and the medium-sized states. His counter-proposals—a Federal Parliament, elected by direct vote, and a conference of ministers—were derisively greeted by the Princes assembled in Frankfurt with the injunction to look at the situation within Prussia (Doc. 75). Yet without Prussia Austria could do nothing, even though the third Germany paid political homage to Vienna. When she made an economic question of it—in 1863, for example, by presenting the alternatives as the commercial treaty with France or the Customs Union with Austria—the outcome was still 'tame' (Doc. 76).

One congress cancelled out the other. The Zollverein negotiations at Munich, with Prussia's success in May 1863, were counterbalanced by the Austrian Congress of Princes in Frankfurt in August 1863 and Frankfurt was more than counterbalanced in its turn by the *Münchner Registratur* in the autumn of 1863 (Doc. 77). The German question came to a standstill.

Now, however, Napoleon III and the storm over the new Danish constitution came, unsolicited, to Bismarck's help. At the end of the year 1863 Napoleon issued invitations to a congress in Paris. He intended to bring about a new political order in south-eastern Europe in accordance with national-revolutionary principles. At the end of 1863 Denmark received a new constitution, whereby the Duchies of Schleswig, Holstein, and Lauenburg were to be incorporated into the Kingdom. Thus, in Germany's view, Denmark broke the London Protocol of 1852 which had linked the continuation of Danish rule with a guarantee of the *status quo* leaving the Duchies with their rights of autonomy intact. The reaction of the German public to the new Danish constitution was violent. Public opinion, highly excited, demanded the independence of the Duchies under the Hereditary Prince of Augustenburg,* who was considered to be the legal claimant to the throne. The Germanic Confederation, under the leadership of the third Germany, decided on Federal Execution.** Holstein and Lauenburg were occupied by federal troops.

These then were the two affairs. In both, Austria was forced to stand by Prussia. Rechberg was obliged to give up any idea of exploiting national ferment in the east: an independent Poland would have inaugurated the break-up of the multi-national state. Likewise, in the Danish question, Rechberg was bound to feel tied by the London Protocol: treaties were the cement which held the Danube monarchy together. Bismarck, following the guide-lines of his policy, opposed any alteration on the eastern frontiers of Prussia or in Schleswig Holstein. Public opinion did not disturb him at all; he had no public sympathy to lose. The Danish affair was a welcome opportunity for him to raise Prussia's position in the European constellation of power. But his proceedings must be legitimate. If Prussia and Austria held strictly to the London Protocol, then Denmark would count as the treaty breaker. Thus the Prusso-Austrian war against Denmark would remain localized

---

* The son of the claimant of 1848, who had renounced his rights. T.
** Military action to enforce a decision of the Federal Diet. T.

and Austria would have to look to Prussia. Bismarck's calculations proved sound.

Rechberg, tired of the medium-sized states' policy of independence, anxious about a further increase in Prussia's power, and afraid of the spread of the national movement, went hand in hand with Bismarck (Doc. 78). The *coup* had succeeded. Austria had forfeited the national sympathies of Germany. At the same time the medium-sized states were isolated— a factor of great importance to Bismarck. Vienna had to follow Berlin's lead.

By December 1863 Vienna perceived the consequences. Bismarck gave notice that Prussia would withdraw from the Zollverein. The resistance of its members to its threatened dissolution was entirely ineffectual, the camp of the third Germany split, and the idea of the Triad collapsed. Whereas Rechberg hoped to come forward to take the Customs Union out of Bismarck's hand, 'Germany' was disposed to accept the new Prussian economic scheme (Doc. 79).

The Prusso-Austrian negotiations for the 'promised' Customs Union were to take place in Prague. Prussia's agreement was still not forthcoming, for Berlin had no wish for a Customs Union (Doc. 80). A Press storm broke loose in Vienna. Rechberg had to recognize that Prussia was not ready to meet his wishes. She had dropped her mask; after the first victory over the Danes at Düppel, the medium-sized states and Austria were again ranged side by side. Prussia's pretensions to hegemony had become clear. It was quite useless for Bismarck to claim that he was optimistic about the 'outcome of Prague'.

Once again the old allies tried, though without much hope, to find a way to succeed against Prussia. Rechberg, with proposals for radically lowered tariffs, tried to beat Prussia on her own ground (Doc. 81). Agreement was again reached at Munich. The medium-sized states, therefore, did not appear at the Zollverein negotiations when they began in Berlin. An attempt was made by a final intrigue to force Prussia to yield. Apart from this, Austria set her hopes upon the negotiations for a truce with Denmark at the London Conference, hoping to regain a free hand there. But all her expectations were disappointed.

In London Bismarck remained reserved and tirelessly

emphasized the necessity for the solidarity of the Powers on the monarchical principle against European revolution (Doc. 82). For the rest, he let Austria become involved in the nego- tiations. As Bismarck had hoped, Denmark put her trust in Britain and rejected independence for the Duchies. So the Conference ended in fiasco—exactly as Bismarck had wished. The war could be continued, without the European Great Powers having any justification to intervene. Austria, however, had to fight on.

A second Prussian success followed. The newly formed inner phalanx of German governments fell again into vacillation. The south-German counter-proposals became more and more 'tame'. Economic factors were stronger than any political aspiration (Doc. 83).

Saxony adhered to the new Prussian Zollverein system and accepted the Franco-Prussian commercial treaty. The Thuring- ian Duchies followed, as did Frankfurt, Brunswick, Oldenburg, Baden and Hesse-Cassel. Hesse-Cassel's step was decisive; for both north and south had struggled to win her. Owing to her geographical position, she was the cornerstone of any German economic system. The adhesion of the southern states would now be only a question of time. Bismarck could, therefore, afford to be patient. He did not wish to overplay his hand. What is more, Rechberg, in the belief that he could turn to advantage the desperate straits he was again in, once more offered Prussia direct negotiations. Bismarck hastened to accept the offer and to propose to Vienna that the two conservative Great Powers should go closely hand in hand against the 'overweening presumption' of the medium-sized states and National Liberalism (Doc. 84). Rechberg accepted these overtures but in return he demanded his Customs Union. Even on this point Bismarck showed himself ready to listen to reason; for he sought, in the impending peace negotiations with Denmark, complete success in bringing home safe and sound a *condominium* of the two Powers over the new Duchies. The sharp conflict of views in economic matters was, therefore, relegated to the background (Doc. 85). King William issued instructions that 'the rejection of the preliminary conditions imposed by Austria should not be positively put into words at *this* moment', Bismarck himself travelled to Vienna, in order to strengthen the alliance for war (Doc. 86).

In the south there was now no further hesitation. Bismarck had decoyed Rechberg with the catch-phrase, 'monarchical principle' and then outplayed him. The third Germany now unconditionally accepted the Prussian commercial system. German economic unity without Austria was no longer in question. As Francis Joseph bitterly recorded, Austria had become a laughing-stock (Doc. 87).

Rechberg was free to go—and he took his leave; Austria's star had set (Doc. 88); the third Germany was powerless. The Liberals had been politically outmanoeuvred, and had been bought off by the virtual annexation (*Anschluss*) of the Duchies. Their economic aspirations had also been realized. The domestic results soon appeared in Germany. The Liberal opposition to Bismarck began to disintegrate (Doc. 89). The *kleindeutsch*, free-trade policy of Prussia had won. *Mitteleuropa*, in Bruck's sense of a league of states under one tariff from Antwerp to the Adriatic, was dead. Instead the road was laid for the further progress of Prussia in power and greatness.

Document 21   Frederick William IV to Radowitz, 23 December 1848
(W. Möring, *Josef von Radowitz, Nachgelassene Briefe und Aufzeichnungen zur Geschichte der Jahre 1848–1853*, Stuttgart, 1922, p. 68)

. . . Our task [that of the Emperor of Austria and of the kings] is to persuade the other princes in the different Circles* of the Empire, to submit themselves up to a point to the kings, primarily for military purposes but also so that the kings may in a sense represent them. The princes or kings must in turn be able to say to the followers of St. Paul (not the apostle, nor the hermit, but the one in Frankfurt**) something like your beloved Schiller said when he wrote in your beloved tragedy *Don Carlos:* 'Cardinal, I have done what I had to do—now do you your part. Farewell.'
    P.S. Here, as a final end, is a little word of confession about the crown which the *Paulskirche* [the Frankfurt Assembly] has for sale:

* An allusion to the Circles, or eight groups of states, into which the Holy Roman Empire was divided for military purposes. T.
** An allusion to the *Paulskirche* (St. Paul's Church) where the Frankfurt National Assembly met. T.

every German nobleman, who bears on his coat of arms a cross or a bar, is a hundred times too good to accept such a diadem moulded out of the dirt and dregs of revolution, disloyalty and treason. The old, legitimate crown of the German nation, not worn since 1806, the diadem by divine right, which makes him who bears it the highest authority in Germany, which men obey for conscience' sake—that crown one can accept if one feels one has the strength for it, and if one's own duties allow it. That crown, however, no one bestows except the Emperor Francis Joseph, myself, and our equals; and woe to him who accepts it, if the price is the loss of a third of Germany and the noblest sections of the German nation. God help us! Amen.

Document 22 Major Huyn to Schwarzenberg, Kremsier, 7 March 1849
(J. Redlich, *Das österreichische Staats- und Reichs-problem*, Leipzig, 1920, vol. 1, Part 2 Additions and Notes, p. 101)

... In obedience to the telegraphic order which came in early [to Kremsier from Vienna] at 7 o'clock: 'We stand by it', Count Mercandin at once gave the command to the President of the *Reichstag**, Smolka, to dissolve it.

While the two gentlemen were conversing I ordered a company [of soldiers] march into the castle. It occupied all the entrances to the offices in strength and the rest, a half company, were marched into the courtyard opposite the main entrance. The main gate was then closed so that people could only pass through one at a time and the only way open for Members who came later was the way to the office of the Executive and the Treasury.

The second company was consigned to barracks, but covered the gates of the town in strength and sent frequent patrols through the side-streets.

Notorious characters were watched as much as possible. The manifesto of the Emperor was finally affixed to the gate of the castle.

Between 8 and 9 o'clock the Members of Parliament arrived and were very astonished at the new look of the Parliament's place of assembly. A few were pleased, others bitterly angry, venomous, but all accommodated themselves: power had made its impression ...

---

* This elective Parliament had been sitting in Vienna since 22 July 1848 as a result of the events following the fall of Metternich on 13 March. It had been moved to Kremsier in November after the accession of Francis Joseph and the advent of Schwarzenberg. On 4 March 1849 a new Austrian constitution was enacted in Vienna. T.

Document 23 Declaration of Dahlmann and 65 others of his party on quitting the National Assembly, 21 May 1849 (P. Wentzcke, *Die erste deutsche Nationalversammlung und ihr Werk*, Munich, 1922, p. 378)

... With the decision of 28 March of this year the constitution-making of the National Assembly was completed. The signatories below are convinced that this constitution was the only formula, attainable in the given circumstances, for a peaceful solution and a reconciliation of the interests and rights of the various German races, states, and dynasties ... Guided by this conviction, the signatories have so far co-operated in all the decisions, which by the appropriate constitutional means and through public opinion could have brought each individual state to recognize the constitution of the *Reich*. Most recently they co-operated in the decision of 4 May which introduced registration for elections to the first Parliament under the constitution. To their deep grief events have assumed a different complexion and the hopes of the German nation, so near fulfilment, seem likely to miscarry. On one hand, though faced by the very great dangers threatening the Fatherland, four German kings, including the Prussian king himself, have declined the formula of mediation between the conflicting principles threatening our times which the *Reich* constitution offered. On the other hand, a movement of violence has arisen, actually nothing to do with the *Reich* constitution, yet threatening one of its most important sections: that concerned with its supreme head. This movement has arisen in those very states which have already recognized the constitution. Both sides appeal to the arbitrament of force, while the provisional Central Power* declares that effective action for the execution of the *Reich* constitution lies outside its functions and duties. Finally, since 10 May, a series of decisions has been taken by a new majority in the Assembly, which are, in part, impossible to execute and, in part, quite contradictory to the course pursued by the earlier majority to which the signatories belonged. In this position of affairs, the National Assembly has only one choice, *either*, by setting aside what has so far been the Central Power, to tear asunder the last common, legal bond between all German governments and peoples, and to foment a civil war, whose beginning has already shaken the foundations of all social order, *or* to renounce the execution of the *Reich* constitution by means of an act of legislation and to do so in co-operation with the provisional Central Power. The signatories have considered the second of these two evils the lesser for the Fatherland ...

* i.e. the provisional Central Executive Power embodied in Archduke John and the ministers he appointed. It was set up by the Frankfurt Assembly on 28 June 1848. T.

Document 24   Frederick William IV to his people, 1851
(H. Pross, editor, *Dokumente und Materialien*, Frankfurt-am-Main, 1963, p. 178)

Making the German question their pretext, the enemies of the Fatherland have planted the standard of revolt first in Saxony, a neighbouring state, then in single localities in south Germany. Some deluded persons in some parts of our country have, to my deep grief, allowed themselves to be swept along to follow this standard in open revolt against legal authority, in order to overthrow both the divine and human order.

It is incumbent on me to make a public address to my people at this serious and perilous time.

I could not give an affirmitive answer to the German National Assembly's offer of a crown because the Assembly did not have the right to bestow the crown, which it offered me, without the agreement of the German governments and because it was offered to me on condition that I accepted a constitution which was incompatible with the rights and the security of the German states.

I sought in vain to reach an understanding with the German National Assembly and exhausted every available means to do so . . .

When the Assembly quitted the ground of justice, law, and duty by decisions which all honourable men fearlessly opposed; when it accused us of breaking the peace because we afforded help to our hard-pressed neighbour and did so victoriously; when it summoned men openly to resist us and the governments which joined with me in not accepting the pernicious stipulations of the constitution—when the Assembly did those things, it broke with Prussia. It—or its majority—is no longer that congregation of men upon whom Germany looked with pride and confidence. A large number of members voluntarily withdrew, when the first step was taken along the road to illegality. By my order yesterday I recalled all the Prussian deputies who still belong to the Assembly. Other German governments will do the same . . . In loyalty and steadfastness I, as King, preserve my faith in German unity, but the hope of seeing it attained through the Frankfurt Assembly has been destroyed by this wanton violence. My government, together with the plenipotentiaries of the greater German states which have associated themselves with me, has taken up the task, begun at Frankfurt, of making a German constitution.

This constitution can and should, in the shortest time, assure to the nation what it rightly demands and expects: unity, embodied in a united Executive Power which will worthily and effectively represent Germany's name and interests abroad; freedom, assured through a popularly elected assembly with legislative power. The imperial constitution deliberated upon by the National Assembly will be the basis of the new constitution and only those points have been altered which, having arisen from party conflicts and concessions, are seriously harmful to the true well-being of the Fatherland. This new constitution will be laid before a Parliament, composed by all the states that are associated in the federal state, to be examined and accepted. Germany trusts in the patriotism of the Prussian government; its trust shall not be betrayed.

There lies my path. Faced with these facts, only fools or knaves will venture to assert that I have ceased to care for the cause of German unity or that I have grown unfaithful to my earlier conviction and my assurances.

Prussia is here to be called upon for the protection of Germany in these difficult times against internal and external enemies and she must and will fulfill her duty. So now I call my people to arms. Let us restore law and order in our own country and in other German countries wherever our help is required! Let us found German unity! Let us protect German freedom from the terrorization of a single party which seeks to sacrifice morality, honour, and loyalty to violent emotion, a party which has succeeded in throwing a net of folly and illusion over a section of the people . . .

Document 25   Schwarzenberg to Francis Joseph, 6 November 1851
(Vienna, Haus- Hof- und Staatsarchiv, PA II, no. 76)

. . . Among the most effective means available to Your Majesty's Government towards the assertion and permanent increase of its influence throughout Germany, must be reckoned its active participation in fostering her common economic interests. The continually growing importance of this aspect of statecraft will entail more difficulty for Austria, as time goes on, in effectually and worthily maintaining her political position as the first Power in the Germanic Confederation and as the basis of the whole European system. This will be especially so, if the Imperial Government continues in the future to remain aloof from general German trade and communications questions, and does not make its voice heard in their regulation. In addition to the great economic advantages which Austria may exchange with the states of the Germanic Confederation in this field, the entry of the Empire into a customs and trade system is important because it would make possible a *rapprochement* and a gradual union of Austria with the other German federal states in commercial policy. This step may also be seen as a political measure, whose scope extends to the relationships of power and influence amongst the great European states . . .

Document 26   Undated and unsigned memorandum on the question of a Customs Union
(Ibid., no. 92)

. . . This Customs Union is a matter of life and death to Austria. She will push it forward with greater energy than anything else and will not blench even at concessions on the purely political field in order to promote it.

If the Customs Union as Austria seeks it is achieved, Prussia's influence will be utterly and completely broken . . .

Document 27   Undated memorial of the Executive of the Central Union for Free Trade
(Ibid.)

. . . Sympathy for the cause of free trade has been vigorously excited in all sections of the population without exception. Austria's tariff plans*, as they have been officially formulated in the published memoranda of Saxony and Bavaria, have shocked even the indifferent and it has become clear even to the most short-sighted what harm their execution must bring to trade and industry and how necessary it is for every man to bestir himself to build up a defence against such a system.

The beneficial and profitable character of a free and unchecked economy—internally and externally—has become all the more clearly and sharply recognized because of the attempts to shackle by new protective duties an economy which is already hamstrung. The anxiety thus awakened is not limited to the wish to repel the new shackles with which we are threatened; there is a wish too to get rid of the old shackles. The call for free trade resounds aloud on all sides. . . .

Only the principle of free trade can form the foundation of the new Customs Union. Only when tariffs are levied purely for revenue will the disadvantages and dangers, to which attention has been drawn in the memoranda that have been submitted, be *basically* remedied or obviated.

Without free trade the Revolution will never lose its hold. On the contrary, it will find fresh tinder and its next outbreak will

* First formulated by Schwarzenberg in September 1849 for a liberalization of the Austrian tariff and the creation of a German Customs Union in five stages. T.

only be the more dreadful. The masses will find in the protection afforded to individuals the ground for claiming in louder and louder tones the right to be protected and maintained in their turn by the state at the cost of the community. If such claims are recognized *in principle* by the administration of the state itself, *the security of private property is endangered. Free Trade is the only watchman and caretaker of private property.* At home one may put production into the hands of monopolists, but consumption can be neither forcibly increased nor forced upon some classes rather than others. The internal economy, therefore, will contract, if the population's consumption is restrained by protective tariffs, proportionately to the expansion which it may at first have experienced, when such tariffs forcibly opened new markets to it. It will not be long before the internal economy stands at the same low level as before the extension of its markets, and meanwhile the whole population—of course with the exception of a few favoured manufacturers—will grow poorer . . .

From the free-trade standpoint a union of the Steuerverein* with the Zollverein, as both now stand, *cannot* be recommended. The Steuerverein recognizes in its tariff, with few exceptions, the principle of mere revenue duties, and the Zollverein tariff, as is well known, has a markedly protective bias . . .

The matter, of course, would assume a different complexion and a union would inevitably both appear desirable and accord with the nature of the Steuerverein, if Prussia, alone or togehter with the present members of the Zollverein (even with the southern states, provided they gave up their excise duties), were to proclaim in her own interests a free-trade tariff, and to carry through reforms similar to those recently enacted in England—for her own prosperity rather than from considerations for others. *Then,* when a change of system has been completed by Prussia, the free-trade party too would be able to recommend a union between the Steuerverein and the Zollverein.

To influence Prussia in this direction must be the particular effort of that party; to strengthen the Prussian government in this direction, to work upon it by public opinion, to sustain it through the voice of Prussia's own population, oppressed as it is by the present system—that must be the immediate task of the free-trade party.

We must, of course, not fail to appreciate the difficulties that prevent Prussia from going forward clearly along this new path. If, however, Saxony and Bavaria, as members of the Zollverein, which cannot be dissolved until 1854, are even now recommending the

---

* The separate union which Hanover, Oldenburg, and Brunswick had made after the Zollverein had been concluded; deserted by Brunswick in 1840. T.

Austrian plan—that is, a new customs system—no reason can exist to prevent Prussia too from likewise setting up a new system and one in a wholly opposite direction. Through the internal results of this new system Prussia could more easily promote a union [between Steuerverein and Zollverein] than by bargaining and treaties.

To this end, in the double task of frustrating the Austrian plans in Dresden* and encouraging Prussia towards a true free-trade policy the undersigned Directorium will diligently and unremittingly direct all its efforts.

The Directorium

Gutike (Stettin) M. Ellissen (Frankfurt-am-Main) Ross (Hamburg)

Document 28 Handel (Austrian envoy in Stuttgart) to Buol, 15 May 1852
(Vienna, Haus- Hof- und Staatsarchiv, PA II, no. 78)

. . . After a few sympathetic and courteous words addressed to me personally, His Majesty [the King of Württemberg] assured me that he had been very pleased by Your Excellency's letter.

'Count Buol has written me a very friendly letter. I am pleased to be able again to enter into direct and confidential correspondence in this way with the Imperial Cabinet.

'Nothing is altered in my relations with the Austrian Cabinet. I am resolved to go hand in hand with Austria, all the more because Austria and Russia seem to be entirely at one with each other.

'With Prussia I now stand on a footing of politeness, but it is a long way to go from politeness to confidence . . .'

After going further into the reasons for this confession of political faith, in which a significant part was played by feelings of goodwill and dislike towards various persons, His Majesty went on to the Customs and Trade Union . . .

His Majesty, of course, wishes for the Austro-German Customs and Trade Union, but has not yet been able to convince himself that it is *inevitable*, if only our allies hold firm; because Prussia, without endangering to the utmost her financial and political interests, *cannot* give up the Zollverein and the bond with south Germany.

Because, then, the King is not thoroughly convinced of this, and because, from financial considerations, he is continually anxious lest he bring the Zollverein into danger through too definite pro-

---

* After Prussia had agreed to return to the Confederation of 1815, the German governments met in conference at Dresden, December 1850–March 1851, to discuss constitutional reform but reached no decisions. Austria brought her proposals for a Customs Union before the conference (see below, Doc. 36b). T.

nouncements, he is hesitant and slow to follow the way we have indicated to him.

There is one aspect of the question of the Austro-German Customs and Trade Union which should be acceptable to the King and accord with his purposes: that is, its political aspect. It is clear to him that the independence of the smaller German states will be endangered if, through the solution of the question in a Prussian sense, Austria is forced out of Germany. But to ward off this disagreeable event requires moral courage, and this the King does not possess. The fear, that the financial ruin of Württemberg must be the result of Prussia's undoubted obstinacy, is even more powerful with him [than his fear for Württemburg's independence] . . .

Document 29   Memorandum on the imperial Austro-German Customs and Trade Union by von Bruck, 30 December 1849
(Merseburg, Deutsches Zentralarchiv, AA II, Rep. 6, no. 1176)

The Imperial Austrian Government, penetrated by the conviction that the question of the Customs Union between Germany and Austria must be brought to a satisfactory solution in the interests of the permanent prosperity of states and peoples, has given serious and mature consideration to this important subject and has formulated certain principles . . . in order to open the way to a solution. As can be seen from them, there is no question of a mere commercial *rapprochement* of Austria to the German Zollverein. What is proposed is the construction, so far as is practicable, of a new, common foundation for economic relations and for the whole economy of Germany and Austria, in order to bring about the merging of their mutual interests. A mere approximation of tariffs, however desirable it has so far appeared, or a mere treaty to facilitate trans-frontier trade and to improve its supervision (to which all previous tariff negotiations between Austria and Prussia have been limited) can no longer satisfy the needs of the peoples or the urgent interests of industry and trade. The limited plans for the improvement of trade, that have so far been drawn up, do not offer sufficient scope to take all needs into account, or to make room for a lasting development of production and trade. So as not to raise those modest plans again, Austria has urgently attacked the task of *radically reforming her whole customs system*—in circumstances of great difficulty and amid the continued vibrations of the most violent political convulsions. Her final aim, clearly acknowledged and resolutely pursued, is, apart from her own prosperity, the complete association in customs and trade of herself with the whole of Germany.

In order to broach the prospective union at once and so that similar trade relations to those established within her empire may be practically applied abroad, Austria proposes that a minimum of mutual concessions be negotiated through the Customs Commission, about to be summoned, and that the following be stipulated:

(a) Mutual *duty-free* exchange, both in import and in export, of *many* home-grown *raw materials* and *foodstuffs* and of many domestic *semi-manufactured goods** provided that for the latter adequate tariff protection be obtained on the frontiers of the territory of the Customs Union against countries not belonging to it.

(b) Duty-free transit through the German states to Austria, and conversely.

(c) A radical and mutual relaxation of the military watch on the frontiers.

(d) Regulation of river navigation and reduction of river duties.

(e) Regulation of the common post, railway, telegraph, and steamship lines.

There remains, in conclusion, only one important question to discuss, namely: to whom should be entrusted the task of broaching, conducting, and concluding the work of customs unification? The simple, natural answer is suggested by the federal relationship itself. *It should be entrusted to the appropriate federal commission of the German Federal Diet.* Its competence in this most important question is certainly acknowledged in federal law . . .

The Imperial Government, moreover, acknowledges that, as always and everywhere in federated states, so in the present most important case, *voluntary action* must be foremost in accomplishing the great work of customs unification. But it is also firmly and completely confident that all German governments are ready to co-operate to the utmost of their ability and that they will therefore take these proposals at once into the most serious consideration, subjecting them to the most exact and exhaustive examination. For these proposals are directed to the creation of a firm and indissoluble bond between all German states, to the secure foundation of the prosperity of their peoples and to the inauguration of a new and wholesome situation in Germany. They are proposals without whose

---

* Schwarzenberg's original proposal of September 1849 (see above, p. 70) described five stages in which his plan might be realized. The crucial lowering of duties on *manufactured* goods was only to begin in the second stage and not be completed until final juncture with the Zollverein in the fifth stage. T.

essential realization any lasting, social, economic, and political contentment of Germany will be impossible. By contrast, if they are favourably received they will, without doubt, immeasurably increase the prosperity and strength of Germany and Austria. The best chance of compromise for differences and disputes lies in the economic field or in a conception of German policy based on economics. Here may even be found the key to any useful regulation of Austrian and German relations in general.

Document 30 E. Wächter (under-secretary in the Württemberg Foreign Office) to Handel (Austrian envoy in Stuttgart), 6 March 1850
(Vienna, Haus- Hof- und Staatsarchiv, PA II, no. 75)

... Guided by the strongest wish that the negotiations to be opened on the subject [of a Customs Union] may lead, through the sincere co-operation of all the state governments, to a firm and lasting union embracing the whole of Germany, the government here will most readily accept the prospective invitation to take part in a meeting* to be instituted to that end and, in association with the other governments participating in the Zollverein, it will make the furthering of that purpose the object of its most eager endeavour.

This government believes that it may indulge the hope that it will be able to derive the utmost profit from the harmonizing of the commercial policy (of which it has always been the spokesman in the Zollverein) with the principles indicated by the Imperial Austrian ministry as its guide-lines for the revision of the customs tariff...

Document 31 Note by Delbrück,** 6 March 1850
(Merseburg, Deutsches Zentralarchiv, Rep. 92, Nachlass Delbrück, II, 6)

In the evening from 7.30 to 8.30 with von Bruck. He was delighted to see me here. I brought a personal recommendation from Herr von der Heydt. *He:* Co-operation with von der Heydt for the welfare of the whole; I, in Austria; he, in Prussia. Allusion to the great

* Schwarzenberg had refused to negotiate with Prussia as spokesman for the Zollverein and opened negotiations with Bavaria, Württemberg, and Saxony separately. He did not want a treaty between Austria and the Zollverein. T.

** Delbrück had been sent to Vienna to negotiate on the basis that Austria must sign three treaties: with the Zollverein, with the Steuerverein and with states outside both; and that she must not negotiate separately with individual members of the Zollverein. T.

4

difficulties; once one was in a position to go forward, one had to go through with it. *I:* Compliment on his activity. *He:* Difficulties greater in Austria than in our country, where much had already been achieved; resistance on all sides. *I:* But also time in which to master the difficulties. *He:* Yes, at one time years were spent in discussion. The limits of the functions of the Minister of Trade. *I:* It is exactly the same in Prussia: Conflicts with the Ministry of Finance. *He:* Of course . . . Allusion to the political complications between Austria and Prussia. Assurance that it would be recognized that it was in the interests of Austria that Prussia should be powerful and strong against revolution from within and storms from without. One will come to terms with Prussia politically eventually, but time presses and the economic union must be pushed forward, in order to reach political union. It was from this standpoint that the proposals had gone forth. The article in the *Wiener Zeitung** had only been bait, in order to make the idea palpable to the business world. He was delighted that Prussia had shown herself acquiescent; the question of form was not within his competence. *I:* The question of form included matters of substance. *He:* Under the Tariff Treaties, Saxony and Bavaria would have to be drawn in. *I:* The distinction between Tariff Treaties and Commercial Treaties; only the latter concerned us now. *He:* In Austria we must insist that the Customs Union should be established immediately by treaty. That was said in the memorandum. *I:* But the memorandum had a new treaty in view. *He:* Yes, but new only in its detail . . . *I:* But they were the essential things. We could not have our hands tied for a long time ahead . . .

Document 32   Schwarzenberg to Prokesch-Osten (Berlin), 21 July 1850
(Merseburg, Deutsches Zentralarchiv, AA II, Rep. 6, no. 1176)

The Imperial and Royal Austrian Government has twice, on 30 December 1849 and 30 May 1850, approached all the states of Germany and in particular the Royal Prussian Cabinet. In detailed memoranda it has made plain its eagerness to conclude a Customs Union between Austria and Germany . . .

Disregarding this, the Royal Prussian Government did not find itself able to decide to acquiesce in the Austrian proposals . . .

Convinced that what is evidently of permanent truth and value will make a way for itself sooner or later, the Austrian government continues, unwearied, its efforts for the Customs Union . . .

---

* Bruck had first ventilated the idea of the Customs Union in the *Wiener Zeitung*.

All expectations are now focused upon Prussia's decision. May this memorandum contribute to turn this decision in a direction favourable to the great interests that are at stake. One ought to speak plainly here about the incalculable responsibility with which Prussia will charge herself, if she makes no response to these expectations and if she again declines to negotiate on an Austro-German Customs Union or tries to change the proposal into one for minor easements of trade. The advantages which Germany and Prussia herself may expect from such a Customs Union, cannot be too highly rated. The great market that would be opened up, the complementary industries in the several states strengthening and stimulating each other, the greater power ... intellectual unity ... similarity of interests—all will bring contentment to the various members of the German nation. Neither should it be forgotten that a moment in world history more favourable to the realization of the Austro-German Customs Union than the present is scarcely likely to occur. This is a moment when the endeavour for greater unity is so vigorously manifested that particular interests opposing it will be easily overcome, and when the events of 1848 and 1849 have brought all established things into flux and created new, malleable forms ...

Document 33   Bruck to Schwarzenberg, 16 June 1850
(Vienna, Haus- Hof- und Staatsarchiv, PA II, no. 75)

... Austria has, above all, one thing *to prevent, namely that, at the Conferences of Cassel*, the Zollverein, due to expire at the end of 1852, should be renewed before the Austro-German Customs Union is irrevocably settled on a sure foundation.* Such a renewal would bind all the German states for twelve years longer to Prussia's will in all national economic affairs. If Prussia were to see her supremacy assured for so long a time, she would scarcely be persuaded to enter the Customs Union with Austria—even though it offered the most convincing economic advantages—and to share, to that degree, her supremacy with her. The matter would, however, stand quite differently, if the renewal of the Zollverein were put in question by several of its members, or if it were made dependent upon the previous achievement of a Customs Union with Austria; for rather than endanger the intellectual and economic supremacy that she has gained through the Zollverein, Prussia would prefer an attempt to share it with Austria ...

At the Cassell tariff Conference, however, Austria has to protect other interests than the negative ones so far mentioned. She has to

* The general conference of the Zollverein states sat at Cassel from 7 July to 2 November 1850. It was interrupted by the political disorders in Hesse-Cassel and was resumed at Wiesbaden in January 1851. T.

strive that the Austro-German Customs Union shall be seriously and thoroughly discussed there; that principles, harmonizing with the Austrian proposals, shall be laid down for these discussions; and that time and place shall be fixed for a general Austro-German tariff conference; or, if this cannot be the aim, she should see that one or two of the states of the Zollverein are empowered to enter into negotiations with her in the name of the whole body . . .

In order to support this proposition, all the advantages will have to be circumstantially described. The advantages that Germany might expect from such a Customs Union would be: the moral unity which the same tariff and commercial laws, the common administration of these affairs, and an unobstructed internal economy would stimulate; closer political links; a large market; complementary industries in the various states, strengthening and stimulating each other; greater power and still greater standing abroad; the multiplication of shipping routes and a most remunerative overseas trade; finally, the satisfaction of the just wishes and expectations of the nation, to whom would be assured all the advantages of German unity without the dangerous disadvantages to particularist interests. Perhaps one might also mention that Austria herself, notwithstanding the political differences still outstanding, unreservedly offers her hand to help forward this unity, because she does not wish to withhold these advantages from the nation any longer and because she hopes to succeed through this unity in settling agitation on other matters . . .

Document 34   Undated note by Delbrück
(Merseburg, Deutsches Zentralarchiv, AA II, Rep. 6, no. 1177)

The discussions of the matter at the Conference* yielded a satisfactory result. According to the contents of the report drawn up by the plenipotentiaries . . . no inclination was anywhere shown to enter into a treaty relationship with Austria such as entailed any sort of obligation to enter a Customs Union with her. The overwhelming majority of the governments of the Zollverein unconditionally acceded to the [Prussian] proposals . . .

A glance back over the course of the discussions [with Austria] shows that right from the beginning up to the present moment the Royal Government had held on firmly to two positions and won for them the agreement of her associates in the Zollverein:

1. In any reorganization of the trade relationship between Germany and Austria, one must start from what is *legally* and de facto

---

* At Cassel, see above Doc. 33. T.

established. This reorganization can, therefore, be brought about only by negotiations between *the Zollverein as a whole*, on one side, and Austria, on the other.

2. These negotiations should have as their object, not a *Customs Union*, whether now or later, but *a commercial treaty*, albeit one drawn up on the broadest basis . . .

Document 35 Agreement between Austria and Prussia at Dresden*
(Vienna, Haus- Hof- und Staatsarchiv, PA II, no. 92)

Record of a conversation between Schwarzenberg and Mautenffel, 23 February 1851.

AUSTRIA	PRUSSIA
Agreed.	1. Both sides recognize full equality of rights in the Confederation. Without prejudice to this, Austria shall remain first in rank.
Austria proposes instead of points 2 or 3 of the Prussian proposal the following form of words: All documents on reaching the Federal Diet shall be first laid before the Austrian representative, who, after he has had them registered, shall have them sent to the Prussian representative. The latter shall have them circulated. The plenipotentiaries will be instructed to come to a confidential understanding with each other as to the handling of the documents received and the action to be taken on them. The authority of the Presi-	2. Both Great Powers shall undertake in common the direction of federal business in such a manner that it shall be conducted by the representatives of the two Parties in the Federal Diet. 3. All documents on reaching the Federal Diet shall be first laid before the Austrian representative, who having noted on them the date of arrival, shall have them sent to the Prussian representative, whereupon the latter shall have them put into the Order of Business, An understanding shall be reached between the two representatives on the handling of

* The Punctation of Olmütz, 29 November 1850, provided for a Conference of ministers at Dresden (see above, p. 46). When the proposals made there for reform failed, the states of the Erfurt Union resumed their places in the Federal Diet (12 May 1851). T.

dent for the time being to give the casting vote, in the event of an equality of votes, shall not be used by either Great Power against the other.

. . .

This is made necessary by an alteration in the Order of Business. The Imperial Cabinet is ready to support any reasonable agreement on this matter.

This shall be supported unless any serious objections are raised against it by the other members of the Confederation. The Austrian representative shall, of course, also sign in his capacity as President of the Federal Diet.

Austria proposes the following form of words for 8, 9, 10, and the concluding sentence:

8. When envoys are to be sent from the Confederation to foreign Powers the representatives of Austria and Prussia shall attempt to agree on the person to be proposed beforehand.

9. During the absence of the Austrian representative, the exercise of the office of President belongs of right to the Prussian representative. Should both the

individual matters and the conduct of proceedings in the Diet's sittings. Differences of opinion shall be decided by each of the representatives in turn, each turn to last a month. In the same way the casting vote of each in turn shall decide, whenever there is an equality of votes in the Federal Diet.

. . .

6. The representative of Austria and the representative of Prussia shall each propose to the Federal Diet the name of a secretary to take the minutes. Their nominees shall act alternately.

7. The written diplomatic correspondence between the Confederation and other countries shall be done in the following form:

The Germanic Confederation and in its name

The Imperial   The Royal
Austrian Envoy Prussian Envoy

8. When envoys are to be sent from the Confederation to foreign Powers the proposal for it shall be made in the first instance by Austria, in the second by Prussia, and thereafter by the two in alternation.

9. In the absence of the representatives of one or the other, the one present shall automatically replace the other in all his functions.

Austrian and Prussian representatives be absent, the representative of the state next in rank shall take over the presidency.

Austria and Prussia shall earnestly commend the above understanding to the acceptance of their fellow members in the Confederation.

10. Should both the Austrian and Prussian representatives be absent, the representative of the state next in rank shall take over the presidency.

Austria and Prussia engage to introduce the above agreement as a joint proposal for the discussion of federal acts and the arrangement of federal business and to support it as strongly as they are able.

Documents 36a and 36b The Customs and Trade Union with Germany

36a Schwarzenberg to Buol (Dresden),* 31 January 1851
(Vienna, Haus- Hof- und Staatsarchiv, PA II, no. 92)

... In these documents the Customs and Trade Union with Germany, which has become a political doctrine to Austria, is firmly kept as the aim to be consistently striven for. The sanction of the federal legislative authority will be claimed for the Union in principle, and the way to its realization will be sketched in its main outlines, without a binding character being ascribed, from the outset, to individual proposals.

The Imperial Cabinet cannot recommend the advancement of this affair to Your Excellency with sufficient urgency. The political importance of the economic unity of Austria with the Germanic Confederation is, incontestably, far higher than its economic importance. The occasion of the revision of the federal constitution now being undertaken, in the circumstances actually prevailing in Dresden, affords perhaps the strongest position that will ever be offered to us—strongest against the attempt to remove economic questions from the competence of the Confederation and so put them outside our influence. In Dresden the basic laws of the Confederation are to be revised. This important task will not necessarily depend upon the successful execution of the understanding over details ... With regard to economic interests, as with regard to political reorganization, the Dresden assembly has only to answer the question: what stipulations are to be adopted in the revised basic laws of the Confederation?

* Buol, later Austrian Minister President and Foreign Minister, see above, p. 48, represented Austria at the Dresden Conferences. T.

This is the question to be laid before the third commission* of the Conference: the enclosed draft of instructions contains everything necessary for an exhaustive discussion of the subject.

*36b   Instructions   for   Ministerialrath   Dr.   Hock   (Dresden),   31
    January 1851*
    (Ibid.)

1. . . . You are to proceed in full agreement with Count von Buol Schauenstein . . .

2. . . . Above all you are to work to the end that these subjects may be really thoroughly treated at the Dresden Conference, decisions taken and suitably recorded in federal laws . . .

3. The purpose of your mission is to bring into existence a Customs and Trade Union between Austria and Germany . . .

Document 37 Zimmermann (Prussian *chargé d'affaires* in
    Hanover) to Thun,** 24 January 1851
    (Ibid.)

. . . I shall give my sincere opinion. I understand very well that Austria can set out to demolish the Zollverein and that Herr von Bruck's project serves this purpose. In so far as the project loosens the Zollverein and makes the German population discontent with it as a system, I quite like and value it. But I cannot wish for its actual execution. I should prefer it to remain suspended as an ideal hovering in the German clouds. I know the subject of tariffs, from its *political* side, pretty exactly. I fear that Austria will provoke the whole of Germany against her, if she brings the big Customs Union into being; for she, no more than Prussia, can satisfy extreme economic desires. Up till now the cry, particularly from south Germany, has gone up loudly against Prussia (an outcry always strikes the man at the top) although the south-German states have received many millions from the Zollverein treasury, which they did not put into it. In the future [if the Union is made] this cry will go up against Austria—and twice or three times as loud because Austria will not give them millions for nothing in return . . .

* On Austria's initiative a federal committee had been set up, during the Dresden Conferences, to discuss trade, tariffs, navigation, and transport. T.

** Friedrich, Count von Thun, Austrian representative at the Federal Diet, 1850-2, Austrian ambassador in Berlin, 1852, and in St. Petersburg, 1859-63. T.

Document 38 Prokesch-Osten (Berlin) to Buol, 31 August 1852
(Ibid., no. 80)

. . . The strength of Prussia's position against the seven states,* who are petitioning her about the Zollverein, is made clear by her threat that, unless they conclude and sign the renewal and enlargement of the Zollverein within fourteen days, she will negotiate no further with them. That means: 'You need the Zollverein; I do not; if I am to be good enough to grant it to you, then sign my terms.' The *Kölnische Zeitung* is right in saying, 'It is very plain that a true standstill depends solely on the forbearance of Prussia.'

The illusion that they can evade the issue by an independent position between Austria and Prussia and the childish calculation that they can bring about the appearance of a breach, find their due reproof in this well-conceived Prussian answer to the ambiguous declaration from Stuttgart. What will the states do now?** Probably the ministers will come together again and will find out that they have to press in Vienna for fresh concessions, until at last nothing remains of our achievements . . .

Document 39 Chotek (Munich) to Buol, 29 October 1852
(Ibid., no. 79)

' . . . As I have said,' the Minister*** continued, 'my one anxiety is that the movement of the pro-Prussians in south-west Germany, which I have just mentioned, will be only the preliminary to a political constellation, which is not beyond the bounds of possibility.

'Everyday Prussia seems more ready to flirt with Liberal principles. All the signs in recent times point that way and she will evidently be strengthened in this direction by Britain.

'At the same time and not unconnected with this, the fear seems well-founded—as to the Berlin Cabinet's attitude towards the present position of tariff and trade affairs—that it will yield itself totally and blindly to free-trade principles. The beginning of this would naturally be accompanied by still louder British applause than that

---

* The medium-sized states, who were members of the Zollverein, Bavaria, Württemberg, Baden, the two Hessen, Saxony, and Nassau, had attended a conference on tariff and commercial questions in Vienna (January to April 1852), refused to negotiate with Prussia except as a unit, and tried to keep the way open for eventual agreement with Austria. T.

** They in fact capitulated soon afterwards. The renewal of the Zollverein was signed on 8 April 1853 after an Austro-Prussian treaty had been signed on 19 February. T.

*** Baron von Neurath, Minister of Foreign Affairs in Württemberg.

given to the political, pro-Liberal moves I have mentioned. Prussia, enclosed by all the inland countries bordering on her frontiers, would give herself out as a British entrepôt on German soil, in order to make two kinds of propaganda: in the political sphere, Liberal; in the economic, free-trade propaganda . . .'

'But what', Baron von Neurath continued, 'should our attitude be, in face of the possibilities I have mentioned, which threaten us from Berlin? The interest of the dynasty, like that of the country's prosperity, our political interests, like our true national-German interests, all imperiously demand that, in face of such a dangerous posture of affairs, we should turn away from Prussia towards Austria.

'We must gratefully yet sadly acknowledge that, when the late Prince von Schwarzenberg, whose death we deplore, deflected the question of unification to the economic field, the Imperial Austrian Court raised the true German standard in the grand sense of the word. To rally to this standard, particularly from the standpoint of maintaining our independence, we fully recognize is in the interest of us all."

Document 40 Report of the Württemberg Central Office for Industry and Trade to the Württemberg Ministry of Finance, 17 December 1851
(Stuttgart, Württembergisches Hauptstaatsarchiv, E. 222, Fach. 193, no. 1164)

. . . We have now reached a point in our most respectful recital, where the alternatives are self-evident: whether it is advisable for Württemberg to renew the Zollverein with Prussia or to strive for a Customs Union with Austria.

In our judgement there is no third course. If the state of affairs is such that a complete fusion of the two trade groups is not to bring lasting salvation for the other states, because each of the two chief Powers, on account of its particular economic and financial interests, is going to exert itself to obstruct and weaken the other's influence over the rest of the Zollverein states and, indeed, to seek to force it entirely out—then nothing remains for the other states except to take a stand likewise upon their own interests and to take their decisions from this standpoint.

In their provision for the prosperity of the other states, of which Austria and Prussia up to now have given practical proof, we find no motive for special sympathy towards one side or the other. What the renowned statesman, Pütter, said in the middle of the last century, when the Emperor requested a money contribution for 'the honour, prosperity, and progress of the whole German nation', can perhaps be applied to Austria and Prussia: 'the advantages of the Empire are specified, but ours are taken for granted.'

In making her decision on this matter Württemberg will, similarly, take her own advantage into consideration. We, on our side, are not in doubt about the course to advise between these alternatives. Württemberg's trade-route goes in the main towards the North Sea. Württemberg, Baden, and the industrial part of the state of Bavaria are connected with the North Sea by the most advantageous lines of communication. These states mainly look to that route for the sale of their industrial products to countries overseas. A breach of the tariff links with Prussia, who rules the Rhine for a long stretch on both banks, would cause the most damaging disturbance of trade. The Rhine shipping-route is, of course, free. We need not, however explain in detail how the traffic on this route, despite its freedom, could be burdened and hindered by all possible kinds of vexation from police and tax officials; how, in particular, the great timber trade from the Black Forest could be displaced and given its death blow.

So . . . during the eighteen years that the Zollverein has existed, contacts in trade have become so many and the interests of the businessmen have so interlocked with each other, that the tearing apart of these countries, which have economically grown together, would be accompanied by the most damaging effects upon industry and trade and connected with enormous losses of capital. No time could be more unsuited, moreover, for such disturbances and losses to be sustained, than just this present period, when the transition from small industry to large-scale factory manufacture is being completed and when, for that very reason, so many handicraftsmen are readily inclined to ascribe blame to the governments for the consequences of natural economic development and to demand from the governments measures of assistance which could cause the most injurious stagnation without helping the trades that have been hit.

The removal of the Austrian tariff barrier in a year or two would offer no adequate compensation for all this dislocation. In order to be able to do business successfully and on a big scale with a country hitherto shut off, the habits, the tastes, and the needs of the people of that country must be investigated, their business customs ascertained, and a knowledge of persons gained. These things cannot all be done in a hurry. A long period of years must elapse before the inhabitants of the two countries can fit in with each other's ways. But if it should really come to profit-making, Württemberg and Baden do not come in the first rank in relation to Austria, partly because they are too far from the centre of the Austrian state, and only linked by indifferent means of communication with it, and partly because countries such as, for example, Saxony, which are industrially more advanced, would quite definitely get in first—Saxony even now is the country in the Zollverein from whom, next to the Prussian Rhine Province, Württemberg has to sustain the severest competition. Württemberg has now overcome the greater part of the dangers from this foreign competition. This disadvantage would occur all over again if she were to break loose from the Zollverein . . .

Moreover, it must also be said that gradually an active trade of some significance has sprung up quite recently between the south German states, particularly Württemberg, and north Germany, particularly Prussia.

We bear in mind not only the great merchantmen going down the Rhine and the great loads of grain and milled corn going there at certain times, but also the considerable quantities of lacquered wares, of straw-plaited goods, chemicals, jewellery, and apparel, shoe-leather and leather luxury goods, and fine cutlery and especially paper despatched to Rhenish Prussia and to other provinces of Prussia too. Our considerable paper manufactures have a large sale in north Germany and could not continue without it on their present scale.

To these economic reasons for remaining in the Zollverein there is to be added a consideration of commercial politics, which certainly seems to us not unimportant—we mean the variation in the degrees of power possessed by the states it unites. Were Austria to enter the Zollverein, with her population of 38 million (not counting Parma and Modena) she would be stronger than Prussia and the other German states taken together, and more than twice as strong as the states without Prussia . . . This superiority in power would fall the more heavily in the scale, the greater Prussia's following among the Zollverein states. It could easily, therefore, happen that those states which broke away from Prussia and attached themselves to Austria would sink, in matters of commercial policy, to an appendage of that great state, without power and without influence. It is different in relation to Prussia. The medium-sized and small states of Germany . . . have a population of $15\frac{1}{2}$ million, only, therefore, half a million less than that of the whole Prussian state. The significance of the medium-sized and small states taken together will guarantee them a stronger influence on the conduct and course of the Zollverein's affairs as against Prussia than they would ever attain in union with Austria or even in union with Austria and Prussia together. Quite apart from this the great similarity of the internal situation of Prussia to that of other German states makes co-operation between them essentially easier, and Prussia finds a very cogent argument for concessions to the three south-German states in the advantages their market affords to Rhenish-Prussian and Westphalian industrial products . . .

Document 41   Extract from the *Constitutionelle Zeitung*, 9 April 1852

. . . Prussia was able to give up the Erfurt Union and return to the Federal Diet, because the Confederation of 1815 is simply an international league in which a state of Prussia's power and standing may hope to be able to assert its independence even against a majority of smaller states. Prussia, however, can never comply with the Austrian demands in commercial policy without denying the whole political position she has up to now held, and without consenting to her own 'mediatization'.* Prussia must, therefore, make it her resolve in commercial policy to maintain the Zollverein's power of free self-determination, which is independent of any Austrian veto. However painful she may find a separation from the Confederation of 1815 and the disturbance of the long-accustomed relationships in many parts of the country and branches of industry, even so in this question of political life or death, Prussia will be obliged, quite decisively, to prefer a north-German, but independent, Zollverein to a greater Customs Union dependent upon Austria . . .

Document 42   Bismarck (Frankfurt) to Manteuffel,** 15 February 1854
(O. von Bismarck, *Gesammelte Werke*, vol. i, no. 473)

. . . We are the better swimmer in both cases and to *each* [Austria and Russia] a welcome ally—as soon as we are ready to give up our isolation, such as it is, and our strict neutrality*** and when we are in a position to lay down our conditions of support; but at present it would be difficult to avoid the appearance of anxiously soliciting the association. Great crises are the weather which Prussia's growth demands—so far as we use them fearlessly, perhaps even unscrupulously. If we wish to continue to grow, we must not be afraid to stand alone with our 400,000 men, especially so long as the other states are fighting each other; and so long as we, by taking sides with each of them, shall still do better for ourselves than by an immediate and

* A technical term used in the Holy Roman Empire to describe the absorption of a small state in a larger one. T.
** Otto, Baron von Manteuffel, Prussian Minister President, 1850–8. T.
*** i.e. in the Crimean War, 1854–6, of Britain, France, and Turkey against Russia. T.

unconditional alliance with a partner so unready for war and so much without honour as Austria. In any event, the value of our support rises with the advancing complications and we shall be given more in return for it later on than now . . .

Document 43   Kabinettsorder of Frederick William IV to Minister of State and Finance Minister von Bodelschwingh, 10 May 1856
(Merseburg, Deutsches Zentralarchiv, Rep. 89H III, Deutsches Reich, no. 11, vol. iv)

. . . Austria will not hesitate to offer the smaller states a *praecipuum* [a reward in advance]. The course the south-German states will take seems scarcely in doubt—because of their leaning towards Austria and because of the exaggerated notion prevailing in south Germany of the importance of the Trieste and Danube traffic. Prussia will appear as the state by whose selfish attitude all attempts at German unification are shattered; and Austria will have attained the goal which she has sought, with all available means, since the restoration of the Federal Diet.

I declare it, therefore, a political necessity that we should proceed at once with a lowering of the Zollverein tariff on a scale that Austria will not immediately be able to imitate.

Until now we have limited ourselves, in revising the Zollverein tariff, to the alteration of single stipulations. Such piecemeal alterations always harm one interest or another without bringing any compensation and can therefore never go very far. They have in addition further disrupted our tariff system, already shaken by the alteration in the level of prices since 1818.

This course of piecemeal advance, which in our experience satisfies nobody, and is in no way suited to attain the aim now before us, must be abandoned, and a comprehensive reorganization of the tariff attempted, so that in one operation the whole tariff may be brought back to the principles established in 1818. This is the task with which I hereby charge you; I await your report upon its execution. You will leave undiscussed the question of need in individual cases; for there is no more unsound basis than this. The most important section of those interested, the consumers, have no voice in that sort of discussion and three or four producers manage to carry more weight in it than the whole nation . . .

Document 44 Bismarck (Frankfurt) to Manteuffel, 26 April 1856

(O. von Bismarck, *Gesammelte Werke*, vol. ii, no. 152, p. 138)

. . . Vienna's policy has made Germany suddenly too small for us both. So long as an honourable arrangement over the influence of each in Germany is not reached and executed, we shall both plough the same narrow furrow, and, just so long, Austria will remain the only state to whom we continually lose and from whom we *could* continually gain . . . We have . . . a great number of conflicting interests, which neither of us can give up, without renouncing the mission in which each believes for itself; they are, therefore, conflicts which cannot be peacefully unravelled by diplomatic correspondence. Even the most serious pressure from abroad, the most urgent danger to the existence of us both, could not in 1813 nor in 1849 forge this iron. German dualism has for a thousand years, off and on, settled our mutual relations by internal war, and since the time of Charles V, it has done so at regular intervals once a century. In this century, too, war alone will set the timepiece of history at its right hour.

I do not intend by this reasoning to reach the conclusion that we should immediately direct our policy to bringing about the *decision* between Austria and ourselves in as favourable circumstances as possible. I only wish to express my conviction that we shall be obliged, sooner or later, to fight Austria for our *existence* and that it does not lie in our power to evade the fight, because the course of events in Germany can have no other outcome. If this is correct, which, of course, remains more a question of faith than knowledge, then it is not possible for Prussia to take self-denial to the point where she puts her own existence at stake in order to protect the integrity of Austria—in what is in my opinion a hopeless struggle . . .*

Supposing we should be victorious against a Franco-Russian alliance, what in the end should we have fought for? For the maintenance of Austria's superiority in Germany and the pitiable constitution of the Germanic Confederation. We cannot possibly exert our last ounce of strength for that nor even set our own existence at stake for it. Were we to seek, however, in co-operation with Austria to put through alterations to the Germanic Confederation in our favour, we should fare as we did in 1815 . . . Every deceit would be practised, now as then, in order to prevent Prussia from reaching a higher standing in Germany and to keep her under the pressure of

---

* The Crimean War was over, the Treaty of Paris signed, and a Franco-Russian *rapprochement*, threatening Austria in Italy, beginning. T.

her geographical position and the unfavourable Federal Constitution . . .

In my judgement our position is, like that of one sought as partner
in an alliance, favourable so long as new political groupings do not
distinguish themselves too sharply, so long as their operation remains
diplomatic and a good understanding with the one does not involve a
breach with the others. If it came to the point when a Franco-Russian
alliance with warlike purposes was an actuality, we should not, I
think, join its opponents because we should probably be defeated;
we might be victorious, but we should have spent our blood *pour les
beaux yeux de l'Autriche et de la Diète* . . .

Document 45 Memorandum of Bismarck for Manteuffel,
March 1858
(H. Kohl, editor, *Bismarck Jahrbuch*, vol. ii, Berlin, 1894–9,
p. 129)

. . . Prussian interests completely coincide with those of most
of the members of the Confederation, apart from Austria, but not
with those of their governments. There is nothing more German than
the development of Prussian particularist interests, rightly understood. The policy of most of the governments, which are alone
represented in the Federal Diet, is opposed to ours, just because the
existence and effective operation of the 33 governments outside
Prussia and Austria, is the main legal obstacle to the strong evolution
of Germany. Prussia would, therefore, be in no way disloyal to her
German mission, but on the contrary would regain the opportunity
to fulfil it, if she ceased to attach any considerable value to the
sympathies of the *governments* of the medium-sized states. All endeavours to win *them* over will always be fruitless and cause nothing
but loss of time and energy . . .

. . . Moreover, experience leaves no doubt that complaisance and
assurances of friendship are not the means whereby Prussia may
succeed in living in a friendly, let alone secure, relationship with
Austria. Neither goodwill, nor gratitude for concessions, nor sympathy as between fellow countrymen, nor indeed, any feelings at
all determine Austria's policy. Her interests bid her combat and
diminish Prussia's standing in Germany, so far as it lies within her
power, and yet in the event of war, and against the multiplicity of
the dangers surrounding her, these same interests demand that she
should be able to count on Prussia's full power for support. In this
twofold need of Austria lies the only means for Prussia to put herself
on a clear and sure footing with the south-German Great Power.
Meanwhile each cabinet assures the other almost weekly of friendly

disposition as a fellow-member of the Confederation and of its mutual goodwill . . .

The result of correspondence of this kind is as a rule only to increase resentment and mistrust . . .

The relations of the two German Great Powers to each other would assume a different shape, if Prussia took the decision to put them back on simple, bare principles of mutual self-interest free from the conventional admixture of false expressions of feeling. This would come about if Prussia were to declare to Austria that, given the Confederation's present constitution and the political tendency of the majority of its members, she would limit her participation to the strict execution of her clear obligations; that beyond this she would refuse to co-operate with the Confederation; and any concession to the majority and to its President she would certainly decline . . .*

Document 46 Merck to Ruperti,** 8 October 1859
(Staatsarchiv, Hamburg, 622–1. Nachlass Merck II, 4. Konv. 3)

. . . The weather is magnificent and the wine harvest good. The people are very well off in this neighbourhood, but their mood is bad. Preparations are being made in Germany which will certainly lead to bloodshed between Prussia and Austria. A great, united Germany may be a fine dream, but whether the prize is worth the bloodshed I cannot say. For us older people certainly not . . .

Document 47 Koller (Berlin) to Rechberg,*** 23 June 1859
(Vienna, Haus- Hof- und Staatsarchiv, PA III, no. 66)

. . . Baron von Schleinitz**** must, in my judgement, at this moment find himself perplexed and in a dilemma.

He knows that his plan to play a European role through the peace negotiations***** is meeting with no response from the Imperial [Austrian] Cabinet. On one hand, he must be saying to himself that

---

* The draft breaks off here in the original in the middle of a side.
** K. H. Merck, merchant banker of Hamburg, and Justus Ruperti, merchant banker. T.
*** Johann Bernhard, Count von Rechberg und Rothenlöwen (1806–99), Austrian Foreign Minister, 1859–64. T.
**** Alexander, Baron von Schleinitz (1807–85), Prussian Foreign Minister, 1858–61. T.
***** Prussia offered mediation between Austria and France in northern Italy on 11 June but insisted on co-operation with Britain and Russia. She began to mobilize on 14 June. Peace Preliminaries between Austria and France were signed at Villafranca on 11 July 1859 after Austria's defeat at Solferino on 24 June. T.

with the deployment of the Prussian army on the Main and the Rhine a long armistice will be intolerable and, on the other hand, he cannot reconcile himself to crossing the Rubicon and shrinks from the idea of it. He would like to make Prussia's independence felt, but allows himself to be crippled in action by considerations put forward by Britain and Russia. He will enter upon no binding declaration towards Austria, so that it should not be said that he had been 'taken in tow', and yet—because the present point in time seems favourable for Prussia to play a part as a Great Power and a part in the Germanic Confederation—he feels the need of an alliance. He is unable to welcome the armistice on account of his military measures —though he wants no rash step—and vacillates in uncertainty, from which he hopes to be rescued by a decisive battle in Italy— whether Austria wins or loses—and he will then step forward at the peace negotiations. Prussia's mobilization serves, in his own words, *pour avoir voix au chapitre* [to give her a finger in the pie] . . .

Document 48 The Eisenach Declaration of the German National Union (*Nationalverein*), August 1859
(W. Mommsen, *Deutsche Parteiprogramme*, Munich, 1960, p. 131)

The present dangerous situation of Europe and of Germany and the need to subordinate the demands of political parties to the great common task of German unification, have brought together from the various German states a number of men, some of them belonging to the democratic party, some to the constitutional party, for the purpose of coming to an understanding about the establishment of a constitution for united Germany and about the necessary common course of action for the attainment of that aim. They have agreed on the following points:

1. In the present position of the world we see great dangers threatening the independence of our German Fatherland—these are increased rather than diminished by the peace just concluded between France and Austria.

2. These dangers have their ultimate origin in the faulty constitution of Germany and they can be countered only by a speedy alteration of it.

3. For this purpose it is necessary that the German Federal Diet should be replaced by a firm, strong, permanent central government and that a German national assembly should be summoned.

4. In the present circumstances effective steps for the attainment of this aim can originate only with Prussia. We shall, therefore, work to the end that Prussia may take the initiative.

5. Should Germany in the immediate future be again directly threatened from outside, the command of her military forces and her diplomatic representation abroad shall be transferred to Prussia pending a definitive constitution of the German central government.

6. It is the duty of every German to support the Prussian government according to his strength, in so far as its exertions are based upon the assumption that the tasks of the Prussian state and the tasks and needs of Germany coincide in essentials and in so far as it directs its activity to the introduction of a strong, free constitution for the whole of Germany.

7. We expect all patriots in the German Fatherland, whether they belong to the democratic or to the constitutional party, to place national independence and unity above party demands and to work together in harmony and perseverence for the attainment of a strong constitution for Germany.

Document 49 Koller (Berlin) to Rechberg, 27 October 1859
(*Die Auswärtige Politik Preussens*, vol. i, no. 535, p. 814)

... In the attitude which Prussia as a German Power ... has recently observed, the Liberal direction of the present Cabinet is as unmistakable as a red streak. The evident purpose to which its endeavour is directed consists in this: to set Prussia up as the shield of a blossoming Liberalism to which the future in Germany belongs; to defeat the influence of Austria in this way by a political theory; and to enlarge her own moral influence and, if the opportunity occurs, her material power—perhaps without any anxious regard for legal right. In this connection the saying that 'the Kingdom of Prussia's skin is too tight for it' rings as true as the genuine Prussian wish: 'If we only had a Frederick the Great!' ...

Since the Italian campaign the newspapers and the temper of the people show a malicious spirit against Austria. It is as if by their fits of anger they wished to stifle their sense of the injustice that has been done to true German interests ...

Document 50 The Prince Regent William to Schleinitz, 26 March 1860
(Ibid., vol. ii, part 1, no. 117, p. 263)

The Council in its sitting today under my chairmanship determined to set out clearly the present position of Europe and to survey Prussia's policy in relation to it, to see how it should be shaped in the future. All were agreed that France, with its unpredictable

Emperor, was the Power that was the source of danger to Europe, Germany, and Prussia . . . The nearest ally to whom we have to look is obviously Germany. She is as much affected by France's hankering after the left bank of the Rhine as Prussia and, because of her obligations to the Confederation, as much bound to ward off a hostile attack upon the Prussian Rhine Province as Prussia is to ward off a similar attack upon the Rhenish Palatinate.* At first sight, it seems obvious that Prussia need make no special exertions in this direction, since federal help is reciprocal. Almost all Germany for the last forty years has, however, cherished a hostile spirit against Prussia, and for a year this has been decidedly on the increase. One must admit, therefore, the sad possibility that south Germany at any rate may seek to preserve its neutrality by means of separate negotiations with France, so that Prussia may be left to endure the struggle alone, and be defeated, whereupon the spectral fear that she is out to devour Germany would be laid for a long time to come. It is a matter, then, of finding ways and means to put an end to German animosity against Prussia. By virtue of Prussia's superiority in moral and physical power, this would be easy if Austria, as our antagonist with her own enmity to us, were not also the moving spirit of German opposition. She could be as ready as the rest of Germany to leave her federal obligations unfulfilled, in the event of an attack upon Rhenish Prussia. The necessity, therefore, arises that we should enter into an understanding with Austria such as would make such an extreme eventuality impossible.

Agreement on this prevailed in the Council. Two decidedly different views, however, prevailed about the means to this end. The Minister von Schleinitz developed the view that, since he, with the whole Council, recognized France as the source of danger, any intimate connection with her in order to improve Prussia's position in Germany must be repudiated. Nothing then remained but to give up our hitherto sharp opposition to Austria and Germany, especially in the Federal Diet (though this must not be done with éclat), and then to bring about a defensive alliance with Austria. After this it would automatically follow that Germany would go closely hand in hand with her two Great Powers . . .

The remaining members of the Council declared themselves, for the reasons adduced above, against such an alliance and also against any alteration of Prussia's German policy. Some even urged that Prussia's German policy should be taken to its logical conclusion, that she should not jib at a breach between subjects and governments. (I declared myself most decidedly against this extreme

* Part of Bavaria. T.

course, for I will never play a part in Germany such as that played by
Victor Emmanuel in Italy. This extreme was therefore set aside.)

Since I, in general, acceded to this point of view, I give the following directive for our future policy: we shall continue to follow a course
in the Federal Diet, calculated to keep the Diet within its legal limits
or to bring it back to them. We must sedulously endeavour to take
our stand on the basis of law . . . If we do that, it is quite unnecessary
to enter a special alliance with Austria for German purposes. Should
Austria request an alliance for non-German purposes, it should not
be discussed, until she actually faces an enemy that she is unable to
withstand alone . . .

Documents 51a and 51b   The Force of Circumstances

51a   Koller (Berlin) to Rechberg, 22 July 1859
   (*Die Auswärtige Politik Preussens*, vol. i, no. 502, p. 762)

The force of circumstances at the moment deflects Prussia from
her own specific interests and obliges her to manifest inclinations
for an understanding with Austria. If the exploitation of these
is not delayed too long, it can bring results in things of both great
and less importance, as, for example, in the possible handling of the
question of federal reform which, in normal circumstances, would
not be so quickly brought to fruition . . .

51b   Ladenberg (Munich) to Schleinitz, 9 November 1861
   (Ibid., vol. ii, part 2, no. 419, p. 490)

. . . King Max, his Minister for Foreign Affairs, his representative
at the Federal Diet, his immediate circle, the majority of Bavarian
statesmen, the most eager *grossdeutsch* agitators in the Bavarian
Parliament, are all enthusiastic for the Triad idea or at least for
a plan which will give Bavaria a special position of power in Germany
. . . Bavaria desires to group the medium-sized German states round
herself and to negotiate with Prussia and Austria as the third independent force, counted equal with them in Germany . . . The
Bavarian government will be strengthened in its projects, and especially in withstanding the demands of Prussia, by the temper prevailing
throughout the whole country. No description can do justice to the
antipathy to Prussia prevailing in Bavaria, especially in the Old
Bavarian Provinces. The same spirit of hostility to Prussia prevails
in the upper and lower classes and I am bound to say in the former
almost more than in the latter. Bavarian newspapers exercise the
greatest and most damaging influence in this connection . . . This
picture is a gloomy one, but according to my most conscientious

conviction, completely true and well-founded. There is no sympathy for Prussia in Bavaria, but although we are not liked, thanks to the organization of our Prussian army, another feeling which the South Germans had to some extent lost has again taken hold, that is, respect for Prussia. Despite all Bavaria's hatred for Prussia, despite all her particularist selfishness, if a danger of war from France loomed up tomorrow in Germany, she would certainly be ready to let herself be protected by Prussia and to trust herself unreservedly to Prussia's leadership.

Document 52 Beust's memorandum on Federal Reform, 15 October 1861
(F. F. Graf von Beust, *Aus drei Vierteljahrhunderten*, Stuttgart, 1887, vol. i, p. 291)

... [In federal reform] one must above all keep in mind the character of what is already established and accordingly must remember that the Germanic Confederation is a league of states. There have been many attempts to set up a German federal state [a United States of Germany] yet, from this standpoint, the question whether it is at all possible will always be answered in the negative. This is because of the simple consideration that to set up a federal state would be tantamount to dissolving the Confederation. It is sufficient to draw attention to the fact that the defenders of this idea have only been able to think of its realization in terms of a single leadership in the hands of one Great Power. Quite apart from doubt whether the states, jointly placed under this leadership, would submit to it, the withdrawal of the other Great Power from the Confederation would certainly follow. Nor can anyone, who looks at things with open eyes, be in doubt that the wider league [with Austria] which is part of this plan, could be nothing but an alliance treaty whose duration and execution would, like that of every other political alliance, remain dependent on changing circumstances.

This simple consideration is the foundation of the standpoint, that every attempt at reform that does not take the league of states* as its starting point is impracticable.

The proposal, therefore, of a Parliament arising from direct, universal and popular election is impracticable. Such a national representative assembly, which according to its mandate, would know nothing of the individual federated states, cannot be an institution integrated into a league of states, without either dissolving the league or being dissolved by it. This is the lesson of the years 1848

---

* i. e. as opposed to the United States of Germany. T.

and 1849. The first alternative was intended, the outcome was the second. There is no place for this idea, then, in a plan of federal reform. The idea of a single central government is also impracticable ... For the same reasons, a supreme army command, permanently in one hand, and an exclusive diplomatic representation abroad would seem equally impracticable. These ideas, therefore, do not belong either to the area of federal reform.

Is this to ascribe the character of an absolutely wretched, spiritless thing to the league of states? Is the league of states, to which Germany owes the finest flowering of her cultural life, of her economy, and her prosperity, completely incapable of satisfying the needs of the national sense of community and the development of national power? Surely not. It is only that one does not wish to attain at *one stroke* what must be the work of patient and persistent co-operation and will surely succeed that way ...

Draft Reforms

(a) The Federal Assembly is composed of representatives of the German governments ...

The Federal Assembly meets twice a year, on 1 May and 1 November, for a period of four weeks at the longest. The holding of the meetings takes place, alternately in a city of south and in a city of north Germany (Regensburg and Hamburg). In the first Austria presides and in the second Prussia ...

(b) The Assembly of Representatives is formed from representatives of the Parliaments of the states; Austria sends 30 members, drawn from the several representative bodies of her German provinces; Prussia, 30 members, chosen from the two Houses of her *Landtag;* Bavaria, 10, chosen from the two Houses of her Parliament: Saxony, Hanover, Württemberg, each 6 ... Total, 128 ...

The Assembly of Representatives does not meet regularly. It may only be summoned by the Federal Assembly ...

In the intervals between the meetings of the Federal Assembly, a Federal Executive Power comes into operation. This Executive Power the Confederation places in the hands of Their Majesties the Emperor of Austria, the King of Prussia, and a third Prince of the Confederation, who act as plenipotentiaries for all the remaining states ...

The Executive Power is endowed with the full power of the Confederation for the event of the occurrence of extra-ordinary political crises ...

Document 53 Roggenbach's* memorandum on Federal Reform, 28 January 1862
(*Europäischer Geschichtskalender*, 3rd year, 1862, ed. H. Schulthess, 1863, p. 22)

... First it is our view—and we are supported by the clearest demands of our population and well justified by our most sacred duties—that *the federal unity to be established should not be exclusive and unconditional, but that it should be one within which the independence and sovereignty of the several existing federal states should continue undisturbed over the whole area of domestic legislation and administration* ...

We believe that just because we propose to limit centralization to the *narrowest* area, where there are only common interests and no division into opposing interests, we must be the more rigorous when it comes to establishing the functions and competence of the institutions to which this area is to be entrusted. There must always be enough centralization *to make possible a united, personal, and responsible government* whose executive power meets no obstacle in organizing action, so that it may be in a position to carry through a political plan backed by the whole force of the nation and with all possible assistance from its several parts. However high a value we set on the representation of the states, *we must exclude all federal activity at the topmost level*, or the participation of a college of princes, acting on instructions and without its own power of decision or the capacity to pursue plans already determined. On the other hand, an energetic central government need not prevent the collaboration, in a way the constitution will have to define, of the federal government from being claimed wherever circumstances admit of it. *The only means and the one most apt* for this purpose of *equalizing the interests of the individual states with those of the whole, is the summoning of an adequate assembly, representing the population as well as the governments of the individual states.* It must have within its constitutional competence the power to grant supplies to the central government and hence the power to control effectively this, the highest authority ...

Document 54 Report of debate in the Prussian Lower House, 4 March 1861
(Vienna, Haus- Hof- und Staatsarchiv, PA III, no. 72)

The Member Wagener: ... We are not of the opinion that the established order is incapable of improvement. On the contrary. But we hold that the unity of Germany, as it ought to be striven for, can

* Franz, Baron von Roggenbach (1825–1907), Badenese Liberal Minister for Foriegn Affairs. T.

be established only with the co-operation of the German princes and
through their agency. The method that is now being recommended
to us has been used once before. It caused a fiasco on that occasion
and we are offered no guarantee that the result will be any better
this time . . . From those very circles which made the earlier, illusory
experiment comes the same agitation as before. You will make a
mistake if you judge the temper of the times by the after-dinner
speeches of the 'commercial travellers' of the *Nationalverein* (dissent
from the Right). The German princes will not go voluntarily,
nor will you drive them out. Face to face with the *Nationalverein*'s
aspirations, it is timely to speak too of the German Federal Army
contingents and their loyalty to the German princes. The roots which
the imperial authority of Austria has struck, over the centuries, in
Germany are much too deep to be torn up by a vote of the Prussian
Lower House. We hold federalism to be the only legitimate means to
unify Germany . . .

The Member Vincke-Hagen: It was news to him that the Prussian-
German way to unification had already been a fiasco. This way
had never yet been attempted by the Prussian government. . . . 'If
the Minister for the Interior, who today represents the Foreign
Office (laughter), is regrettably going to repeat the phrase "co-
operation with Austria", then I must reiterate: Austria is not German. She has only 7 million Germans out of 35 million inhabitants.
To go hand in hand with Austria is to co-operate with 28 million
Slavs and others. When Member Wagener called our attention
to General Benedek, he cannot have taken into consideration that
he is a Hungarian. I do not understand how, after the most recent
Austrian constitution,* anyone can still recommend co-operation with
Austria . . . We must urge that each German government observe
a national attitude and that the efforts of each be directed towards
protecting the frontier . . . Whole-hearted sympathy for Prussia
will never be aroused unless we can bring it about that nowhere,
in any respect, does one have it so good as in Prussia' (applause).
That would be as it were the 'egg of Columbus' . . . To promote this
initiative is the affair of both the dynasty and the whole people. If
this is neglected, everything will remain as it has always been; what
will then become of our state defies calculation. He who does not
take time by the forelock, may expect time to pass him by (applause).

* The constitution of 1849 (see above, p. 66) had been revoked on 31 December
1850. Provincial Diets and the *Reichsrat*, partly composed of delegates from them,
still existed. The latter was modified by the October Diploma in 1860 and most
recently by the February Patent (24 February 1861). The tendency of the changes
was to satisfy Czechs and Hungarians rather than Germans. T.

The Minister of the Interior: . . . The Government's policy is not one based on speculative contingencies; it is a fixed, positive, and realist policy, which takes into consideration what at each moment answers to the interests of Prussia and the related interests of Germany. We shall go hand in hand with Austria so long as it is convenient for us and the interests of Prussia demand it and make it desirable. We wish to make Prussia strong internally, so that she can meet the possible dangers threatening from abroad—I guard myself against speaking of precise, immediate dangers. In times like the present, Germany must be on the watch and she can only be so if she co-operates with Austria. I was delighted, therefore, to welcome Austria's [constitutional] development. I understand the 'policy of the free hand' to mean that Prussia holds aloof from foreign transactions and is ready to act when her own interests are at stake . . .

The Member Beseler: We wish to see Prussia as strong as possible in and with Germany. If that is a pro-French policy, then we take the responsibility for being pro-French (Bravo!). We shall not let ourselves be guided by mere sympathies, and shall cast them away—when it is in our interest to do so—whether they direct us to the Rhine or to the Danube. We do not begrudge Austria her rights, but we ask Austria in return not to begrudge us ours. A united Germany is more advantageous to Austria than one struggling for unity. A meeting of princes, such as the Member Wagener wants, is synonymous with mediatization* or absolutism. We want nothing to do with either . . . Away with these fantasies when such universal historical realities are at stake (Bravo! from the right)!

Document 55   Károlyi (Berlin) to Rechberg, 16 March 1861 (Vienna, Haus- Hof- und Staatsarchiv, PA III, no. 72)

. . . The kernel of the situation is contained in the question: 'Will Prussia take the higher standing ground and perceive that if we hold faithfully together, we can look all dangers calmly in the face; or, will she consider this the right moment to secure for herself a place in Germany at Austria's expense?' . . .

I cannot entirely banish the fears that I have permitted myself to amplify in my full report—fears indicating possible attempts to smuggle, so to speak, the seed of certain political concessions into the defensive treaty. Baron von Schleinitz again mentioned an alternating Presidency for the Confederation, particularly in our last conversation, when he appealed to the contents of the Teplitz conversations;** he indicated this point as a difficulty still to be

----

* See above, p. 87, note *.   ** See Introduction, p. 52.

solved before the conclusion of the treaty. I at once most clearly opposed this point of view and referred to His Majesty the Emperor's minute, which plainly expressed refusal of any such concession to Prussia. In arguing for his point of view the Minister, on his side, adduced the letter of the King from Ostend, in which 'it is firmly hoped that the two governments may succeed in finding a *form* for the solution of this question which, without too much trespassing on Austria's dignity, does not leave the wishes of Prussia unregarded, in so far as they are justified by the nature of the situation' . . .

In face of the revival of this old stumbling block, I held it to be my duty to make it quite clear to the Minister that if he had the conclusion of the treaty at heart, he must at once check the emergence of any idea running in that direction; since I had not the slightest doubt that the Imperial Cabinet would not agree to it and to bring forward such a demand would, therefore, inevitably cause the whole affair to fall to the ground . . .

Document 56 Usedom* to Bernstorff, 15 November 1861
(*Die Auswärtige Politik Preussens*, vol. ii, part 2, no. 419, p. 489, note 4)

. . . I replied: I could not find any great interest in such intellectual games,** with no real force behind them. If I know with certainty that nothing will come of a project, it is a matter of complete indifference to me whether it has been described in one way or in another. Baron Beust's present proposals are cleverly made, in so far as they take into account all the different standpoints and seek to press a bribe into everybody's hand. Political centralization, the Triad, division into two, alternating Presidency, National Parliament, Conferences of Ministers, what has existed up to now and what is to come in the future—everything, or at least a fraction of each thing, is to figure in his plan. It is precisely this which makes the thing as useless as it is impossible. The pressure from all sides for national unity has only one rational purpose: to give the Fatherland more strength against foreign states through unified concentration. Such a complicated piece of machinery as Beust suggests will not afford this strength; anyhow in great matters only what is simple is realizable . . .

* Guido, Count von Usedom, is reporting a conversation with von der Pfordten. Usedom was Prussian representative in the Federal Diet, 1859–63, Minister to united Italy from 1863. Pfordten was Bavarian Minister President. T.
** An allusion to Beust's plans of federal reform.

Document 57   Protocol for alliance between Austria and the medium-sized states against Prussia, 29 January 1862 (Darmstadt, Staatsarchiv, Staatsministerium, Konv. 46, Fasc. 3)

In consideration of the ever more threatening posture of affairs in Europe, and particularly in Germany, the undersigned: the Imperial and Royal Minister and Envoy, Count von Blome, entrusted with an extraordinary mission to the Royal Württemberg Court by His Majesty the Emperor of Austria, and Baron von Hügel, the Royal Württemberg Minister of the Royal Household and of Foreign Affairs, in the name of their Exalted Monarchs, have set out the following views and proposals as guide-lines for the common attitude of their governments in the immediate future:

1. The Imperial and Royal Government [of Austria] and the Royal Government of Württemberg will agree to no project for the reform of the Confederation which would exclude Austria from the bonds of the common German constitution and subject the rest of the German princes to any one member of the Confederation. They will consent neither to the foundation of a parliamentary German federal state under unitary direction nor to any other arrangement whereby the diplomatic and military leadership in the non-Austrian part of Germany would be transferred to any single member of the Confederation. They adhere to the preservation of Austria's position and the equality of Württemberg and of the other big states in the Confederation as the condition of any reform of the federal constitution. The two Governments will, therefore, also oppose any proposal by which the diplomatic and military leadership of the federal states would be shared between any two federal governments.

2. The Imperial Austrian and the Royal Württemberg Governments consider it, in the present circumstances, advisable to make proposals on their side, in the matter of federal reform, only if the initiative is taken in this question by another federal state with a project of the kind indicated as inadmissible in clause 1.

3. If such a case should arise, Austria would send out invitations to a ministerial conference. This would meet, even if some federal governments did not take part in it. The following drafts would be brought as proposals before it, but the signatories reserve a closer understanding on their form for the future:

(a) a draft plan to establish a permanent federal executive;
(b) a draft plan for the co-operation of an assembly, composed

of delegates from the federal states, in the enactment of legislation for common German affairs;

(c) a draft plan to establish a federal court;

(d) a draft plan for the extension of the federal system of defence to the non-German possessions of Austria and Prussia.

4. If, as a result of efforts to reform the Confederation or of a refusal to recognize constitutionally valid decisions of the Confederation, a split should occur within it, or if individual members should resign from it, Austria and Württemberg, in agreement with the other federal governments, shall adhere to the federal treaty [of 1815] as long as possible and aim at the restoration of the Confederation in its entirety; but, if it should prove necessary, shall regulate their mutual relations so as to safeguard their independence, autonomy, and free self-determination in the spirit of the federal treaties.

5. In the event of an attack upon Austria in Italy, the Government of Württemberg will contemplate all means of support for the Imperial Government, compatible with neutrality, assuming that there is no occasion for taking the common measures of defence provided for in the basic law of the Confederation. Should France come to the assistance of the Italians, the Government of Württemberg, faithful to its prescribed attitude, will make every effort to bring the Federal Diet to consider such an attack as a threat to Germany according to the terms of article 47 of the Vienna Final Act* and accordingly to take such measures as seem suitable and desirable in the light of the ensuing course of events. The Government of Württemberg will exert itself to support Austria in the conflict and thereby to protect the interests of Germany.

6. The two Governments will, through their envoys in Berlin, present identic notes [to Prussia] in which they will indicate that the plan for the reform of the Germanic Confederation, elaborated in Count Bernstorff's despatch to the Prussian envoy in Dresden of the 20th December, is incompatible with the basic law and forms of the Confederation. The notes will also express a confident expectation that the Royal Prussian Government will give the plan no further consideration.

The two Governments will invite the Governments of Saxony, Hanover, the two Hessen, Brunswick, and Nassau to adhere to this declaration by means of identic notes.

Signed, Blome
Signed, von Hügel

---

* Of 15 May 1820. It was drawn up at a ministerial conference of the German states under Metternich's influence and elaborated, in a restrictive sense, the federal constitution of 1815. T.

Baron von Dalwigk declares, in the name of His Royal Highness the Grand Duke of Hesse, that the Grandducal Hessian Government is in agreement with the principles laid down in the above protocol, and accedes to the agreement contained in it.

Signed, von Dalwigk
Signed, Blome.

Document 58 Bernstorff to Werther (Vienna), 12 February 1862

(*Die Auswärtige Politik Preussens*, vol. ii, part 2, no. 443, p. 575)

We too answer these notes in identic form.

We can see in these measures of the Vienna Cabinet nothing beyond a political move of doubtful value. It is difficult to take seriously prospective negotiations for reform on the principle proposed at the end of the identic notes of 2 February, when one knows how far the views of the cabinets of Darmstadt, Stuttgart, Munich, Nassau, and particularly Hanover diverge from each other on the subjects of the executive and of a national representative assembly, and what reserves have hitherto prevailed in the Vienna Cabinet itself on the solution of these questions. We shall await the outcome of the discussions the more calmly, if the conferences actually take place and we shall willingly leave to the participating governments the unenviable task of making such proposals for federal reform as are acceptable to the others . . .

Documents 59a and 59b The reform of the Federal Constitution

59a   Reuss* (Paris) to Bernstorff, 10 February 1862
(Ibid., note 5, p. 577)

. . . I believed I could use the opportunity to question the Minister confidentially next about the French government's views on German affairs. I said that I must assume at the outset that France could not see with any pleasure German efforts for unification. M. Thouvenel answered that France was very little concerned with what was going on in Germany [in the margin: ?!] because she knew perfectly well that the least intervention of France in the internal affairs of Germany would bring the most heterogeneous elements into immediate unity against her . . . The relations of Prussia with France, although not always intimate, had always been good and France had never had

* Heinrich VII, Prince Reuss, Prussian secretary of legation in Paris, 1854–63. T.

cause to complain of Prussia. Moreover, Prussia, rather than Austria, was called to represent the German idea and he did not understand, therefore, how the medium-sized states, who so readily brought forward notions of German unification, could attach themselves to Austria . . .

59b Bismarck to William I, 1 March 1862
(O. von Bismarck, *Gesammelte Werke*, vol. iii, no. 282, p. 332)

My German colleagues* have received instructions to communicate in confidence to the cabinet of this country the identic notes addressed to Your Majesty's Government on the subject of federal reform; and to take its opinion. As far as I have learnt, partly from Prince Gortchakow** and partly from some of the envoys of the governments concerned, the Imperial [French] Minister has not concealed from their representatives his displeasure at the proceedings of those German governments. He submitted to their consideration the fact that because of the internal condition of Austria, the basis of Germany's power and security rested wholly upon Prussia and that the small German states could not refuse to take this into account, unless they were ready to run the risk of becoming puppets on the European stage without the necessary strength to meet the requirements of the plot . . .

Document 60   Karnicky (Cassel) to Rechberg, 25 April 1862
(Vienna, Haus- Hof- und Staatsarchiv, PA VII, no. 81)

. . . Opinion in this country, now, alas, under the Liberal party, who are setting the tone, is decidedly in favour of the conclusion of the treaty. It sees in it both commercial and political advantages —to be derived from the more intimate connection with Prussia. For that reason most of the industrialists of the country, in reply to the inquiry, addressed to them by the Government last autumn, stated that they were not afraid of French competition and must therefore declare themselves in favour of the lowering of customs duties and the maximum of free trade, which would open the French market to their products.

As far as the Government of this country is concerned, there are many reasons for its hesitation. There are reasons both of an economic and a political nature, which make accession to the contemplated Franco-Prussian treaty seem hazardous. The iron industries,

---

* i.e. the envoys of the other German states at Paris, where Bismarck was Prussian ambassador in 1862. T.
** The Russian ambassador. T.

controlled by Cassel, which will suffer damage from French competition, especially arouse its anxiety. It is, however, the political
side of the treaty that must weigh most in the balance and hold the
Government back from over-hasty decisions. In the present circumstances there is, on one side, the fear of antagonizing Prussia; on the
other, the consciousness of belonging together with her within the
confines of the Zollverein. This feeling is so important and any
dissolution of the latter is considered likely to bring such damage
upon this country, that the Government is very perplexed over this
urgent decision. A hasty declaration of accession on the part of
Electoral Saxony [?sc. Hesse] does not seem impossible . . .

Document 61   The foundation programme of the *Fortschrittspartei*, June 1861
(W. Mommsen, *Deutsche Parteiprogramme*, Munich, 1960, p.
133)

November of this year will see the end of the legislative period
of the present [Prussian] Lower House. At some time during the
course of the year, therefore, the whole nation will be called upon to
re-elect its deputies. The urgent seriousness of the times, our Fatherland's uncertain position in foreign relations, the domestic difficulties
with which the present Lower House has not shown itself competent
to deal, these all, as never before, oblige every Prussian, entitled to
vote, to a conscientious and fearless implementation of his political
conviction by the exercise of his right. In order to discharge this
duty and to give a firm focus in the coming elections to those fellow
citizens who are of the same persuasion as ourselves, we now set out
the following political principles, on which our campaign will be
conducted.

We are united in our loyalty to the King and in the firm conviction
that the constitution is the indissoluble bond which holds Prince and
people together.

As a result of the great and far-reaching changes that have taken
place in the European state-system, we are equally clear that
Prussia's existence and greatness depend upon a firm unification
of Germany, which cannot be conceived without a strong Central
Executive Power in the hands of Prussia or without a common
German representative assembly.

For our domestic institutions we demand a firm Liberal government, which sees its strength in the observance of the constitutional
rights of the citizens, which understands how to make its principles
relentlessly observed by all classes of the official world and which,

by doing so, will win and maintain the esteem of the other German peoples for us.

In legislation the strict and consistent realization of the constitutional *Rechtsstaat* appears to us a prime necessity without qualification . . .

The unexpectedly heavy burdens which were laid upon the country during the last legislative period unconditionally demand that the country's economic forces should at the same time be set free. A revision of industrial legislation, such as has already been formulated in the resolutions of the present Lower House, must, therefore, be enacted.

If these blessings have to be preserved or attained by war, for the honour and power of our Fatherland no sacrifice will ever be too great. But for the sake of the sustained pursuit of such a war, the greatest economy in the peace-time military budget seems to us essential. We are convinced that the maintenance of the militia, the general introduction of physical training for the young, increased conscription of men capable of bearing arms, the two-year period of service—all these offer a guarantee that the Prussian people in arms will be fully qualified for war.

It must be abundantly clear to the most near-sighted, after the history of the last three years, that the attainment of these aims will remain a pious hope so long as a thorough reform of the present Upper House has not been achieved. This objective above all must be energetically pursued as the beginning of all other reforms.

We call upon all those who share our views to elect men who have the principles of the German *Fortschritt* [Progressive] Party close to their hearts, men whose character and attitude to life guarantee that they will acknowledge these principles openly in the Lower House and not let themselves be led astray by considerations of any kind.

Document 62   The programme of the Prussian *Volksverein*, 1861 (W. Mommsen, *Deutsche Parteiprogramme*, Munich, 1960, p. 45)

The undersigned, who hereby constitute themselves the Prussian *Volksverein* [People's Union], proclaim their intention of influencing the coming elections in their favour, and further, of creating for all like-minded men in the Prussian people a focus and an organ for the period after the elections—thereby offering a hand to like-minded men in the wider German Fatherland. They have meanwhile agreed with one mind and one voice upon the following main points:

5

1. Unity of our German Fatherland, yet not *like the Kingdom of Italy by blood and fire*, but *by* the *union of our princes and peoples* and by holding firm to authority and right. No betrayal of our Prussian Fatherland, and its glorious history. *No decline into the dirt of a German republic. No theft of crowns and cheats of nationality.*

2. No break with the past internally within our state. No abandonment of its Christian foundation and the elements of our constitution tested by history. No disturbance of the centre of gravity of our European position by a weakening of the army. No parliamentary rule and no ministerial responsibility established by a constitution. Personal royal rule by divine and not by constitutional right. Church marriages, Christian schools, Christian authority. No abetting of the ever wider-spreading depravity and disregard of the divine and human order.

3. Protection and proper regard for honourable work, for all property, all rights, and all classes. No favour for, or exclusive domination by, money wealth. No surrender of the artisans or landowners to the mistaken doctrines and profit-earning arts of the day. Freedom of the King's subjects to participate in legislation and in the autonomy and self-government of corporations and parishes. Freedom in the maintenance of the protective forces of order. No movement in the direction of bureaucratic absolutism and social slavery by means of a limitless and undisciplined anarchy; nor towards the imitation of the political and social organization which has led France to 'Caesarism'. The development of our constitution in the direction of German freedom, in love and loyalty to King and Fatherland.

Document 63 Károlyi (Berlin) to Rechberg, 22 March 1862 (Vienna, Haus- Hof- und Staatsarchiv, PA III, no. 75)

When one surveys the phases through which Prussian domestic politics have passed since the beginning of the ministerial crisis, one's observations on these matters relate partly to the resignation of the previous ministry and partly to the governmental tendencies, decisive for the immediate future, underlying the newly formed Cabinet . . .

Concerning the new direction the Prussian government is to take—I have already hinted at it to some extent; it consists in reconciliation with moderate Conservatism—the maintenance of an Upper House supporting the government—an attempt to obtain as favourable an outcome of the elections as possible by the influence, so far as is legitimate, of government officials . . .

If, nevertheless, the elections do not succeed (which is, alas, probable, because the number of Schwerin's* liberalizing measures over the last three years has in many ways undermined the reputation of federal officials who are still Conservative)—if they do not succeed the Lower House will be dissolved again, according to the programme now fixed, and a new electoral law enacted by decree.

Even in the political course on which he has by now embarked, the King is willing to attempt to carry on the government with loyal, independent men, attached to *him* personally and to no one else, men of moderately Conservative tendency but energetic character. He is willing to derive as much profit as possible from those in the country still of a 'monarchical' persuasion in order to protect and hold firm the inalienable rights of the Crown against the invasion of democracy. He will attempt to do this without a *coup d'état*, or at least by avoiding any proceeding violating the constitution as a whole, to which he has sworn loyalty. He will seek a form of state dependent on a representative Parliament, and the maintenance of freedom—yet freedom distinct from that of the Manteuffel régime . . .

In every circumstance the new phase can be considered an incontestably better course for the future. The evident resolution to make a stand against the flood of constitutional democracy lies behind it. If democracy is suppressed inside Prussia, its damaging influence on the rest of Germany will also be crippled . . .

Document 64 Rechberg to the Austrian envoys in Frankfurt, Stuttgart, Munich, and Dresden, 26 April 1862
(Ibid., PA IV, no. 30)

As Your Excellency will gather from today's despatch on the subject of the French commercial treaty, the Imperial Government has already considered the eventualities which will result, for itself and for the Zollverein states from the acceptance or, conversely, from the rejection of that treaty . . .

From the political standpoint, moreover, it is evident that a change, even accompanied by dangers and sacrifices, is preferable for Austria to complete isolation in face of a close, exclusive economic union of the rest of Germany under Prussian leadership. It will be necessary, then, for the governments to work against such a turn of things and indefatigably to hold off the accruing political dangers. In addition, public opinion must be stirred up, especially in those classes of society who care little, or not at all, for the continuation

---

* Maximilian, Count von Schwerin-Putzar (1804–72), Prussian Minister of the Interior, 1859–62. T.

of independent governments in the individual states. It must be constantly reiterated in the Press that politically the exclusion of Austria from Germany, far from encouraging the ideal of national unity, will stamp it as a lie and, at the worst, will have the effect of splitting or totally dissolving it . . .

Document 65 Rechberg's memorandum on *Mitteleuropa*, 10 July 1862
(Vienna, Haus- Hof- und Staatsarchiv, PA III, no, 79; also at Merseburg, Deutsches Zentralarchiv, AA II, Rep. 6, no. 1194)

. . . On the basis of careful consideration and investigation the Imperial Government, penetrated by this knowledge, has decided to propose to the governments of the German Zollverein the conclusion of a preliminary treaty for the foundation of a Trade and Customs Union embracing both the Austrian Empire and the Zollverein. The principle of its proposal consists in complete mutual freedom of trade and communications, limited only by the measures made necessary by the variety of systems of internal taxation and the need to maintain state monopolies. In order to make this great league possible, Austria declares herself ready to adopt the Zollverein's tariff and institutions in so far as the Zollverein will not combine with her in a timely revision . . .

While we address to our fellow members of the Confederation the proposal elaborated in more detail in these documents, we permit ourselves to hope that they will see therein an instrument, offered at some cost to ourselves, for the conclusion of closer ties between Austria and the states of the Zollverein instead of the threatened dissolution of the present ones; and that they will see in it a means towards the final attainment, in the field of economic interests, of the unification of the whole of Germany that has been so long our goal. What we offer is only the fulfilment of what Austria, Prussia and the other states of the Zollverein solemnly declared, by the treaty of 19 February 1853,* to be the aim of their common endeavour. It is well known that the Royal Prussian Court has indicated the fact of a general economic progress and the need to associate herself with it, as the motive for her negotiation with France. Nor do we fail to understand the influence of that fact. Our proposal, too, will do justice to that need in fullest measure. Our offer is equally directed to the high purpose of preserving German *national* interests— the very purpose that the Zollverein treaties have expressly placed at the head of their stipulations . . .

* Renewing the Zollverein, see above, p. 83, note **.

Document 66 Bernstorff to Werther (Vienna), 25 September
1862
(*Die Auswärtige Politik Preussens*, vol. ii, part 2, no. 493,
p. 757)

. . . Count Rechberg has too much penetration to be able to believe
that the war which he is waging against us both on the political and
on the commercial field, although it appears to have been initially
successful, will oblige us to abandon our standpoint and to go over
to the uncertain Austrian position. He is too precisely acquainted
with the exact political, financial, and economic position of present-
day Austria and knows too surely that it is not hidden from us, to
reckon on the sustained operation of the present false attitude of
some of the German governments and of public opinion in south
Germany or to connect with it the hope of lasting success.

He may delude himself about the effect of our present domestic
difficulties upon our differences with Austria. Yet here too it is
hard to mistake the truth. Whatever turn the crisis, caused by
the strong feeling of the Opposition in the present Lower House, may
take, in no event will it bring us closer to another view of the un-
restrained hostility to Prussia in which Austria is at present indulging.
As far as our commercial policy is immediately concerned, there
exists among us no difference of opinion worth taking into account
as to the cold and inconsiderate way in which Austria is acting. She
is endangering our interests through her aggression instead of
protecting hers, in conjunction with ours, after previous agreement
with us. Should Austria wish in fact for what is constructive and
possible, particularly for the further amplification and development
of the offer made in the treaty of 1853 (to which, in any event, a
welcoming response is desirable from us), she has gone sadly wrong
in the choice of her present means which can only disturb and
prevent such a wholesome development rather than prepare or
further it. In essentials, exactly the same is true of the purely political
field. If Austria wishes to have in us, on any hypothesis, a willing
partner in the counsels of the European Powers and a companion in
arms in a European war, she must put an end to her agitation
against us and her suspicion of us. She must make up her mind to
clear existing difficulties out of the way in co-operation with us,
instead of ceaselessly increasing them by constantly sowing fresh,
groundless mistrust. She must begin not only to respect our equality
of status and essential equality of rights, but to acknowledge them
and to act accordingly. On such preliminary conditions, but only
so, *we are ready*, as we have always been, *for an understanding* and we
believe we are not mistaken in saying that the gain from such an

understanding would *at least* be as much on the Austrian side as on ours and that further persistence of the present quarrel must become *injurious to the whole of Germany* . . .

Documents 67a, 67b, and 67c   To govern without a budget

67a   Sir A. Malet to Lord Russell, 28 May 1862
   (London, Public Record Office, F.O.30/201)

   . . . Monsieur de Bismarck might be described as 1mo Prussian, 2do through and through Prussian and 3° German through Prussian!

   It may perhaps serve usefully to characterize this Gentleman, if I state to Your Lordship my entire conviction of his high honour and integrity,—that he has a great, perhaps undue contempt of public opinion,—and hardly less of German liberalism and its Leaders,—that he is frank to the verge of imprudence, in expressing his opinions—and has extraordinary command of temper. I think however that scarcely any considerations would weigh with him against the perspective of a territorial rounding off, for Prussia, which is the object of his life, and political aspirations, and it is on this account, that his position at Paris might, in certain contingencies, become fraught with danger to the peace of Europe . . .

67b   From Max von Forckenbeck's diary, 24 September 1862
   (W. Bussmann, *Bismarck im Urteil der Zeitgenossen und der Nachwelt*, Stuttgart, 1956, p. 28)

   . . . The name Bismarck-Schönhausen signifies: to govern without a budget, to rule by the sword at home and to wage war abroad. I consider him a minister most dangerous for Prussia's freedom and prosperity . . .

67c   Speech of Bismarck in the Prussian Lower House, 27 January 1863
   O. von Bismarck, *Gesammelte Werke*, vol. x, p. 153)

   Bismarck: . . . In this address rights are claimed for the Lower House which it either does not possess at all or shares [with the King and Upper House]. If you, gentlemen, by your decision alone, had the right to fix the budget finally in its sum total and in its details; the right to request from His Majesty the King the dismissal of ministers, who did not have your confidence; the right to fix the size and organization of the army by means of your decisions over the state's expenditure; the right, which you do not have according to the constitution, but claim in the address, to control definitively the relations between the state's executive power and its officials—if you had these rights you would in fact be in possession of full power to govern this country. Your address rests on the basis of these claims, if it has any basis at all. I believe, therefore, that I can characterize its practical significance in a few words. This address requires that the royal Hohenzollern House should surrender its constitutional right to govern and transfer it to the majority of this House of Parliament. You invest this demand with the form of a declaration that the constitution is violated when the Crown and the Upper House do not conform to your will. Your reproach of having violated the constitution is directed against the Ministry, not against the Crown, whose loyalty to the constitution you put beyond all doubt. In the sitting of the committee I guarded myself against this very distinction. You know as well as anyone in Prussia, that the Ministry acts in Prussia in the name of, and at the behest of, His Majesty the King and that it put through these very acts of government, in which you claim to see a violation of the constitution, in his name and at his behest. You know that in this connection a Prussian Ministry is differently placed from an English one. An English Ministry, whatever it is called, is a Parliamentary Ministry, a Ministry drawn from the majority in Parliament; but we are the Ministers of His Majesty the King . . .

You find the ground for the violation of the constitution specifically in Article 99. Article 99 runs, if I remember the words: 'All income and expenditure of the state must for each year be proposed in advance and set out in the state budget'. If this were followed by the words: 'which is annually fixed by the Lower House', you would be completely right in the grievances you state in the address, and the constitution would have been violated. But there follows in the text: 'this (the budget), will be fixed annually by means of a law'. Article 62 states with unanswerable clarity how a law is enacted. It says, that for the enactment of a law, for the budget law as for any other, the concurrence of the Crown and the two Houses of Parliament is required. The article, moreover, mentions particularly that the Upper House is entitled to reject a budget decided upon by the Lower House but not agreeable to itself.

Each of these three concurrent rights is in theory unlimited, and each is as strong as the others. The constitution lacks any stipulation as to which of them shall give way, if no agreement is reached between the three powers . . . The constitution then refers to compromise as the way to an understanding. A statesman, experienced in constitutional government, has said that life under a constitution is at any time a series of compromises. If the effort to reach compromise is made fruitless by one of the participating powers seeking to carry its point of view with doctrinaire absolutism, then the series of compromises is interrupted and in its place conflict enters, and because the life of the state cannot stand still, conflicts become questions of power. He who has power in his hands goes forward in his chosen direction, because the life of the state cannot stand still even for one moment . . . You expect the Crown to give way; we expect you to do so . . . It is no new discovery that there is a gap here in the constitution. I myself was present at the transactions for the revision of the constitution. We occupied ourselves for several days in an extremely thorough way with this very possibility which now, after thirteen years, has become an actuality for the first time . . . Theories have been put forward as to the correct procedure, if no budget is enacted; but I will not go into an appreciation of them here. Some say that the previous year's budget, *eo ipso*, continues valid if no new one is enacted; others say, because of the *horror vacui* innate in the law, that gaps not covered by new law are filled according to old law . . . so that, with us, the complete power of absolutism would again have to prevail if there was no state budget. I shall not pursue this theory any further. It is enough for me that the state must exist and that it must not, whatever happens, through an outlook of pessimism, allow the situation to reach the critical point where the flow of money stops . . .

Documents 68a and 68b   The Nation is leaving us in the lurch

68a   Speech of J. Miquel* to the first General Assembly of the Nationalverein, *3 to 5 September 1860*
(W. Mommsen, *J. Miquel*, Berlin, Stuttgart, 1928, vol. ii, p. 190)

. . . [Miquel] then declared: 'We are members of a union [the *Nationalverein*] that does no more than make preparations, without possessing any real power; that seeks only to mould the mind of the nation, and has to set its hopes on the future . . . We have no ability to tell what shock will have to be administered if we are to achieve unity—that is, whether it will be through the help of Prussia, through revolution, or through [the spontaneous action of] public opinion.'

The task of the *Nationalverein* is 'to cause the fruit to ripen for the moment which must surely come'. The main thing is not the

---

* Johannes von Miquel (1828–1901) prominent in the foundation of the National Union (see above, Doc. 48), Prussian Finance Minister, 1890–1901. T.

programme, but that the *Nationalverein* should remain united and push forward its endeavours for national unity . . .

68b   Max Duncker to August von Saucken,* 16 June 1863
(J. Schultze, editor, *Max v. Duncker, Politischer Briefwechsel aus seinem Nachlass*, Stuttgart, 1923, p. 352)

. . . I know that the present mood is bitter and that its sharp point is directed against the person of the King. It is as much so in Berlin as it is where you are. I deny, however, that it threatens the dynasty. The position of our dynasty, which created our state, is different from that of Louis XVIII or Charles X whom our bayonets restored to the throne of France. It is different from that of the Stuarts, who did not make England, but were imported from Scotland and tried to recatholicize that ardently Protestant country . . . You told me yourself that your peasants are loyal to the dynasty. Vincke writes the same from Silesia and I have no doubt that things in Saxony, in the Mark and Pomerania, lie the same way.

You know, from your direct experience of it, how foolish the policy of the *Fortschritt* Party is and how immature the whole method and aim of the Opposition are and you have bitterly deplored this to me. You have always been, as I am, of opinion that a skilful ministry would do the state a service if it declared to this Party: 'Gentlemen, you can't do it that way.' I deplore, as much as you do, that opposition should be entrusted to those in whose hands it is at present, but we cannot shut our eyes to the fact that these very men have succeeded in laying bare the unsteadiness of the movement, now made much of by the Press. Herr Gneist says: 'We are on the horns of a dilemma; the Press having whipped us there, now deserts us.' The gentlemen of the *Nationalzeitung* says: 'The nation is leaving us in the lurch as in 1848.' . . .

Document 69 Bismarck's confidential statement before the Budget Commission, end of September 1862
(E. Brandenburg and P. Rühlmann, editors, *Quellensammlung für den Geschichtlichen Unterricht an höheren Schulen*, Leipzig, Berlin, 1913, p. 4)

. . . Germany looks not to Prussia's Liberalism, but to her power. Bavaria, Württemberg, and Baden may indulge in Liberalism: but Prussia's role is not for them. Prussia must concentrate her

---

* Both Duncker and Saucken were Liberal members of the Prussian Lower House. T.

strength and hold it together for the favourable moment, which has already once passed us by. Prussia's frontiers, as fixed by the Treaties of Vienna, do not favour a healthy political existence. The questions of the day will not be decided by speeches and majority decisions—that was the mistake of 1848 and 1849—but by blood and iron . . .

Document 70   Thun (Berlin)* to Rechberg, 5 January 1863 (Vienna, Haus- Hof- und Staatsarchiv, PA III, no. 83)

. . . I must begin by saying that Herr von Bismarck received me in the most friendly way, I may even say in the warmest way. In his attitude, as in his words, there was not the slightest trace of irritation or strong emotion to be observed. On the contrary, it seemed to me that he had set himself as his main task to moderate as much as possible the unfavourable impression of certain expressions and, without yielding anything in principle or altering his standpoint, to appear as conciliatory as possible in his assertions when expounding the special position of Prussia in Germany and deducing the necessary consequences for the future. He seemed to dwell less than before on 'blood and iron' . . .

No one more than he [Bismarck] considered a true union of Austria and Prussia as the political ideal. The wellbeing of Germany would then be secured, the alliance with Russia as good as concluded and even that with England or France,—yes, perhaps with both—put beyond all doubt. But for such a union the position of each partner must be made comfortable and desirable. It was pertinent to this too that Austria should not continually seek the alliance of the small and medium-sized states—even that of Anhalt-Dessau (this was said humorously)—in every possible way, to the disadvantage of Prussia. Austria must choose, once and for all, between Prussia and Hanover . . .

As for the chances and dangers of a war with France—he should be spared a discussion of that, first because there was no immediate prospect of it, second because they had *the means of restraining France* from it . . .

Herr von Bismarck said: 'I am quite inaccessible to this emotional policy of sentiment; I have no sense of German *nationality;* for me a war against the King of Bavaria or the King of Hanover (he might just as well have said the Emperor of Austria) is just as serious as one against France' . . .

In conclusion he continued: 'And you must give up the idea of a Customs Union. That can lead nowhere.' To my question: 'But why

* Thun had known Bismarck in the Federal Diet 1850–2, see above, p. 82, note **, and had called on him on his way through Berlin from St. Petersburg. T.

not?' he said: 'You might as well make a Zollverein with the whole world.' So speak the defenders of free trade when Germany unity is in question . . .

Document 71   Promemoria by Bismarck, 25 December 1862
(*Die Auswärtige Politik Preussens*, vol. iii, no. 86, p. 136)

. . . I consider it a fixed principle that we shall not renew the Zollverein as *at present* constituted; for the right of disagreement of each individual member cripples commercial legislation as long as the treaties last. The reforms, which are in themselves necessary in the Zollverein, are most closely connected with our needs and aspirations in the area of *German policy*. In the present constitution of the Confederation, there is no point of departure in this area answering to Prussian interests. It has caused the federal relationship to become not a source of strength, but of paralysis for the power and significance of Prussia. The viability and security of the Confederation rest in the main upon Prussia, whereas *we* derive no equivalent advantage from the federal relationship, such as could compensate us for our being bound to it and for our defencelessness, owing to the federal treaties, against the intrigues of our enemies within it. In the event of war, the support of *Prussia* is decisive and to be relied on by the other members of the Confederation; but *theirs* for us is weak and uncertain . . .

The advantages of the federal relationship for Prussia are by all *anti-Prussian* organs wilfully overrated, and our own German feeling explains the ease with which we let ourselves be persuaded that the existence of Prussia would be endangered if she gave up the claim, *theoretically* grounded on the federal treaties, to the support of the other German states.

Conversely, I believe that I do not go too far in asserting that it would be one of the most fortunate occurrences for us if we could free ourselves from the net of the federal treaties. If the Confederation did not exist, the natural relations of Prussia to her less powerful neighbours would spontaneously evolve after the manner of those of Austria to the small Italian states some time ago . . .

Prussia, from the time of Frederick William I to the year 1815, undoubtedly carried more weight in European questions than now. I cannot ascribe this phenomenon exclusively to the personality of Frederick the Great, but rather seek its origin essentially in the circumstance that Prussia's being bound by the federal treaties and her partial merging of her own policy in the policy of the Federal Diet, led by Austria and her other enemies, have substantially impaired her significance as a European Power. The alliance of the

German *Reich* [i.e. the Holy Roman Empire before 1806] was too loose to exercise an analogous influence . . .

There is no doubt that the weight which lies within the Prussian state, whether the Germanic Confederation continues to exist or not, can only be brought fully to bear *by its side* or *outside* it. All Prussia's aspirations in the area of German policy tacitly take this premiss as their point of departure. The road to their realization has been opened by the Zollverein. This institution, upon which the common customs system of its members rests, would afford in the present circumstances the most effectual basis for the common handling of the economic and eventually of the political interests of the German states. The judgement of His Majesty the King will determine the time when a programme in this sense can be published. But we cannot long postpone . . . coming forward. Even if the Zollverein remains, as up to now, appointed only to be the vehicle for the customs system, we cannot, as already mentioned, retain it as at present constituted. The alterations to be undertaken, whatever specific form they may take, must aim at introducing *majority* decisions binding on the minority and at establishing an *assembly representative* of the peoples of the Zollverein states. To this assembly would fall the task of mediating in the disagreements between the governments and of replacing the need to gain the agreement of all the Parliaments in the individual states. One can foresee that proposals of this kind from Prussia will meet lively resistance from many of the Zollverein governments. This resistance is not likely to be broken, except by excluding those who take part in it from the new Zollverein which we shall establish.

I believe I can take it for granted that our action must be essentially directed to realizing our intentions, as far as possible, for the period after 1 January 1866, without letting ourselves be deluded by apparent successes in the interval. This interval will in all circumstances be filled by diplomatic conflicts over the shaping of the period following 1865. In these conflicts Prussia's position will be strong in proportion as our treaty relationship to France appears lastingly assured or irrefragable.

The commercial system to be created by the treaties of France with England, Belgium, Prussia, and Switzerland has a significance which makes it almost impossible for the majority of the Zollverein states not to adhere to it eventually . . .

Document 72   Bismarck to Werther (Vienna), 9 April 1863
(Merseburg, Deutsches Zentralarchiv, AA II, Rep. 6, no.
1195)

... I have drawn the attention of the Imperial [Austrian] ambassador (who fully acknowledges, as I do, the great importance of trust and sincerity between our respective Cabinets) to the fact that friendly relations between us cannot be attained more easily, or be more securely safeguarded, than by striving first of all for similarity of views and aspirations in the *purely political* field. I said that an understanding here could be reached without impairing the independent development, which each state is obliged to assure to the special and established interests of its subjects in the economic field. I observed that to mix the two matters—to transfer commercial and industrial interests to the political field or contrariwise—might make a sincere understanding more difficult. Such an understanding in one field alone could be extremely easily attained, without the same prospect being temporarily or permanently offered in the other field ...

Document 73   Bismarck to Werther (Vienna), 28 April 1863
(O. von Bismarck, *Gesammelte Werke*, vol. iv, no. 79, p. 114)

... I turn next to commercial policy. Count Rechberg draws special attention to Austria's having acquired a right by the commercial treaty to enter tariff negotiations with the Zollverein states individually and to our refusing the exercise of this right. I must reject the accusation ... Moreover, she [Prussia] adheres to her repeatedly expressed view that the entry of the Imperial state [Austria] into the Zollverein is for both sides, in practice, unrealizable. Neither this view nor other considerations, however, preclude us from believing a considerable *rapprochement* to be possible, in commercial policy, between Austria and the Zollverein. We see no hindrance to such a *rapprochement* in our treaty with France. On the contrary, we believe that on the basis of that treaty, further reliefs and stimulation could very reasonably be afforded to trade with Austria ... As far as the purely political field is concerned, I fully share Count Rechberg's regret at the divergence of views, which has prevailed for years between the two Cabinets on many important questions of domestic federal policy, and I should welcome an understanding about them as in everybody's interest ...

Documents 74a, 74b, and 74c   The Congress of Princes

74a   Prussia's reply to Austria's invitation to the Fürstentag *in Frankfurt, 1863*
(Ibid., no. 109, p. 151)

The Emperor of Austria has invited His Majesty the King on the 16th instant to an assembly of German sovereigns in Frankfurt-am-Main to deliberate on the reform of the Confederation. His Majesty considers preliminary conferences of ministers more practicable and would agree to them. His Majesty, however, declines the aforesaid invitation to the assembly of sovereigns in Frankfurt-am-Main . . .

74b   Holograph letter of Bismarck to Thile,* 4 August 1863
(Ibid., no. 110, p. 151)

Enclosed is His Majesty the King's reply, which goes to Vienna today, to the Emperor's invitation to Frankfurt, the official report of which I will send tomorrow. Without waiting for the second document, the first is to be communicated as quickly as possible to our legations in Germany . . . We shall be silent, as long as Austria is. If Vienna publishes the news, then our public line must be that the Congress of Princes is impracticable and that *consultative* delegates to the Confederation are insufficient and that we favour *directly* elected representatives instead of delegates.

74c   Telegram of Bismarck to the Ministry for Foreign Affairs, 9 August 1863
(Ibid., no. 111, p. 151)

The Congress of Princes must not be taken tragically by our Press; rather [it must be taken] as a contrivance for the celebration of the Emperor's birthday; an over-hasty move in the style of the identic notes; but no officious** resentment against Austria; the predictable results to be discussed with well-disposed scepticism.

* Karl Hermann von Thile, Under Secretary of the Prussian Foreign Ministry. T.

** The diplomatic jargon of the day expressed degrees of formality with the words 'official', 'officious', and 'unofficial'. T.

Document 75 Election address from a joint assembly of the Prussian *Volksverein* and the *Patriotische Vereinigung*, 15 September 1863*

(W. Mommsen, *Deutsche Parteiprogramme*, Munich, 1960, p. 47)

The dissolution of the Lower House, has placed us once again before the voting urns. Neither Party motives nor Party purposes have determined us to enter the electoral struggle afresh. We follow the call of His Majesty the King and we obey it with all the loyalty and devotion which our duty as subjects and the seriousness of the situation require . . .

We are, moreover, confident that among the majority of our people Prussian patriotism is stronger than the arts of an unpatriotic democracy . . .

Let us hold firm, therefore, to all that His Majesty the King wishes to see protected and maintained as his inherited and constitutional prerogative, in particular to his position as Commander-in-Chief of the army of his people. Let us hold firm to the position of power which Prussia enjoys in Germany, which, since it was the fruit of the blood and sweat of our fathers, cannot be impaired by the attempts of misguided foreign statesmen. Let us hold firm to the strength and prestige of our army, which is Germany's sword and Prussia's brazen wall. Let us hold firm to right at home and abroad and enter the electoral fight with the design of vindicating, for friends and foes alike, the view that it was not just for appearance's sake that we lately celebrated the memory of the great deeds of our fathers.

Since the days of Frederick the Great, Prussia has never been content to be second of the two first Powers in Germany. She must always be the first.

Document 76 Minutes of the preliminary deliberations by the plenipotentiaries of Bavaria, Hanover, Württemberg, the two Hessen and Nassau on the renewal of the Zollverein Treaties, 12 October 1863

(*Die Auswärtige Politik Preussens*, vol. v, no. 540, p. 802)

The plenipotentiaries of the above-named Governments, who have met here today at the invitation of the Royal Bavarian Government, have recorded the result of their discussions and their views in the present Minute, which shall be laid before their Governments for further consideration and for decision.

* The German original misdates this document. T.

1. Several plenipotentiaries expressed their conviction that the maintenance of the Zollverein should remain the steadfast aim for which their Governments should strive . . .

In order not to surrender this high interest and to safeguard the prospective extension of the Zollverein to the rest of the German states, the assembled commissaries considered it desirable to oppose to the Prussian proposal (with reference to the Zollverein's character as an institution established for all Germany and to the central stipulations of the treaty), a motion for the immediate opening of negotiations with Austria on the basis of her proposition of 10 July 1862 [see Doc. 65]. They considered it further desirable for the Governments here represented to speak for, or to support, this motion in the most conciliatory way, but yet with the utmost exactitude and clarity . . .

5. If the motion, . . . thus acknowledged to be necessary, should meet decided resistance from the other Governments of the Zollverein; or if the Berlin negotiation should fail to attain the aim acknowledged in paragraph 1 as that of their common endeavour— the decision as to their further action was reserved for the Governments here represented, but the hope was expressed that they would be ready to allow deliberation in regard to the most practicable understanding over their future common procedure to take place elsewhere . . .

Documents 77a and 77b   Austria *and* Prussia

77a   Kalchberg to Rechberg, 6/7 October 1863*
(Vienna, Haus- Hof- und Staatsarchiv, PA IV, no. 31)

. . . Sympathy is felt for us. As far as wishes go, it is Austria *and* Prussia, but Austria pushed a little aside; yet should it be a question of Austria *or* Prussia—and how easily, indeed how probable it is, that it will come to this—then there will be *sincere* regrets and sorrow, but Prussia's standard will, nonetheless, be followed . . .

77b   Kalchberg to Rechberg, 8 October 1863
(Ibid.)

. . . Hesse-Cassel, whose plenipotentiary, however, is to express himself in rather colourless language, will go with Hanover. Darmstadt and Nassau, at least their Governments, seem certain [to support Austria], although much sympathy for Prussia prevails there, among the population and in the Civil Service, because of the agitation of the *Nationalverein*. . . .

---

* Head of section in the Austrian Ministry of Trade. T.

Document 78 Circular despatch of Bismarck to the Prussian envoys at the German Courts, 29 November 1863
(O. von Bismarck, *Gesammelte Werke,* vol. iv, no. 174, p. 220)

... The position of the Imperial Austrian and Royal Prussian Governments is fixed by the treaty which both, in common with France, Great Britain, Russia, and Sweden, concluded with the Crown of Denmark on 8 May 1852 in London, after preliminary terms* had been determined in discussions with Denmark during the year 1851–2. Both Governments consider these agreements, taken together, an inseparable whole to which the London Treaty provided the concluding piece. Now that the event, which this treaty envisaged, has actually occurred, both Governments are ready to execute the treaty, if the Crown of Denmark on its side carries out the preliminary terms of 1851–2. Their implementation formed the condition precedent of the signature of the London Treaty by Austria and Prussia ...

Document 79 Philippsborn** to Bismarck, 29 February 1864
(*Die Auswärtige Politik Preussens,* vol. v, no. 549, p. 818)

I respectfully inform Your Excellency that we have had another sitting of the Customs Conference today.

Bavaria has now modified her motion, so that she is ready to join at once in deliberations with us on the tariff. Thus she has *given up* her insistence on preliminary negotiations with Austria.

In the same way, Württemberg, though making more fuss about it, has drawn even *closer* to our position.

Hesse-Cassel has quite come over *to our side,* accepts our tariff, accepts the French treaty, but wishes in connection with the latter, that we should make the attempt we have ourselves offered to make in Paris, and has agreed that negotiations with Austria shall only take place after it. Hesse-Cassel reserves the right not to give her final decision until she has surveyed the matter as a whole. Thus *Hesse-Cassel has separated herself from Hanover*—as her plenipotentiary tells me in confidence—because the Elector [of Hesse] has seen, from the last Hanoverian declaration, that Hanover thinks only of her *praecipium* [reward] which until now he had not wished to believe. From now on the conferences will make progress. The current is favourable.

---

* The reference is to promises made by Denmark to the Austrian and Prussian governments to gain the sanction of the Estates of Holstein before the enactment of a constitutional settlement in the Elbe Duchies. T.

** Director of the commercial policy section of the Prussian Foreign Office. T.

Document 80   Promemoria of the Prussian Finance Ministry
and the Prussian Ministry of Trade, 9 March 1864
(Merseburg, Deutsches Zentralarchiv, AA II, Rep. 6, no.
1195)

... Our present commercial interests, the starting-point of our
commercial policy, may be summed up: the maintenance of the
Zollverein's autonomy, the execution of the treaties with France,
... and the introduction of such reliefs in trade with Austria as are
compatible with these premisses and with our financial interests.

The maintenance of the Zollverein's autonomy excludes the
Customs Union with Austria, even in its modified form ...

Prussia cannot accept the propositions of 10 July 1862; nor
can she renounce the execution of her treaties with France. She
is not only formally bound by these treaties—and the present
political situation particularly indicates that she would do well
to observe the obligation she has contracted—but she must always
recognize in them the expression of the commercial policy which
meets her interests ...

It is obvious that Prussia cannot, without denying the principle
itself, make a basic exception to it in favour of the Imperial Austrian
state, that is, of a state with more than two-thirds of her territory and
almost two-thirds of her population outside Germany ... The
more decidedly the [free trade] movement grips [Austria], the easier
will her understanding with the Zollverein be ...

Signed by Bodelschwingh and Itzenplitz;* given by Bismarck on
10 March to the negotiator in Prague, Geheimen Finanzrath
Hasselbach.

Document 81   Report of Rechberg to Francis Joseph, May
1864
(Vienna, Haus- Hof- und Staatsarchiv, Administrativ
Registratur F 34 SR 3r8, Karton 40)

The negotiations, which Your Majesty's Government has conducted for fully two years, to prevent the Franco-Prussian commercial treaty from applying to the whole area of the Zollverein
and to avert from Austria the disadvantageous consequences of
permanent exclusion from all share in guiding Germany's commercial policy, have reached the point when I must respectfully beg
the favour of a decision as to Austria's further commercial policy
at home and abroad.

* Ministers respectively of Finance and Trade. T.

First, so far as relations abroad, that is with the governments of the Zollverein states, are concerned, Prussia, in spite of her political relations with Austria, which are friendly, has deliberately continued to proceed in such a way as to make it impossible for the Imperial Government ever to realize the Customs Union, which by the treaty of February 1853* was set as Austria's and Prussia's common aim. Prussia has already significant results to show along this path . . . Despite its lack of reciprocity, the French commercial treaty has silenced all opposition in Prussia itself and, by its approach to the free trade system of the western Powers, has clearly won favour for itself in the Kingdom of Saxony and the Thuringian states, in Brunswick and Oldenburg. Moreover, the temper of the Parliaments in the medium-sized and southern states, in Bavaria, Württemberg, both Hessen, Nassau, etc., has quite turned in favour of the treaty and the maintenance of the Zollverein despite it. It is only the governments in the last-named states and still more their princes personally who, for political reasons and in order to counteract the sole dominance of Prussia in economic matters, continue their opposition and seek support from Austria. Hanover and Hesse-Cassel still offer for this reason to persevere in opposition . . . It is the only resistance north of the Main. Prussia does not owe these great successes only to her progressive industrialists and to their consciousness that they can stand up to competition from abroad. She owes them too to the consistency and single-minded direction with which the Berlin Cabinet, whether Liberal or Conservative statesmen hold the rudder, steadily uses the implementation and extension of the Zollverein as the foundation and guide-line for Prussian power in Germany and thoroughly exploits it against Austria. Finally the correctness of the economic principles, which have guided Prussian commercial policy, has very substantially contributed to her successes. It has been a policy of breaking free from artificial assistance to protect particular branches of industry, and has favoured the free exchange of the products of the soil and of manufacturing industry in natural competition.

These principles . . . have latterly made further progress in Austria too . . . Unfortunately the present Austrian draft tariff appears, to most of the governments friendly to us, still insufficient in its lowering of duties and approach to the system of the Franco-Prussian commercial treaty. These governments desire a further considerable reduction of duties to make it possible for them and for us to prove to Prussia that no economic barrier lies in the way of a German-Austrian Customs Union and that, therefore, only unjustifiable political

* The treaty of alliance, see above, p. 83, note **. T.

motives dictate her wish at all costs to exclude Austria from participation in the Zollverein and from leadership of the economic interests of Germany.

Document 82   Bismarck to Werther (Vienna), 14 June 1864 (*Die Auswärtige Politik Preussens*, vol. v, no. 147, p. 220)

. . . *We consider the Danish conflict as essentially an episode in the fight of the monarchic principle against European revolution. We take our rule of conduct in handling the Duchies' problem from our appreciation of its effect upon that great question of the day. If the good understanding between the monarchs of Prussia and Austria and their active energy can satisfy justifiable national needs, that is, those felt by the respectable sections of the nation, the revolution will be deprived of the pretexts from which it draws its strength. From the outset the present Prussian Government has been guided by this conviction in its handling of the Danish question.* Up to now our success has been according to our wishes, and I am convinced that in Vienna, as well as here, the good influence which the two German Powers have exercised over the public situation in Germany as a whole, by their common and energetic action, will be felt. A glance at the present position of Germany, compared with what it was six months ago, is sufficient to enable one to appreciate it. We believe we may also record with satisfaction a substantial progress of Conservative feeling within both monarchies. In Germany, this is a matter not merely of public opinion, as it finds its expression in the daily newspapers. The position of the German governments themselves has become essentially different and they are now no longer in danger of being driven into the current of revolution . . .

We have found a bond in this joint action on the military and political fields of whose firmness and permanency we are convinced.

This is great progress, its significance goes far beyond the present moment, and we record it with satisfaction.

But the *decisive* success has not yet been attained and our work has not reached a conclusion. In order to make firm the position gained, we need a conclusive and lasting success . . . All old quarrels will find new nourishment in the complaints each is making against the other and anarchy will once more raise its head in Germany, while trust and respect abroad, which depend upon the solid combination of Austria and Prussia, will again be lost, if people are not convinced that the two Powers, when united, face foreign

* . . . * Bismarck's addition.

Powers aware of their unity and sufficiently conscious of their strength . . .

Document 83 Louis II of Bavaria to Schrenck,* 20 August 1864
(Munich, Hof- und Staatsarchiv, Allgemeine Staatsarchiv, Ministerium des Handels, no. 9693)

The course taken by the negotiations for the renewal of the Zollverein fills me with serious anxiety. From your reports I have obtained corroboration of my view that Bavaria has no choice other than to form a Customs area of her own, in which she could *perhaps* still count on the co-operation of Württemberg, or else to comply with the Prussian demands for unconditional acceptance of the Franco-Prussian customs and commercial treaty.

However well-founded all the considerations are which you have brought forward against the latter alternative, and however much I recognize that Prussia's superiority, at least in the field of commercial policy, will be confirmed for the future by it, I yet believe that we must decide for it. In her commercial policy Bavaria has been deserted by the other German states or will shortly be deserted, as one can now acknowledge with certainty. In my view, it is not obvious how far the consequent isolation of Bavaria and Württemberg can serve any useful purpose. The separation of their customs area from the rest of Germany is too unnatural for one to hope to build a tolerable, durable situation upon it. We should rather assume that the Government would sooner or later be forced, by the powerful interests involved, to rejoin the rest of Germany. It is shown by experience that Bavaria always has to give way sooner or later. But her surrender, if Prussia had once united herself with the rest of Germany and thereby won a strengthened position, would not be facilitated by greater complaisance from Prussia. An *unconditional* surrender on Bavaria's part, it seems to me, on the contrary, would be the only way, of eventually healing the split, and the longer the resistance, after which surrender happened, the more painful it would be. In addition, I believe that Bavaria's isolation, if only on account of the Palatinate, is not viable. I believe that the Government would gain the support neither of Parliament nor of our business houses for a continuation of its present policy to the point of separation from the Zollverein . . .

As for the moment when Bavaria should decide for the hard step

* Karl, Baron von Schrenck, Bavarian Minister President, Foreign Minister and Minister for Trade, 1859–64. T.

of yielding to Prussia: I can well appreciate the importance of the reasons why it has so far seemed advisable to you to wait until the end of next year, by which time the general political situation may have turned to our favour. Yet it seems to me that one can only speak of a *possibility*, not of a *probability* of this. There exists little prospect of things in Austria taking a turn more favourable to the medium-sized states or offering any hope of actual success . . .

In these circumstances, I have asked myself whether it would not be advisable to begin negotiations with Prussia without delay and to summon Parliament towards the end of September to approve the *punctation* to be agreed upon with her . . .

Document 84   Bismarck to Werther (Vienna), 6 August 1864
(O. von Bismarck, *Gesammelte Werke*, vol. iv, no. 454, p. 525)

. . . A true German and Conservative policy is only possible when Austria and Prussia are united and take the lead. From this high standpoint an intimate alliance of the two Powers has been our aim from the outset.* We see in its pursuit an earnest of the durability and fruitfulness of firm combination. We consider combination, though it is true both Powers and even all Germany already owe important successes to it, from a wider standpoint than that of the moment and as the means to consolidate the successes we have won. We consider combination (such as the joint action in waging war which is our immediate political purpose) as the foundation of an enduring unity and as the basis of a firm and healthy evolution of German policy in the future, and we have seen Austria's welcoming response in the *same* light. We consider the uncontested leadership of Germany by her two Great Powers as a peremptory requirement both for Germany and for the two Powers themselves. This leadership alone can guarantee to the complicated body of the Confederation, in itself little suited to action, a firm and assured attitude towards foreign Powers, and secure to it that influence on European politics which the nation justly demands. ** If Prussia and Austria are not united, politically Germany does not exist. If they are united, leadership belongs to them of right and in undertaking it they do no more than fulfil their duty to themselves and to the rest of Germany. At the same time, if they do so, but only if they do, they gain an increase in their own strength and security.** This natural relationship existed to a certain extent before 1848. Unfortunately events have since caused it to be almost forgotten. Quarrelling between

* The allusion is to the Austro-Prussian alliance, 6 March 1864, for the Schleswig Holstein question and their joint war upon Denmark, January to October 1864. T.
** . . . ** Holograph addition by Bismarck.

Austria and Prussia has left some of the smaller states unsure, and made others presumptuous . . .

If we hesitate or weaken on the path we have so far trodden, or even if we tread with too great circumspection, timidity or disunity will be thought to impair our resolution. Courage will be found for majority decisions, to which we *cannot* conform, and the collapse of Germany will be brought about by an absurd effort to cause the European policy of two monarchs, powerful and victorious in arms, to be taken along in the wake of a few unarmed small states whose whole significance consists in the misdirected courage of their Parliaments and newspapers. If, on the contrary, we come forward firmly and energetically,* the other German states will hardly venture to bring about majority decisions. They will not fail to understand the fruitlessness, indeed the danger of such decisions, as soon as the two Powers face them in clear and united resolution. They will conform as soon as they see the firm will of Austria and Prussia . . .

Document 85   Bismarck to Balan,** 26 August 1864
(Merseburg, Deutsches Zentralarchiv, AA II, Rep. 6, no. 1196)

I return to Your Excellency the enclosed report on the negotiations with Austria over customs and commercial relations. I have signed it and placed it before the King. His Majesty has been pleased to declare himself in general agreement with its gist. In consideration, however, of the present political situation and having regard to the conversations which took place at Schönbrunn with Count Rechberg, he has commanded that the preliminary conditions put forward by Austria should not be bluntly rejected but that the discussion of the questions should be carried over into the negotiations, about to be opened, without in any way yielding the principle . . .

* The beginning of the sentence is Bismarck's holograph addition.
** Hermann Ludwig von Balan, Prussian representative in Copenhagen, 1859–64; when war broke out, served in the Prussian Foreign Office; a close ally of Bismarck. T.

Document 86   Draft of a treaty to be concluded between Austria and Prussia over Schleswig-Holstein-Lauenburg and Lombardy, 24 August 1864
(Ritter von Srbik, editor, *Quellen zur Deutschen Politik Österreichs*, Berlin, Oldenburg, 1937, no. 1768, p. 271)

By order of their Royal Sovereigns, Their Majesties the Emperor of Austria and the King of Prussia, the undersigned depose herewith that the conversations which took place at Schönbrunn between Their Majesties on 22, 23, and 24 August have led to complete understanding on the following points:

1. The two Courts will watch in common that the question of sovereignty in the Duchies of Schleswig, Holstein, and Lauenburg shall not be brought to a hasty solution, but be kept open until such time as the two Courts, after a thorough testing of the various relevant claims, consider it ripe for a definitive decision . . .

3. If, before the definitive arrangements over the Duchies, complications should arise to disturb the state of possession of the Great Powers, the Royal Prussian Court binds itself to [work together with] the Imperial Austrian Court to the end that both the peace treaty of Zürich* shall be executed, and that Lombardy shall be reunited with the Imperial state.

The Imperial Austrian Court on its side, in the event of the attainment of this aim, will renounce in favour of Prussia its share of the rights to Schleswig, Holstein, and Lauenburg which the Crown of Denmark has ceded to Austria and Prussia jointly,** and will communicate its agreement to the union of these three Duchies to the Prussian monarchy.

Document 87   Rechberg to Bismarck, 17 September 1864
(*Die Auswärtige Politik Preussens*, vol. v, no. 278, p. 407)

. . . You will grant me, honoured friend, that a fair acknowledgement, made without disloyalty to the Confederation, that Austria and Germany[1] belong together, forms one of those basic conditions, without which Austria cannot feel at home in the alliance—if the term is allowed—with Prussia. I venture to assert that in this truth rests the answer to your question—as to what inexplicable magic lies hidden for us in the mere words 'Customs Union'. The value of

* Between Austria on one side and Sardinia and France on the other, December 1859, providing the restoration of deposed rulers to the Italian duchies as well as for the annexation of Lombardy to Sardinia. T.
** In a preliminary form in the armistice of July 1864 and definitively by the Treaty of Vienna, 30 October 1964. T.

these words, I grant you, is an imponderable thing, but the value of our identity as a German Power[2] is itself something imponderable. The opinion has been often expressed that the Customs Union can never be carried through. I have no practical means of proving it wrong. The view, however, that the Customs Union will inevitably be achieved, sooner or later,[3] is just as irrefutable. The present question whether Austria will surrender[4] the right to make a Customs Union, and so acknowledge that, for commercial policy, she does not belong to Germany,[5] it is my duty as an Austrian Minister, to answer in the negative. What would one have said in 1815 to a proposal that essentially consisted in the exclusion of Austria from a general German Customs and Trade association? What would one have said to a stipulation that Austria should not have any preference in trade and intercourse over the foreigner? If we insist on our claim to a Customs Union, it is not because Prussia has signed article 25 of the February treaty*—though one is not setting a good example if one reduces one's word of honour to a mere turn of phrase[6]—but rather because Austria is a German Power and cannot admit that a common German[7] institution should be completely[8] closed to her and that she should be treated as a foreign state[9] by her fellow members in the Confederation. You say that we should not let slip the practical benefits of the commercial treaty by chasing the will o' the wisp of the Customs Union. From the Austrian standpoint, upon which I operate, the matter appears in another light. I naturally present to you only the Austrian standpoint. When you tell me that you must not prejudice the economic interests of the country by political considerations and that your colleagues fear to be restrained by negotiation with Austria from advancing towards a more wholesome commercial policy, I can only appeal to the consideration that Austria too is going calmly to work at tariff reform and that it will never be possible to show that Prussia's industrial and commercial progress depends upon the rejection of our proposals . . .

Marginal Comments by Bismarck

(1) Theory!
(2) A phrase, more Power than German
(3) !
(4) 1853 has passed
(5) To the Zollverein
(6) It was no longer and it is just such turns of phrase that I wish to avoid
(7) It is not

---

* See above, document 81. T.

(8) No!
(9) Is Mecklenburg or Hamburg [who were not members of the Zollverein] a foreign state?

Document 88 Blome (Munich) to Mensdorff,* 29 October 1864
(Vienna, Haus- Hof- und Staatsarchiv, PA IV, no. 33)

... Your Excellency takes over the conduct of affairs at a sad time and at a moment when Austria's reputation abroad, alas, is too low. I will not presume to point out the origins of this regrettable fact to you who are much better able to survey them than I, but perhaps it will afford you some little interest to know the unprejudiced (as I believe) judgement reached here, outside Austria, from a conscientious observation of things.

Our influence has sunk, not for the reason that we have embarked upon this or that specific course, nor because we have fought for Denmark's integrity, nor because we are allied to Prussia, or have opposed the Liberal opinions of the day—for none of these reasons. We have lost reputation and sympathy just because we follow no specific policy. One day we play the card of the *Fürstentag*,** the next that of the presiding Power [in the Confederation]. [We have lost reputation] because we are no longer credited with the necessary firmness to strive persistently for either a traditional or a new aim. We are seen to vacillate; we are no longer feared; we are, therefore, less popular. Lasting popularity is never won by concessions to public opinion. The policy of the *Fürstentag* was a great one—had we carried it through energetically and consistently. We dropped it. It would be an egregious mistake, in my opinion, to return to it now, or a variant of it, and only to court the alliance of the German medium-sized and small states. The medium-sized states will always come to us when they need us, and they can only need us when we are powerful. They on their side afford us no support, as 1859 showed. We must now turn the alliance with Prussia to good account . . . Of course Bismarck has hitherto taken the lion's share of advantage from that connection; of course Prussia will always seek to drive us out of Germany; we can only fight Prussia if we combine with France and, since we do not wish to do that, our task is to prevent Prussia from falling into her arms. It will be easy for us to counteract the disadvantageous results of the commercial treaty with France if we decidedly turn to the system of free trade; for the future belongs to it and we cannot

---

* Alexander, Count von Mensdorff-Pouilly, Austrian Foreign Minister, 1864–6. T.

** See above, p. 61. T.

escape it. We shall also find in it the most effective means of fusing England's interests with ours. Moreover, England is neither an active ally nor a decided enemy. Russia, for years to come, will have to observe a passive attitude. Our course in relation to Italy, and especially Rome, is so prescribed by tradition, principles, feeling, and interests that we cannot abandon it without utterly ruining ourselves. In Germany it is time to cease to meddle and muddle [English in original]. Where we neither wish to bite nor can do so . . .

Document 89   Speech of J. Miquel during the discussions of the Executive Committee of the *Nationalverein*, 30 October 1864

(H. Oncken, *R. von Bennigsen: ein deutscher liberaler Politiker*, Stuttgart, 1910, vol. i, p. 652)

. . . In practice we had first to agitate for the restoration of the constitution in Hesse-Cassel, and who achieved this and was the only one who could? Bismarck. Who restored the Zollverein? It happened under the government of Bismarck. Who frustrated Austria's project of reform? Bismarck. Who freed Schleswig Holstein? Bismarck. Make no mistake, I am far from scattering praises indiscriminately upon Bismarck's ministry. Bismarck may have done what he did reluctantly, [but he did it in Prussia's interest and, therefore, in Germany's too;] since in all great questions Prussian and German interests coincide. Confronted with such lessons, such achievements, to show the capacity of a united Power to get things done, do you wish us to abandon our programme, to abandon the ideal of a united Central Power?*

---

* Metz, Schulze-Delitzsch, and Miquel led the defence of the main position of the *Nationalverein:* that the essential basis for united Germany was an imperial constitution with a Central Executive Power, an electoral law, and a formulation of basic rights.

III · GERMAN UNITY. ONLY A QUESTION OF TIME

THE leading statesman in Berlin had no time to rest on his laurels after the victory of the Prussian cause. Count Pouilly-Mensdorff, Stadholder of Galicia, had become Foreign Minister in Vienna. His first political measures showed that he was ready to draw the right conclusions from the bankruptcy of Rechberg's policy and to do so with decision. Either he must consolidate the alliance with Prussia or he must reach a *real* understanding with France. Like his close adviser, Baron von Biegeleben, Mensdorff believed that an understanding between Austria and France was possible, since both states were 'absolutely and essentially' interested 'in the federal organization of central Europe'—that is, to put it bluntly, in acting together to check Prussia's will to power and to territorial consolidation. At the same time more 'constitutional features' were to characterize Austrian policy. In the Schleswig Holstein question Austria would support 'the Augustenburg solution': the two Duchies to become a state of the Confederation on their own account with a sovereign government. Vienna hoped to attach the medium-sized states and public opinion to Austria by this anti-Prussian policy[1] (Doc. 90).

Unlike his Ministers, Bismarck was disturbed by the possibility of Austria's leaving an alliance that up to now had been so profitable to him. He, therefore, pressed forward the commercial negotiations that had been begun in the autumn of 1864 and, as far as possible, minimized every cause of conflict with Vienna. He proposed a cautious policy of understanding in questions of administration in the new Duchies. Yet the atmosphere remained tense. Agreement could be reached neither in the commercial question, nor over the administration of the Duchies. Points of conflict were ever more sharply discernible. Bismarck had no idea—however conciliatory he was—of letting the Duchies become independent under Augustenburg. The common administration of the new Duchies remained a 'chimaera of discord' (G. Mann).

In May 1865 a meeting of the Prussian Crown Council considered whether the German question, which was now essentially the Schleswig Holstein question, would not be better and quicker solved by 'blood and iron'. Yet the man who for a generation had demanded this method, now forbade it. He did so because he patently believed that Austria's position was really so isolated that a peaceful compromise *à deux* would now be possible with her (Doc. 91).

Austria, indeed, gained support for her policy in the Confederation and Prussia was hated, but even Austria's diplomats assessed this support scornfully. Even co-operation between Vienna and Paris remained merely an academic proposition. Prussia had more factors in her favour. 'Caesar on the Seine' was stimulating national movements in Italy and Germany and hoping to reap a political success as arbiter among the European nations (Doc. 92). Britain was well-disposed to a strengthening of the centre of Europe. The European balance of power could only profit from it. Finally since 1859 and 1863, Russia had been grateful and well-disposed towards Prussia. Prussia was restrained by no Great Power's ill-will. On the contrary, she had an extremely free hand in Germany at this time. Yet Bismarck had still not assured the Prussian position by treaties. He desired to do this and realized that he must make no mistake in doing so, lest after all he should not be able to avoid bloodshed and a battle for predominance in Germany. He needed a little more time for diplomatic preparation. He now began this by the aid of commercial negotiations with Italy. He knew how to tear apart the *entente* between the medium-sized states and Vienna; for the Zollverein would have to go with Prussia (Doc. 93). It was enough merely to gain time. He had no wish to precipitate a crisis.

There were, however, still other reasons that made it possible for Bismarck to procrastinate in the first months of the year 1865. They were reasons of domestic and economic policy. Industry and trade were again expanding in 1865. New commercial treaties were on the point of being signed. The economic integration of the Zollverein into western Europe had

helped to overcome the depression [of 1863]. Political economists and chambers of commerce unconditionally supported
Prussia's policy. 'Politics are dying and economics *alone*
claim to annex the vacated territory.'[2] Thus here too calmness,
method, and time were the prerequisites of policy.

Last not least the Democrats in Prussia despite eloquent
opposition 'had never forgotten that they lived in Prussia'.
Even if Herr von Bismarck was no Cavour and could never
become one, a large section of the Liberal camp acknowledged
in 1865 that 'unification must be contrived by using the reputation and strength of an actual Great Power [Prussia] and by
bringing economic means to the task'.[3] That meant nothing less
than that the Liberal opposition was dissolving. The policy of
the New Era had been abandoned—especially by the business
world. The Liberals were now ready even to sanction the
budget for 'the wild man' [Bismarck].

Was Bismarck to check this movement by a war?—by a
war, which if it were begun too soon, could end in a *débâcle*
for Prussia? He did not do that. Rather he now came to terms
with Austria. [By the Convention of Gastein] in August 1865,
Vienna—crippled by a financial and domestic crisis—agreed to
the administrative separation of the Duchies: Holstein for the
Emperor, Schleswig for the King, while Lauenburg was bought
by Berlin. The first step towards annexation had been taken.

Although conflict was avoided by the agreement of Bad
Gastein, Austria and the Confederation were once more the
losers: Austria, because she had again failed to solve the
German question as an affair within the exclusive competence
of the Confederation; the Confederation, because, relying on
Austria, it had come out strongly for Augustenburg (Doc. 94),
and was once more betrayed or duped. Roggenbach, the
Badenese Foreign Minister and spokesman for the Liberals of
Germay, resigned.

Thus Gastein could only provide a respite. The causes of
conflict smouldered on. It was now that the specific preparation
of arms and search for alliances began (Doc. 95). Vienna
wanted to iron out what was done at Gastein; Prussia to
make sure of revenge for Olmütz.

At the beginning of 1866, when Vienna again presented the
Augustenburg solution to Prussia, Berlin answered in a belliger-

ent tone. In Vienna the Crown Council demanded that
Austria should stand up to Prussia. Yet the economic position
of the monarchy was wretched, and war a thing of doubtful
value. For what would be gained if Prussia were defeated?
Bismarck would fall and another New Era would follow in
Prussia—a New Era of which *Kleindeutschland* would still be the
political aim. Yet even if Austria did not accept war, her
German policy would be as bankrupt as ever. So preparations
for war were made 'on paper' as the Emperor commanded
(Doc. 96).

Prussia armed too. Public opinion was prepared for the
duel (Doc. 97). Austria hoped for the support of Bavaria,
Württemberg, Saxony, and Hesse-Darmstadt. Even Baden
joined Vienna. Yet Austria turned hither and thither and still
hoped to come to terms. Prussia gained cover for her rear
from Russia and Italy. Austria had to face, therefore, war on
two fronts. She continued to arm, however much she valued
peace and however much she offered to come to an understanding. Each side saw in a military success the guarantee of
its political system (Doc. 98).

After the spring of 1866, Austria increasingly gained the
support of the Liberal public. Bismarck could not count for
sure on a reconciliation with the Liberals and with the medium-
sized states. Yet he tried to bring it about. He submitted a
proposal for reform to the Confederation in Frankfurt. This
looked to the constitution of a Parliament elected by universal,
equal, and direct suffrage. But Frankfurt declined. A Parliament was certainly desired, but not one elected by universal
suffrage. Unity was certainly wanted, but it was German
unity that was sought and not a 'Greater Prussia', with its
hated Minister at the head of an illegal régime.

When the economic regression that was to characterize
the end of the year began to threaten in the summer of 1866,
uncertainty and wavering anxiety marked the policy of the
medium-sized states. Meanwhile the European Great Powers
continued in their attitude of reserve and indifference towards
Germany's future. Bismarck acted accordingly. He seized the
chance at once when Vienna rejected Napoleon's offer to act
as mediator in the question of the Elbe Duchies, and when
Vienna called instead for its regulation by the Germanic

Confederation (Doc. 99), Prussia considered this a breach of the Gastein Convention and invaded Holstein. Thereupon the Confederation mobilized. Prussia in turn declared the Federal Act of 1815 broken, resigned from the Confederation, appealed to the German nation (Doc. 100), and went to war (Doc. 101). Now arms, after all, were to decide who should be master in Germany. Bismarck was confident of victory, whatever domestic resistance he might encounter (Doc. 102).

The Stock Exchange in Berlin was by no means so certain of victory; there was speculation, to Bismarck's rage—in view of the united German opposition to Prussia—in a victory for the Danubian Monarchy. But this was a fundamentally mistaken bet. As expected, France stood neutral and Napoleon awaited the outcome. He counted on a long war of exhaustion. This too was a miscalculation. Prussia without much difficulty and with small forces occupied north-west Germany and assured her western flank. That was the first stroke, executed with unexpected speed. In addition Italy went hand in hand with Prussia and the Southern Slavs offered her their services. Moltke directed the principal attack of the Prussian troops on Bohemia. Here the decision came very quickly. On 3 July 1866 the bulk of the Austrian, Saxon and Württemberg troops were faced at Königgrätz (Sadowa) and—with luck— defeated (Doc. 103). This decided everything. What would Bismarck do now? Would he march on Vienna? Would he conclude the war, as King William wished, with a Roman triumph? Nothing of the sort! He judged the victory of Prussia in the light of the power constellation in Europe. What use would a total Prussian victory be, if it caused Russia and France to join together? What use would the immediate unification of Germany be, if the Great Powers by armed force made this increase in Prussian power a matter for renewed conflict? What he wanted and what the Prussian victory could bring him he had already outlined before Königgrätz: offensive and defensive alliances with all the German states, the establishment of a German Customs Parliament and the linking, for purposes of foreign policy, of the German states to Prussia; in short, no annexations, no dictated peace. Prussia, in Bismarck's judgement, 'could not digest Munich and Stuttgart from Berlin'.[4]

Vienna, after the defeat at Königgrätz, begged Napoleon to intervene and he, taken by surprise and chagrined by the quick Prussian victory, and cheated of the office of arbiter, accepted the mission (Doc. 104). Bismarck did not decline his good offices. Napoleon, though with a sour mien, accepted Bismarck's terms, which after the Prussian victories included annexations after all. They were: the exclusion of Austria from the Confederation, annexations in north Germany, the absorption of Schleswig Holstein, and an independent South-German Confederation.

Prussia and Austria then came to terms with surprising speed (Doc. 105). On 27 July 1866 peace preliminaries were signed in Nikolsburg (Doc. 106). Bismarck was content. He had forestalled a French intervention; and had avoided giving offence to Russia without the optimum gains for Prussia being endangered by foreign political pressure. These gains would be: extension to the line of the River Main, and a wider league between north and south to cover the whole of Germany, with a common Federal Diet, a common economic policy, and a mutual guarantee of each other's territories. Bismarck had acted true to Prussia's fundamental principle: 'Our power only finds its limit when the supply of Junkers to fill official places gives out.'

The King and the military element were, however, not so pleased with the peace preliminaries. King William wished for further 'punishment'; the military men for security; they wanted, for example, Bohemia and Saxony. Bismarck was able to impose his will. Later historians have interpreted his restraint from annexation and his abstinence from all idea of 'punishment' as great moderation. In doing so, they have directed their attention too much to the actual treaty with Austria and forgotten that with her exclusion from the Con-federation, with the annexation of Schleswig, Holstein, Hanover, Hesse-Cassel, Nassau, and Frankfurt, and with 'the chaining' of Hesse-Darmstadt,* Saxony, and the Thuringian Duchies to Prussia, an aim had been attained 'so great that no one could have entertained it when the war broke out'.[5] In addition the south German states were ready in 1866 at once

---

* The reference is to the part of Hesse-Darmstadt, north of the River Main, which was ceded to Prussia.

6

to ally themselves to the north. The Prussian victory had brought about a temporary change of opinion in the south. Bismarck exploited this change and concluded secret military alliances with the southern states in August. He did not, however, wish to go any further. He declined an immediate absorption of the south. He did not wish to make France his enemy (Doc. 107).

Bismarck stopped short primarily because he believed he could carry through the establishment of Prussian hegemony in Germany, without complications with France, by other means. These means were also the traditional factors in his policy. They were the development of the military agreements, the conversion of the Zollverein into a Customs Parliament, and constitutional preparations for final unification. He now wished to rule *with*, and not *despite*, the constitution. The armed victory had had other effects in Prussia than merely the strengthening of the special position of the army and of the dominance of Prussia in north Germany.

At the very outbreak of war all political ill-temper and strife disappeared in Prussia. There was no more opposition to be seen; on the contrary, the elections, which took place during the campaign, brought a landslide in favour of the Conservatives. The Left lost over 100 seats and the Conservatives won them (Doc. 108). The two groups were now equal in strength. Bismarck could set about making *his* peace with Parliament [i.e. the Prussian *Landtag*]. He begged for an indemnity, begged that the Prussian Parliament would sanction his governing without a budget and in retrospect declare that his policy since 1862 had been right (Doc. 109). The Liberals had their 'Rhodes'. Not all of them 'leapt',* but the majority none the less made their peace with Bismarck, and acknowledged that he had been right (Doc. 110). The *Fortschritt* Party was thus split. To the right of the old Party a new political organization arose which after 1867 called itself the National Liberal Party (Doc. 111). The National Liberals were liberal in that free trade, the rule of law, and the constitutional state

---

* The Greek proverb, in its Latin form (*hic Rhodus, hic saltus*, here is Rhodes, here is your leap) was a commonplace of German Latin textbooks. It is applicable when someone is asked to do on the spot what he boasts of having done elsewhere. T.

were their aims. They were national because they strove before all else for the unity of the *Reich* as a state based on power. They wanted to be 'in opposition' only when it was necessary; and to be 'on the watch but loyal'. Their standing ground was 'reality'; they found support throughout Germany; and Bismarck was their idol.

The Conservatives too broke up. To those on the right, Bismarck was wrong to seek an indemnity at all. They feared constitutional and federal arrangements and, even more, the dissolution of Prussia in *Kleindeutschland*. Finally they saw that equal, direct, and secret voting, which Bismarck wished to introduce into the new north-German constitution, meant the beginning of the decline of their political power. Bismarck was now a revolutionary to them; it seemed political folly to them to yield in the moment of victory abroad and at home (Doc. 112). Among the Conservatives there were, however, professors to whom Germany's greatness was of more value than 'legal squabbles' (G. Mann), industrialists, bankers, merchants, and Liberal Silesian noblemen, who knew their interests would be better cared for by Bismarck than by the Old Conservatives. Thus there arose to the left among the Conservatives a second party for Bismarck *sans phrase*—the Free Conservatives (Doc. 113).

'The time for ideals has passed' (J. Miquel). The Prussian Catholics, despite their *grossdeutsch* inclinations, also recognized this. The majority of them, including Ketteler, now too made their peace with Bismarck. Only radical Democrats, the *grossdeutsch* and extreme anti-Prussian elements left over from the Parliamentarians of 1849 were now out-and-out opponents. They wanted neither Habsburg nor Hohenzollern. Their voices, however, provoked no echo (Doc. 114).

In Prussia the ship of state remained set on Bismarck's course, despite opposition from the right. The achievements of the one-time country-bumpkin Junker, the derided Prussian Minister President, had become national necessities. This view was taken so long and so far as it paid. The dominance of the south-German florin was destroyed. The Prussian *taler* provided the German monetary standard. Berlin broke away from the Frankfurt Stock Exchange (Doc. 115).

Reassured thus by the new political parties, and with his

eye on south Germany, Bismarck set about constructing the north-German house and so arranging it that the south Germans could move in when they wished (or must) and the Great Powers, especially France, would not be able to oppose it. The constitution was drafted with this object. It is only intelligible as something instinct with political aims, improvised 'with elastic turns of phrase, apparently meaningless but in fact having wide implications' (Doc. 116).

Knowing what he was doing, Bismarck harked back to the traditions of the *Paulskirche*.* The franchise for the new North German Parliament was to be universal, equal, and secret; the new representative assembly was to be called the *Reichstag*. These traditions had served their purpose when once that had been decided. The constitution was really to be a compromise— a compromise between the people and the princely governments. But for a [true] compromise two parties equal in strength are needed. There were no such equals in 1866 and 1867. What counted was the power of Prussia, which had bidden the new Confederation come into existence. This was one important fact; Bismarck's own position was the other. It was, then, a matter of securing the power of the state and not allowing Prussia to be dissolved in the north-German nation. What counted was not the people, but the state; not the majority, but traditional authority; not the fundamental rights of men, but the right of the state. The new *Reichstag* did not acquire such sovereignty as had been ascribed to that of 1848. It was to *co-operate*, to co-operate in shaping tariff and commercial policy, and the communications system, in standardizing the currency, weights and measures, and in drafting civil legal procedure. The *Reichstag* was to sanction expenditure for army and navy, but the army's special position was not to be impaired. The representative assembly was not to have any direct influence on the executive and especially not on foreign policy. There were to be no responsible ministers. Government was to be the business of the *Bundesrat*. This was a meeting of the representatives of the individual state governments, not of representatives from the state Parliaments.

Finally, sovereignty in the new German state was to be vested in 'the allied governments'. [If the power of the *Reichstag*

* See above, p. 40. T.

followed one German tradition], this followed a second—the federal, the tradition of Metternich's day. For the *Bundesrat* was nothing else than the Federal Diet of 1815. In contrast with the Frankfurt arrangements of 1848, the presiding power —Prussia—had quite different formal and actual rights [from those of the presiding power—Austria—of 1815]. Nothing could happen against Prussia's will. Yet the structure of the constitution was such that the south-German princes could be part of the sovereign power and that the Parliaments of the individual states were not dissolved in the *Reichstag* (Doc. 117). Competition, then, all round. This was precisely Bismarck's aim. The possibility of playing off one interest against another—*Reichstag*, state Parliaments, governments, princes, and people, each against the other—guaranteed the power of Bismarck, Prussian Minister President and Foreign Minister.

The basic structure of the constitution was not altered after the draft had been put before the constituent *Reichstag* for its discussion. The Liberals, after hard discussion, gained for the *Reichstag* more influence in voting money and were even able to gain for it an indirect influence on foreign policy. Bismarck had even to accept one 'responsible' Minister. Everything and yet nothing was gained by that. The Chancellor alone, not his colleagues, was 'responsible' and it was left uncertain to whom he was responsible. He was certainly not responsible to Parliament; for he did not need its confidence in order to govern. He was, rather, responsible to the hereditary President of the Confederation—the King of Prussia and, later, Emperor—for the latter nominated and dismissed him and did this without regard to the will of the majority in Parliament.* The authoritarian state thus remained unimpaired. The deciding power in this state were the princes and, under them, the nobility, the army, the civil service and those political Parties which observed their loyalty as their subjects. The Chancellor stood above the Parties. He needed them, but

---

* Bismarck had in mind, rather, the sense of the word 'responsible' as it was used in Prussia by those who, like Stein, opposed Frederick William III's system of *Kabinet* government. 'Responsible' meant 'responsible for', so that it should be possible to point to a named individual instead of a faceless group as responsible for a decision. It did *not* mean 'responsible *to*', so that the person or body to which he was responsible might dismiss him. T.

they needed him far more, if they were to have any political influence. Everything, however, depended upon the monarch, the President of the Confederation.

So it remained until 1918. Thence the legacy was handed down still further. The Weimar constitution, by the introduction in principle of the parliamentary system, altered, it is true, the structure of the constitution, but at the same time it left the way open to a retrograde evolution—back to the system of the authoritarian state. The constitution, as it was accepted in 1867 by an overwhelming majority in the constituent *Reichstag* of the North German Confederation, was a veritable monster. It met, however, the needs not only of Germany's complicated internal structure, but also of her economic structure. Finally it satisfied the momentary political needs of the Prussian Minister President of the day.

While the constitution was being debated and accepted in the spring of 1867, relations between north and south Germany had rapidly cooled. After the Prussian victories in the summer of 1866 Bismarck, using the favourable fact of armed victory, had vigorously set about throwing his bridge over the Main and binding the south Germans—despite French opposition— to the north. This he succeeded in doing by the secret military alliances (Doc. 118). The next step, however, was patently more difficult. Baden alone wanted, without limitations, a settlement which would go beyond these military claims upon her. Her geographical position, her fear of the French, and her economic interests led Karlsruhe to press forcefully for absorption in the North German Confederation (Doc. 119).

The situation was more complicated in the three other southern states. The Liberal *bourgeoisie* in Bavaria was for immediate entry into the North German Confederation, if only for economic reasons. At the end of 1866, however, its views were becoming more and more overshadowed by those of the Old Bavarians, the Conservative, royalist, landed, Catholic supporters of an independent, self-dependent, Bavarian policy. Despite their disillusionment in 1866, they still thought Vienna a 'pleasanter' ally than Prussia, which meant 'the rule of the sword', and 'Prussian Caesarism'. They defended themselves against any compounding with the north and even forced von der Pfordten's successor, Prince Hohenlohe Schillingsfürst, to disclaim his plans, that had become known, for an understanding with the north. All they allowed him to do was to introduce a reform of the army's structure to conform with the Prussian model—Prussia had won here—and to try to make Bavaria the leading Power of 'the other Germany' organized as a southern confederation (Doc. 120).

Bavaria's western neighbour, however, would not have this. Württemberg, like Bavaria, had given her support to the military alliances with Prussia, but that was all. The traditional *grossdeutsch*, democratic, Swabian opposition then again awoke. As in Bavaria unequal partners allied with each other: the Democrats and Conservatives. Whereas, however, the Catholics in Bavaria believed they could learn military drill from Prussia, but still remain economically independent, the Württembergers thought the other way round: economically they would look north, for the Zollverein had brought them nothing but advantages; militarily they thought they should remain independent, so as to be still masters in their own house politically.

In Hesse-Darmstadt the upper *bourgeoisie* strove for entrance into the North German Confederation. The government, however, held back—essentially for reasons of foreign policy. Baron von Dalwigk, the Hessian Minister President, saw Hesse as the connecting link in a possible Franco-Austrian alliance rather than as a Prussian outpost against France.

In 1867 Dalwigk's calculation was no bare theorizing. France showed less and less inclination to allow Prussia to act on a long rein in her policy. She saw with unmitigated mistrust the establishment of the North German Confederation and Bismarck's policy of courting her. Napoleon III still expected Prussian support in a policy of compensations, such as Bismarck could venture on. As in 1866, Bismarck could only hope he would be able to restrain Napoleon III and meanwhile try to come to terms with the south as quickly as possible (Doc. 121). Yet this was easier said than done; for Austria had again become active. Baron von Beust, the former Minister President of Saxony and opponent of any increase in Prussia's power, now conducted Austrian policy. Meanwhile the monarchy had carried through a reform of government and given the

Hungarians autonomy in the eastern half of the Empire.* Hungarian interests became more and more influential at Vienna. Although the Hungarians by no means favoured a policy of revenge against Prussia—indeed they owed their position to the Prussian victories—they represented a policy which was in the long run directed against her. For the Hungarians were farmers and wanted to export and so favoured free trade. At the same time Austria experienced—in contrast to the Zollverein—an economic upswing. Aided by French capital, Austria caught up in industrial development (Doc. 122). That meant von Beust could now lower the tariff and come to an understanding with Paris in the economic field. It fairly soon became apparent that Austria hoped to create a counterpoise to Prussia by means of a Franco-south-German-Austrian customs *rapprochement*. It was self-evident (Doc. 123) that Beust, like Napoleon, would support any anti-Prussian movement in south Germany and any plan for an autonomous confederation. There was a choice for German development between, on the one hand, south-German strivings for unity and, on the other, a north-German-Prussian policy of attracting states to itself.

What was Bismarck's attitude in face of this taking sides in south Germany and Europe? He played a double or even three-sided game. He kept France at bay; he sought an understanding with Austria in both the political and economic fields; from Russia and England—using the weakness of one and the imperial policy of the other—he sought cover for the rear (Doc. 124). He advised Baden and the National Liberals to be patient; he depicted Prussia to the south as a satiated state (Doc. 125), but tried to conclude a military convention with Hesse-Darmstadt. Finally, he used Hohenlohe in Bavaria as the lever for his German policy.

Hohenlohe wished to establish a southern military confederation following Prussia's example. This met Bismarck's ideas half-way. A military alliance with a southern confederation would be the first bar to Franco-Austrian conspiracies. He, therefore, supported Hohenlohe (Doc. 126); showed himself affable to Württemberg and drove Baden, who struggled against them, to accept Bavaria's proposals. Baden was to be

---

* i.e. by the *Ausgleich*, or Compromise of 1867. T.

the connecting link. The convention thus came into being. Bismarck rejoiced. He emphasized, in face of Old Conservative scepticism, the necessity of coming to terms. Prussia saw herself on the way 'to bringing about for all Germany what she has brought about for herself' (Doc. 127).

Bismarck at once sketched the outlines of a close North German Confederation and a wider German league (Doc. 128),[6] and urged the south to go hand in hand with the north even in non-military matters. 'The north should be ready to enter an agreement with the south because this would answer to the interests of both.' Having signed the military alliances, Bismarck now wanted agreement on economic matters or the economic unity of Germany under the Prussian sceptre: that is, a German Customs Parliament. He reminded Dalwigk, Varnbühler, and Hohenlohe—the south-German Minister Presidents—of his power to dissolve the Zollverein at six month's notice (Doc. 129), so that they might know where they stood and how seriously he took economic unity. He also let the south know that this question would only be solved '*either* by the formation of a Customs Parliament in which the German states would have to have their part, *or* by the sending of representatives *ad hoc*, whenever tariff and trade questions were discussed, to the [North German] *Reichstag*'.[7]

Bismarck was sure, that the affair would develop in Prussia's favour. He, therefore, allowed Hohenlohe a free hand to go forward, and even supported him because he considered his political plans aimed at entry into the North German Confederation. Bismarck, however, was mistaken. Bavaria would have nothing to do with merging herself in Prussia or with a Customs Parliament. Hohenlohe only wanted a wider confederation on *grossdeutsch* lines. The negotiations, which Hohenlohe allowed his intimate associate, Tauffkirchen, to conduct, aimed at the revival of the old Triad idea. Hohenlohe hoped to be able to use the opportunity of strained Franco-Prussian relations over the question of compensations and he also succeeded in concluding a Bavaro-Württemberg convention. Bismarck was furious and rejected every south-German demand. He informed Bavaria and Württemberg that Prussia was '*still* in a position to be able to enter any European alliance she chose'.[8]

Napoleon III, undesignedly, again aided Prussia to escape from a dilemma. During these events, he had been directing his efforts to the annexation of Luxemburg. France offered to buy this Duchy from Holland. Prussia would only accept the transaction provided her part in it remained concealed. Holland, however, publicly inquired what the Prussian attitude was, so Prussia was compromised. The south and Austria reacted at once. Beust and the particularists hoped to be able to foment and use the mistrust, thus aroused, against Prussia (Doc. 130).

Bismarck, however, turned the game to his favour; broke off the negotiations with France (Doc. 131), denied to Holland that he had any responsibility for Luxemburg and enflamed the *Reichstag* into a clear glow of nationalist feeling and excitement over the ravishing of a member of the Germanic Confederation. Europe found itself on the edge of war (Doc. 132). Prussia did not, after all, come to blows with Bavaria. Indeed, Bismarck used their differences at once—as the means to draw Austria to Prussia (Doc. 133). The alliance with public opinion and with economic interests completely answered his purpose as the leverage to bring the south to the north.

When Bismarck and Napoleon reached an understanding on Luxemburg in London—Prussia renounced her right to garrison the fortress of Luxemburg but Luxemburg remained (until 1918!) in the Zollverein—the usefulness of Hohenlohe's plans was exhausted. Even the Austrians let Hohenlohe and his plans alone. They had been built on sand. Economic interests directed the south towards the north. Württemberg and Baden released themselves from the convention into which they had entered with Bavaria and were now ready to sign a permanent alliance with the Zollverein states without a veto (Doc. 134).

In June 1867, the southern states agreed to the Prussian proposals. A Customs Parliament and a Customs Federal Council [*Bundesrat*] were the Prussian-dominated institutions of the new Zollverein. The whole *Reich* had 58 votes in the Customs *Bundesrat* and of these Prussia had 17. The Customs Parliament was elected by universal, direct, and equal suffrage so that the more thickly populated, monarchic north dominated it. It was now essential for Prussia to implement these new arrangements, before France and Austria found them-

selves side by side in energetic opposition to her. This co-
operation could not be prevented; for France now at last drew
the right conclusions from Prussia's attitude and sought an
entente with Austria.

As early as August 1867, Francis Joseph and Napoleon III
met in Salzburg. Both monarchs set their hopes on an alliance
against Prussian hegemony; but their interests were too different for that to be realized. France wanted to bind herself
most strictly to Austria for the one purpose of opposing the
'Prussification' of Germany. The Hungarians were against
that. Moreover, opinion in Austria was not simply and bluntly
anti-Prussian. The majority wanted to wait, let France and
Prussia fight it out and then play the part of *tertium gaudens*
(Doc. 135). Beust, therefore, waited. France, on her side,
betrayed no wish to afford support to what Beust wanted, which
was an anti-Russian policy for Austria in south-east Europe.
They reached agreement on one point only: that south Germany should be supported 'in maintaining an independent
and, when necessary, resistant attitude towards Prussia'.[9]

During the Salzburg conversations, Bismarck preserved the
most pained reserve (Doc. 136). He had to put a good face
upon a bad situation—one so bad that it could entirely frustrate
his own policy. Prussia, it is true, gained as a compensation
Russian and British goodwill. Bismarck, however, in order to
get it had had to disclaim any intention of extending the
political and military hegemony of Prussia in Germany.

Everything now, as so often, depended upon economic
factors. Bismarck acted accordingly. The North German
Confederation had been created; the Ministers [of the states]
had agreed to the parliamentary remodelling of the Zollverein; national feeling in the south had abated. Prussian
policy could now be directed to objects which expressed the
wishes of interested men in north and south, the ideals of the
new Parties and the ideas even of the *Nationalverein*. She
sought the basis of political union, in other words the reassur-
ance of Prussia's position of power, by urgently fostering
economic links and the setting up of institutions common to
north and south (Doc. 137). Bismarck now gave up his oscilla-
tion between the political and commercial organization of the
north-German leadership. Rudolph von Delbrück, the soul

of resistance, in the fifties, to the Austrian plans for a Customs Union, was summoned to be head of the new north-German Central Executive, and so the decision was taken (Doc. 138). The economic foundations of political unity were laid in cooperation with the Parties. There could be no expectation, however, that unity would be directly achieved. Bismarck devoted himself to a liberal policy of fulfilment in the north. Circumstances must be allowed to develop.

His policy was now to wait. He could, indeed, do nothing else. The south-German Parliaments accepted the new treaties instituting the Customs Parliament, but were not prepared to meet any Prussian wishes beyond that. Vienna and Paris at once recognized their opportunity, launched with great verve plans for a southern confederation and strengthened the south-German resistance to an all-too-speedy 'Prussification' (Doc. 139). The opposition against Prussia rose again. The south knew what lay at the end of the journey, but wanted to regulate its pace for itself (Doc. 140). Bismarck nevertheless judged the stormy Parliamentary debates in the south with forebearance. The Chambers of Commerce, the export industry, anticlerical Protestants, rich merchants, military men, and army officers, it was clear, demanded entry into the North German Confederation. So everything turned on the elections to the Customs Parliament (Doc. 141). If Prussia once had the Customs Parliament, 'the child would scream' and it would then 'be known to be alive'.

Bismarck was once more disappointed. The north thought it had already won the game and counted on the south resigning itself to defeat (Doc. 142). The election campaign for the Customs Parliament began in the south in December 1867 and January 1868. Both groups, particularists and Prussians, mobilized their last reserves (Doc. 143). The outcome of the elections was a catastrophe, despite all Bismarck's exertions and hopes (Doc. 144). Everywhere, in Baden, Württemberg, Bavaria, and Hesse, the supporters of union on a *grossdeutsch* basis, the clericals and the old families won. The south decided with a great majority against the nationalists (Doc. 145). What had been achieved satisfied the south: the bounds which the treaty of 8 July 1866 had set to the competence of the Customs Parliament were not to be crossed.

Bismarck could start no new measures by means of the Customs Parliament. On the contrary, the south-German opposition strengthened the position of Saxony and the other sovereign states of the North German Confederation (Doc. 146). Bismarck could only allow his King to open the new Customs Parliament with a fine speech. Meanwhile north and south, Liberals and Conservatives, Catholics and Protestants were already at odds over the question whether the Parliament might present an address to the Prussian King, which expressed a wish for the unification of the whole Fatherland. Despite the unity now achieved in economic matters, there was a long way to go before political unification could be attained. Here the south determined the way to proceed. Bismarck could only readjust himself to the new situation (Doc. 147) and hope that the national and economic development would make progress. Even in this respect overcast weather seemed to lie ahead.

France and Austria drew closer together. Plans for a Catholic economic union fluttered on Bismarck's writing table; rumours of a triple alliance between Italy, Austria, and France disturbed him. France opened a lively phase of active foreign policy aimed at success. Beust felt no 'contentment' in seeing Austria surrounded on all her frontiers by Prussian helmets.[10] He revived Austria's traditional activity in south-east Europe. He grew more and more reserved towards Prussia. During 1869, diplomatic relations with Berlin became increasingly cool (Doc. 148). Bismarck indeed sought stronger contacts with Russia and Britain, but he could only gain compensating support from them by supporting their interests in the Balkans. He had neither the wish nor the ability to do this. Prussia could offer Russia help only where German affairs were concerned. Bismarck had to stop short in his course. All he could do was to put out threats which bound him to nothing (Doc. 149).

Nor was there any success to be discerned in the south. Parliamentary elections in Württemberg (and later in Bavaria) confirmed the anti-Prussian direction of the elections to the Customs Parliament (Doc. 150). Men voted 'German' as against 'Greater Prussian'. The Democrats in Württemberg mocked: 'The Greater Prussians are drawing in their claws.'

'German-Austria', they said, 'is again a Power.' 'We defend ourselves against Greater Prussia in order to save ourselves for Germany'[11]—that was the electoral cry in the south.

Bismarck had to practise a policy of procrastination. In Berlin bitter disappointment prevailed over the fruitlessness of the Customs Parliament. The south refused every proposal for tax reform. Bismarck, however, needed tax reform. The budget, owing to the wars, had fallen into deficit and his allies since 1866, the National Liberals, refused for the first time to co-operate with him. They would accept no tax reform without political compensation in the shape of constitutional reform. This Bismarck declined. The budget question made clear the limits of his Liberal policy. He could not give the Liberals a constitutional state without entirely losing his association with the Conservatives. So at the beginning of 1869 there reigned in Berlin—in the words of the Austrian ambassador, Count Wimpffen—'a complete calm'.

An impulse to the *speedy* evolution of the German question could only come from outside; since quick transition, within a few years, to political unity would completely cut across the slow course of development in the economic situation. Bismarck was not prepared to put the clocks forward (Doc. 151), but he exerted himself nonetheless to develop the situation so that he would be able to exploit it in action at the right moment for Prussia's course towards her objective 'the more distant aim, the unification of Germany'. In practice this meant not taking Baden too soon into the North German Confederation. The Liberals, in a motion in the *Reichstag* in the spring of 1870, had demanded her admission. Practical policy was not the policy of the people who understood nothing about foreign affairs. Practical policy meant waiting until Prussian interests could be linked with nationalist enthusiasm without the monarchic, authoritarian order in Prussia taking harm. For this chance Bismarck waited (Doc. 152).

Document 90   Blome (Munich) to Mensdorff, 8 December 1864
(Vienna, Haus- Hof- und Staatsarchiv, PA IV, no. 33)

... I shall certainly endeavour to win influence over Pfordten*
and I can scarcely go wrong if I take him by his boundless vanity for
this purpose and strike at the side of his mind that is always vibrating
in him. Anyhow I shall need a little time before I obtain his confidence to the same degree that I possessed that of Schrenck; for,
since his nomination as Minister, he has unfortunately been so
unwell that he has not yet seen anyone of the diplomatic corps.
His health gives cause generally for justifiable anxiety. Any mental
excitement—his choleric temperament often creates such excitement—brings immediate physical suffering, which owing to his
heart trouble is not of a kind that can be disregarded.

It affords, moreover, a lamentable spectacle to see from close-to
how narrow the horizon of these statesmen of the medium-sized
states is. Pfordten, who undoubtedly, because of his intellect and
knowledge, occupies a prominent place among them, cannot
detach himself any more than the others from doctrinaire attitudes
and always bestrides the professors' lame horse of abstract legal
theories. All political considerations are sacrificed to the standpoint
of theory and power-political relationships are totally misunderstood.

The Duke of Augustenburg** enjoys such popularity in the
Liberal circles of Germany and in the [Bavarian] Lower House
only because a cause which derives its right from the year 1848
would gain ascendancy [if he came to power]. I doubt whether it
would be possible to force a Conservative government on Augustenburg if only because the Conservative elements in the Duchies,
such as Plessen and others like him, will never attach themselves
to a Prince who is so little esteemed. Nevertheless, I grant that
it is only a matter of secondary importance to us who rules up there
[in Schleswig and Holstein] so long as the peace of Germany is not
disturbed. *Il n'y a rien qui réussisse comme le succès* says the proverb:
thus Bismarck has in the end gained the victory in Germany and,
in the nature of things, gained it partly at our expense. Yet we
shall never win back the sympathies we have lost by fruitless efforts
to withstand Prussia, however well-intentioned ...

* Ludwig, Baron von der Pfordten, Bavarian Minister President and Foreign
Minister. He had earlier held the same positions in Saxony. T.
** Claimant to the Duchies of Schleswig and Holstein, who had, however,
renounced his right.

Document 91   Note by Moltke of the meeting of Ministers, 29
   May 1865
   (*Die Auswärtige Politik Preussens,* vol. vi, no. 101, p. 179)

   ... Minister President von Bismarck:

   There are three courses:

1. It will probably be possible to execute peaceably the minimum
demand* with certain modifications, if the oath to the flag is given
up. To charge the Duchies with 80 or 100 millions** will be considered by public opinion in Prussia as a retreat.
2. Compensation for Austria and a financial settlement with the
claimants by Prussia. His Majesty will not allow any surrender of
territory, therefore [this is] not to be further pursued.
3. Open annexation which will probably lead to war against Austria.
In this case France and Russia would be likely to observe benevolent
neutrality. War with Austria sooner or later is probably anyhow
not to be avoided; for Austria has again adopted the policy of
suppressing Prussia. Russia has given us to understand that she will
defend the rights of the House of Oldenburg should the Augustenburg claims succeed.

   One cannot *proffer the advice* to His Majesty to make a great war
upon Austria. The decision thereto can only derive from His
Majesty's free conviction. Then (in that case), however, one would
gladly follow him in it.

   The Finance Minister expressed cautious agreement, recommended a peaceful settlement.

   The War Minister declared himself decidedly for annexation.

   Count Itzenplitz very decidedly in favour of it.

   Von Raumer particularly emphasized that this was a duty
towards the Duchies. A protectorate led the Athenians only to the
Peloppenesian War; incorporation was better. Count von Lippe
justified this by the legal decision of the Crown lawyers.

   Von Selchow also very decidedly for the maintenance of our
rights.

   Count Eulenburg [also supported annexation] with the addition,
that it was not therefore necessary to proclaim it.

   The Crown Prince took an opposite point of view. Annexation
would lead to civil war in Germany and the intervention of foreign

---

   * For the complete separation of the Duchies of Schleswig and Holstein from
the Danish monarchy. Since 1864 they had been occupied on a provisional basis
by Austria and Prussia jointly. T.
   ** As their share of the joint Danish national debt. T.

Powers. The Hereditary Prince* was out-and-out Prussian and ready to accept the Prussian terms.

Von Bismarck protested against regarding war with Austria as civil war. If war with Austria in alliance with France was struck out of the diplomatic dictionary, no policy at all would ever be possible for Prussia. Only by a war against Austria could Prussia gain anything. Austria had always sought the French alliance and even now would accept it in the very hour that France agreed to it.

Count Eulenburg pointed out the ambiguity of the Augustenburg acceptance. Every single article left a door open. His Majesty finally asked me what the opinion of the army was. My personal conviction is that annexation is the only beneficial solution for the Duchies, as for Prussia.

The gain is such a great one that very considerable sacrifices must be made as well as the chances of a war be tolerated.

I cannot speak for the opinion of the army, but what I know and have heard of it is for annexation.

I have had to ask myself whether Prussia can take on the struggle against Austria. It would lead us far too far if I went into details here, but as the outcome of my investigations I can declare that, besides the excellence of our army, numerical supremacy can be attained at a decisive point, if the section of our militia, the second call-up, which does not serve for garrisoning the fortress [Kronborg] on the front line, goes into the field with the main army—otherwise not.

The Minister President then observed that the way to peace diverged very sharply from that to war . . .

Document 92   Blome (Munich) to Biegeleben, 9 March 1865
(Ritter von Srbik, editor, *Quellen zur deutschen Politik Österreichs*, Berlin, Oldenburg, 1937, vol. iv, p. 591)

You seek comfort from me, by dear Baron? You cannot be serious, for basically you see much more calmly into the future than I. I should rather let myself be heartened by your confidence, because, without support, I can hardly resist the uneasy impression that we are again about to fall between two stools and to sit on the floor in that beloved position with which we so successfully made ourselves familiar in the Crimean War and during the Polish question . . . I take as my point of departure the fundamental consideration that the maintenance of Denmark was an Austrian

* Son of the Duke of Augustenburg, who was not bound by his father's renunciation, see above, p. 153, note **. T.

and therefore a German and, in the last analysis, a European interest. In my opinion, an increase in Prussia's power in one form or another became inevitable from the day when the Duchies were forcibly torn from their natural association with the northern island Kingdom. There was nothing much left for us to do but to put a good face on a bad situation ... We seem to me perfectly justified in rejecting the last Prussian proposals;* for 'mediatization'** is incomparably more dangerous than annexation pure and simple. The latter is equally horrifying. The question is whether there is a third possibility. You put your finger on the wound when you suggest that we have a better instrument in our hand to frighten Prussia than Bismarck has for us—namely: the Messiah Imperator [Napoleon III]—the key to this as to all the puzzles of the present day. Now I assert that we no longer possess this instrument first, because, as experience shows, you will never persuade the important person [Mensdorff] to use it; secondly, because unfortunately they know that very well in Berlin where Bismarck, with the most irritating calmness, can reply to any possible threat of ours of this kind in the well known phrase 'terrorization cuts no ice'. Moreover, would Caesar III, if he had the choice, really rather play the game with us than with Prussia? I doubt it. As you yourself suggest, he is growing old and prefers to conquer provinces without, rather than with, war. It now turns out that we may indeed offer him the prospect of winning the German Rhineland by fighting but that unfortunately Prussia may peaceably cede it. Our only hope [that Prussia will not herself promise the Rhineland to Napoleon] rests in William's self-styled character as an honourable man and his proud declaration, 'a German village—they shan't have it'. But William has already been brought to accept much which he at first rejected. It is said, for example, that he is now already half convinced that his hereditary Brandenburg claims are well founded. You will grant me that Bismarck in any case has more chance of forcing him into the French alliance than we have of forcing [Mensdorff] into it. But such extremes apart, what means of pressure are available to us to make Prussia yield? If Bismarck should now peremptorily declare: either annexation or half-sovereignty or unlimited continuation of the *provisorium*, so that annexation may come of its own accord—what then? Refer the matter to the [Federal] Diet? Do not smile. A man like Pfordten can still harbour such illusions. Majority decisions, protests, proto-

---

* On 22 February 1865 Prussia had communicated the terms on which she would accept an Augustenburg solution or an Augustenburg vassal state.
** See above, p. 87, note *. T.

cols, warnings—vain dust! The dissolution of the Confederation?
Bravo! An out-and-out gain for Prussia! Federal Execution? Do
we really want to make war on Prussia for North Schleswig's
sake and set Europe aflame? Not so. The Emperor's entourage
thinks of that least of all and no one in Austria wants a war except
perhaps against Piedmont for the sake of Venice. What is the
point of resisting? Do we seriously think we can persuade a Bismarck with honeyed words or frighten him with hard ones? I
cannot help saying that the worst evil always seems to me to be to
bark without biting. The fruit of this system of half-heartedness is
unfailing: first, to make defeat, the splendid way we have been
tricked, all the more obvious because of our final surrender and so
to ruin Austria's moral influence in Germany all the more fundamentally; the second result is to annoy our opponent by our
clamour or at least to offer him a wonderful pretext at the next
opportunity to bite without barking. See Russia after 1856 . . .

So I am resigned and would propose to deliver Germany over to
the German Piedmont? Stop, not so quick, if you please. I acknowledge that we have conducted an ignominious campaign, but
that is a reason, it seems to me, for at least covering up our losses
by good policy instead of giving them an even more calamitous
shape. I believe Austria's influence could thus be rescued. Austria
lived down 1805 and 1809 and from 1815 to 1848 was at the head of
Europe. Why? Because from 1809 to 1813 she wisely held back
until the storm was over. If we were to strengthen ourselves internally (which unfortunately we don't do) and were to intervene skil-
fully in the next general conflagration, which will probably flare
up within the next two years from an Italian cause, Prussia
would fall back again into insignificance. As things now stand, we
can conclude no new alliance with the son of lies and—to his own
people—the father of conventions on the Seine. Our task is to prevent
Prussia from throwing herself into his arms . . . So, my dear Baron
I reason—right or wrong—here in my Bavarian solitude far
from the focal point of the state chancery in which all the rays of
European policy meet. My judgement is certainly quite one-sided
and I gladly submit it to your longer experience and clearer
insight . . . Let us put our hopes then in Prussian stupidity and
build upon Austria's proverbial luck. The latter is an article in all
our creeds and I need it as much for my policy as you undoubtedly
reckon upon it for yours . . .

Document 93   Wolckenstein (Stuttgart) to Mensdorff, 17 June 1865
(Vienna, Haus- Hof- und Staatsarchiv, PA VI, no. 29)

... First, so far as the recognition of the new Italian state by the Zollverein states is concerned, the Minister observed that he thought that he had clarified and precisely defined his basic standpoint by the declaration he made to the second Chamber ...

'For this reason alone', Herr von Varnbühler said, 'I vote against the Prussian proposal.' '*Moreover, Württemberg*', the Minister continued, '*cannot isolate herself in the field of trade policy*. We cannot separate ourselves from the other German states which surround us. *We must do whatever Bavaria or Saxony does* ...'

Document 94   Note of Pfordten (of Bavaria) on his meeting with Beust (of Saxony), 12 August 1865
(*Die Auswärtige Politik Preussens*, vol. vi, no. 243, p. 323)

Question I: If Austria and Prussia come to an understanding over a *provisorium* [in Schleswig Holstein] that we regard as disadvantageous, can we come out against it?
Only in the Press.

Question II: What ways and means are at hand in order to bring about a final decision?
Furtherance of our motion [in the Diet] at Frankfurt, should the need arise, with a minority decision.

Question III: For the definitive solution two cases are conceivable:

i. Austria maintains the rights of Augustenburg. How is Prussia to be persuaded to yield to that?
(a) By agreement to her demands in so far as this is possible within the law of the Confederation.
(b) By a conciliatory step on the part of the Duke.
(c) By an initiative of Austria in the Confederation in the way discussed, i.e. either by drawing up a programme or by formulating a motion for the recognition of the Duke.

ii. Austria abandons Augustenburg. What should we do?
(a) If the majority of the Confederation supports us, form a new Confederation of the medium-sized states with a Parliament.
(b) If only the minority supports us, protest and declare that we consider our task for the time being at an end.

This was agreed with Baron Beust, 12 August 1865.

Document 95 Bismarck to William I, 20 March 1866
(O. von Bismarck, *Gesammelte Werke,* vol. v, p. 412)

During a conversation just held with the Italian envoy, and in connection with my statement approved by Your Majesty yesterday, I made the following suggestion:

That we should conclude a treaty of friendship, cast in general expressions of goodwill, in itself binding neither of the two Powers to anything definite, but containing a promise to enter into negotiations for a specific war alliance as soon as one of the two Powers should consider that it had to conduct a war. In order that, in such a case, no further time should be lost in negotiations, the text of this second treaty should be agreed upon at the time of the conclusion of the first (the one drawn up in general terms). Its signature should, however, be withheld and either Your Majesty's representative in Florence or the Italian envoy here be provided with such full powers that, on the outbreak of war, it would only be necessary for both governments to agree by telegraph on 'yes' or 'no', to put the plenipotentiary in a position to conclude with the Minister of the other state . . .

Document 96 Protocol of a meeting of Ministers, drawn up by Belcredi, approved by Francis Joseph, 21 February 1866
(Ritter von Srbik, editor, *Quellen zur deutschen Politik Österreichs,* Berlin, Oldenburg, 1937, vol. v, p. 202)

In the chair: the Emperor.
Present: Mensdorff, Belcredi, Esterházy, Frank, Majláth, Larisch, Komers, Wüllerstorf, Haller, Kussevich.
. . . V. Conduct necessitated by the threatening attitude of Prussia in the Schleswig Holstein question. The threatening attitude, which Prussia has recently assumed in the Schleswig Holstein affair, His Majesty observed, raises the question whether we should calmly look on at these demonstrations or whether the honour, dignity, and security of Austria do not demand that such warlike preparations should be made as shall enable us calmly to face all eventualities, however serious. He admittedly shared the view that no sufficient occasion existed for such a deplorable event as a clash between Austria and Prussia; on the other hand, one must probably take into serious consideration the fact that the Prussian army was at present much more ready to take the field and that the railway network there would greatly facilitate its despatch to the chief strategic points, whereas our army had been reduced to the utmost limit of an army on a peace footing and to bring it up to its full

complement would require a great deal of time. Count Mensdorff also expressed the view that there was no occasion in the present foreign relations of the Empire for an event so difficult to gauge in its consequences as war; that, moreover, one could not tell where fate could drive the Government in Prussia, given the complications of the internal situation there, the position of the Government *vis à vis* the Lower House and the impossibility that such a situation could persist much longer ... Count Esterházy observed in this connection that the fate of Schleswig in particular did not concern the Germanic Confederation, but the fate of Holstein* did. He was expressing his opinion bluntly that any wavering on our side, and still more any concession, would entail the most damaging consequences for our own Fatherland. We must show our teeth. It was the task of our diplomacy so to define our attitude that our allies in the Germanic Confederation could have no doubt at all about our views and our conduct ...

The Finance Minister, Count Larisch, and the Minister of Trade, Baron von Wüllerstorf, urged a peaceful solution, if at all possible, because, if events should take a warlike turn, the repercussions upon the finances and the economy of the Monarchy would have immeasurably disastrous consequences. The Hungarian Chancellor von Majláth mentioned the assertion of an important Prussian emissary that in the event of war Prussia could rely on Russia and Italy. He was also of opinion that any warlike demonstration on this side was to be avoided as long as possible but could not hide the fact that if Austria should ever be involved in a war, none could be more popular than one against Prussia. The Minister of State, Count Belcredi, agreed with Count Esterházy in thinking that it was the government's duty to inspire our fellow members in the Germanic Confederation with confidence in our policy. At the same time, one must not hide from oneself the danger that, precisely in this question, democracy stood behind the German governments and drove them forward. Precautions must, therefore, be adopted to see that any action taken should be that of the legal Government and not that of democratic revolution. His Majesty expressed, in conclusion, the opinion that he agreed with the view that he should leave warlike preparations for the time being aside and should continue to seek the maintenance of the honour and dignity, as well as of the interests, of the country by diplomatic means. The preparations, moreover, could all be made on paper ...

* Schleswig was not a member of the Germanic Confederation, but Holstein was. T.

Document 97   Károlyi (Berlin) to Mensdorff, 22 February 1866
(Vienna, Haus- Hof- und Staatsarchiv, PA III, no. 91)

... So far, during the whole course of the Duchies question, the
differences between the two Powers have been limited to the Cabinets. They have now been transplanted to the field of public opinion.
An ominous silence reigns while the Prussian Cabinet at this moment
is meeting. I should like to think that this artificial exaggeration of
the danger by public opinion formed an essential part of the calculations and actions of Count Bismarck. If the purpose of his policy
is to bring the Duchies question quickly to a definitive solution in a
specifically Prussian sense, it is to his interest to win public opinion,
through the Press and similar manifestations to an increasing extent
for this aim; to excite it in this direction; to identify the honour
and the interests of Prussia with such a solution; to call into being
such tense public feeling and to drive relations with Austria to such
an acute crisis that no other solution than a definitive one should
seem open to Prussia and that finally the force of events should
irresistably thrust the situation to the ultimate consequence, a
casus belli ... As a result of my last impressions, I am clear that
Count Bismarck no longer intends a mere attempt at intimidation
for the attainment of his purposes (he may have limited himself
to this in the various previous phases of the Gastein Convention),
if he does not succeed, at least in a partial furthering of his policy.
He holds that the time has come to mount a great Prussian action
abroad and, if it can be done in no other way, to appeal to the
arbitrament of war, and he thinks that circumstances are favourable
for this. Such an action has been from the beginning the goal of his
political career. It would suitably quiet his ungoverned and unscrupulous, but daring, thirst for achievement.

Count Bismarck considers the annexation of the Duchies, or
something approaching it, a matter of life and death for his political
existence and he seeks to make it appear such for Prussia too. After
such a success, especially if it were attained by means of a fortunate
war, the Government would more easily master the internal strife.
Its end without the diversion of war would be subject to the most
critical difficulties; for it is absolutely inconceivable that King
William could bring about legal recognition of the principles
represented by his Government without a *coup d'état*. His Majesty
is supposed to have positively refused his consent to the *coup d'état*,
which Count Bismarck may well have recommended. The most
effective, indeed the only means, of bringing about a sudden change
internally must thus be sought in the field of foreign policy. It is
such points of view which guide Bismarckian policy.

As to the disposition of the King towards Austria, I heard recently that His Majesty is pretty excited and considers the situation a serious one. How far Count Bismarck has succeeded, or will succeed, in winning His Majesty for his extreme policy is precisely the question on which the whole future depends. I need not say that a forcible solution goes most decidedly against the grain with the King. Yet His Majesty is easily accessible to personal influences and is especially sensitive to illusions about supposed injuries to Prussian honour etc. The influence on His Majesty of Count Bismarck in alliance with one or two high-up military personalities must be ceaselessly active in this direction. . . .

Document 98   Blome (Munich) to Mensdorff, 20 May 1866
(Ibid., PA IV, no. 36)

. . . The material fruits of victory will of course be small, but it is the moral gains from it we need. They will make amends for Magenta and Solferino. Trust in Austria's star and the strength of Austria's resolution will be revived. If, next, instead of a long peace a series of wars were to follow, that too would have its good side: it would hold off the Revolution. *Inter armes silent*, not *leges* (that's not necessary) as the Latin proverb wrongly says, but talk of constitutions, *loquaces revolutionarii*, which by incessant legislation would simply make the observance of any laws difficult. Without a war there is only the prospect of insecure peace or Revolution. The perspective of further wars has, therefore, little terror for me. Nor do I fear to pass for inhuman; for revolution costs more streams of blood and undermines prosperity more fundamentally than war and—which is often worse—it destroys the moral strength of the nation which war, contrariwise, raises. If we need war, but, on the other hand, ought not to attack, we must oblige the enemy to attack by using means, which because they remain strictly within the bounds of the law, cannot be made a reproach to us . . .

I had an audience today with the old King Louis who repeatedly called out: 'Now don't attack! Magnificent, the temper in Austria! Congratulate the Emperor! Splendid! Quite different from Prussia. Bravo. But don't attack! And don't sacrifice the Rhine, not that. Bismarck and Cavour are base thieves. King William unintelligible —a weak head. I have just come from Nice—the feeling quite Italian, not at all for France. Baden is pitiable. Always was. No mentality. But don't attack! . . .'

Documents 99a and 99b   War, we need war, only war

99a   Blome (Munich) to Mensdorff, 29 May 1866
  (Ibid.)

God be praised and glorified! So we make progress in the Holstein affair! ... Mistrust towards Austria will disappear, right-
thinking people will attain a majority in the Chamber and the
Governments will be strengthened in their opposition to Prussia.
It will even be impossible for Pfordten, in Paris or elsewhere, to go
for a compromise with Prussia for the sake of his beloved peace.
This declaration of ours, which alas! cannot be delivered before
next Friday, must be published as soon as possible. Our interests
demand it. Bismarck is unfortunately still too weak to forge a
cause of war from it. His position becomes more untenable from day
to day owing to the cost of Prussian mobilization which becomes
constantly more burdensome. If only the financial exhaustion of the
Prussian government and people does not bring him down! Then we
should have peace and a Parliament, that is, Austria's exclusion from
Germany. War, we need war, only war. The Congress is a humbug
and a misfortune into the bargain. Perhaps it may serve to let us
see more clearly into Napoleon's intentions, but surely it will delay
the outbreak of war and spoil our position in Italy ...

99b   Conversation of Bismarck with Miquel,* 1866
  (O. von Bismarck, *Gesammelte Werke*, vol. vii, p. 118)

... In the evening in the beer-house Miquel recounted a conversation with Bismarck in 1866. It was the end of May and Miquel had
come from Hanover to Berlin to find out where he stood. Abeken,
his only acquaintance, told him that it was certain there would be
war. In the evening Bismarck had Miquel asked whether he would
not come to him. Miquel insisted on a written invitation (as that
time it was considered a sin to go of one's own accord to Bismarck)
and received one. After he had waited in an ante-room, over-
crowded with every possible person, he called on him at night at
one o'clock. Bismarck: 'Now, how are things in Hanover? I have
just concluded an alliance with your kingdom through Stock-
hausen.' Miquel: 'Had you concluded ten treaties with him, the
King of Hanover would not go with you, he will not respect the
alliance.' Bismarck: 'That is just my opinion, on that we are at
one. But you and yours *shall* help me. We cannot do without
Hanover. She has always been on our side: in the Seven Years'

* See above, p. 114. T.

War; in 1813. We cannot let Hanover, since it lies between the two parts of our monarchy, stand against us. We must occupy it if it votes against us in the Confederation.' Miquel: 'Yes, but we cannot support you, if you break the constitution like that.' Bismarck: 'How otherwise can I deal with the King. Don't trouble yourself now about the constitution. Later on when we have won our victory, you shall have your fill of constitutions. Would you be so good, when you get back to Hanover, as to go to Count Platen and say, if he won't support us I must occupy Hanover, we are strong enough even without him?' Miquel: 'I shall be glad to do it, but it won't help, for we must speak plain today. Platen considers Your Excellency a fool.' Bismarck: 'I cannot be offended with him for that, but I tell you, we shall yet realize our aim, a short campaign in Bohemia and we shall checkmate the Austrians and the thing is done. It is your national duty to stand by us.' Miquel: 'We should not go through with it.' Bismarck: 'Then I tell you, we have not the least need of you' . . .

Document 100 Prussian proclamation 'To the German People', Saturday, 16 June 1866
(H. Kohl, *Dreissig Jahre preussisch-deutscher Geschichte 1858–88 in amtlichen Kundgebungen*, Giessen, 1888, p. 90)

The Germanic Confederation for half a century has represented and promoted, not the unity, but the fragmentation of Germany. It has long lost the confidence of the nation and for the foreigner it counts as a guarantee of Germany's continuing weakness and powerlessness. Now, over and above that, it has been abused in order to call Germany to arms against one of its members: the very member who by its proposal for the calling of a German Parliament had taken the first and decisive step to satisfy the demand for national unity. The federal constitution affords no ground, neither a good reason nor an apparent pretext, for the war against Prussia sought by Austria.

The decision of the 14 June, when a majority of the members of the Confederation passed a resolution to arm against Prussia, finally violated the federal constitution and abolished the Confederation.

All that remains is the basis of the Confederation: the living unity of the German nation. It is the duty of governments and peoples to find a new means of [constitutionally] expressing this unity and one with the strength to last.

Prussia has the further duty, linked with this, of defending her independence, threatened by the decision of 14 June and the arming of her enemies. The Prussian people offers its total strength to perform this duty. In doing so, it proclaims its decision to take up the struggle for the national unity of Germany hitherto thwarted by the self-interest of individual states.

Immediately on the dissolution of the Confederation, Prussia, therefore, offered to the governments a new alliance based on simple provision for mutual defence and participation in the national struggle. She sought nothing beyond the preservation of peace and, for this purpose, the immediate calling of a Parliament.

Her hope that this just and moderate demand would be met has been disappointed. Prussia's offer has been declined. Prussia is, therefore, obliged to act upon her duty of self-defence. At such an hour, Prussia can tolerate neither enemies nor doubtful friends on her borders or within them.

When Prussian troops cross her frontiers they do not come as enemies of the people. Prussia respects their independence and hopes to deliberate on the future destiny of our German Fatherland together with their representatives in a German national assembly.

Let the German people, with this high aim in mind, come forward in confidence to meet Prussia. Let it help to promote and make secure the peaceful development of our common Fatherland!

Document 101   Bismarck to Manteuffel,* 9 June 1866
(R. Sternfeld, 'Ein Brief Bismarcks an Edwin von Manteuffel', *Historische Zeitschrift*, vol. cxviii, 1917, p. 251)

I was acquainted with your conviction, expressed here when you had occasion, that for political, military, and financial reasons we must take on the war quickly and wherever opportunity offers. I saw to it, therefore, that my telegram conveying your instructions should prompt you to act in that sense. I expected important news from you in the course of yesterday. Information about the friendly tone of the music on both sides of the military *chassés-croisés* does not harmonize with the feeling *here* which expects news from you of the first cannon shots. You say: 'To take possession would be confusing as an act of force.' I answer you in Deveroux's words: 'Friend, it is now *time* to make a noise!' If you don't do it, you will not only frustrate my European plan out of military courtesy but you will find no one, apart from the Württembergers, in the army who any longer understands your behaviour. Every three days costs us 2 millions which we shall not have in our possession to give much longer; for we do not, like Austria, live at the expense of our

* General Edwin von Manteuffel, Prussian governor in Holstein. T.

creditors. Every three days brings to Austria 5,000 more men of the army of the Confederation. In all parts of Europe the wind lies in our favour. People *expect* us to act. *Today* they would find it natural, perhaps in a week's time they would not. Three days ago we communicated the situation to the friendly Courts. They will now ask questions about our campaign of politeness in Holstein. I had hoped that in consideration of all these factors you would play the part of [General] York* [and take the law into your own hands]; now you have to act on the precise orders of the King, and if you don't carry them out as quickly as our *policy taken as a whole* demands, Your Excellency will do Prussia great harm. Should we fall back again into the bog of half shares and the condominium [with Austria], it would be difficult to recover at the right time so favourable an occasion for war as the present one . . .

Document 102 Conversation of Bismarck with the journalist, Vibort, 4/5 June 1866
(O. von Bismarck, *Gesammelte Werke*, vol. vii, p. 118)

. . . 'Sir,' [Vibort said to Bismarck], 'it is my object to keep the French public as well informed as possible over everything that happens in Germany. Allow me, then, to talk to you with complete frankness. I gladly acknowledge that Prussia appears at present to follow aims in her foreign policy which are congenial to the French nation in a quite extraordinary way: the aims, that is, of finally freeing Italy from Austria and constituting united Germany on a foundation of universal suffrage. But does there not exist between your Prussian and your German policy a flagrant contradiction? You proclaim that a National Parliament is the only source from which Germany can arise new-born, the supreme power alone capable of realizing her new destiny. Yet meanwhile you treat the Lower House in Berlin after the manner of Louis XIV when, horsewhip in hand, he entered the Paris *Parlement*. We in France do not concede that a relationship is possible between absolutism and democracy and, to speak frankly, in Paris public opinion has not taken your project of a National Parliament seriously. It is seen only as a well-thought-out stratagem of war. It is generally thought that you are the kind of man, who, when you had used this tool, would break it into pieces again as soon as it became troublesome and useless to you.'

'Upon my honour,' replied Bismarck, 'you go right to the heart of the matter. I know that in France I enjoy the same unpopularity

* Prussian Field Marshal who by acting without orders precipitated Prussia's entry into the 1813 coalition against Napoleon. T.

as in Germany. Everywhere I am made responsible for a situation which I have not created. It has forced itself upon me as upon everyone else. I am the scapegoat of public opinion, but I don't trouble myself about that. I pursue my aim with the quietest conscience—an aim which seems to me right for my state and for Germany. As far as the means are concerned, I use those which, for the want of any others, offer themselves. There is much to say about the internal situation of Prussia. In order to judge it impartially one must know and study the particular character of its population from its roots. Whereas France and Italy, each in its own way, represents a great society which is animated by one mind and feeling, in Germany by contrast individualism reigns. Each man lives here in his own little corner with his own opinion, always full of mistrust towards the Government and his neighbour. Each man judges everything according to his own personal point of view, never according to that of the whole. Self-interest and the need to contradict are developed among the Germans to an inconceivable degree. Show him an open door—he will prefer to insist upon going through a hole in the wall rather than through the door.' . . . 'People celebrate', he continued, 'the victories of Frederick the Great, but when he died they rubbed their hands for joy to be free from a despot. Together with this contrariness there yet prevails a deep attachment to the dynasty. There is no Prince, no Minister, no Government which will ever be able to get the better of this inclination of the Prussians to individualism. Yet they all cry from the heart "Long live the King" and when he commands they obey.'

'Nevertheless, Sir, one hears that discontent may lead to revolution, one day.'

'The Government has no need to fear that and, indeed, is not anxious about it. Our revolutionaries are not so terrifying. Their hostility exhausts itself principally in accusations against the Minister, but they have respect for the King. It is I who am the evil-doer and I alone who provoke their anger! With somewhat greater impartiality you would acknowledge that I have acted as I have, because I could not act otherwise. Given the present position of Prussia in Germany and *vis à vis* Austria, we *need* an army. In Prussia it is the only force capable of being disciplined. The Prussian', Bismarck continued, 'who had an arm cut off on the barricades would be ashamed to go home and his wife would laugh at him as a silly fool. But in the army he is a soldier worthy of admiration and fights like a lion for the honour of his country. . .'

Document 103   Extract from the diary of the Baroness
Spitzemberg
(R. Vierhaus, editor, *Das Tagebuch der Baronin Spitzemberg*,
Göttingen, 1960, p. 69)

8 July [1866] Until today it has been impossible for me to recall
the days that have just gone by partly for lack of time, but chiefly
because I have been in too sad a mood to write down what I should
like for ever to forget. On 3 July there took place between Josefstadt
and Königgrätz the battle of Sadowa in which eight Prussian
army corps gained a great victory, after a hard battle, over five
Austrian army corps. The retreat soon degenerated into a mad
flight so that the enemy gained an endless number of prisoners
and 116 cannons. 70,000 men on both sides were killed, drowned
in the Elbe, wounded, missing, or taken prisoner. In short, Austria
has perhaps never before suffered such a frightful defeat. In addition, a few days later she gave up Venice to France and entreated
Napoleon to mediate for an armistice between herself, Italy, and
Prussia. Negotiations have, therefore, been conducted of which the
result is still in doubt. Meanwhile the Prussians advance in Bohemia
and Moravia, meeting no resistance, for the northern army seems
completely broken up and dissolved. Clam-Gallas, Henikstein, and
Krismanič have been brought before a court martial; for it seems
that irresponsible mistakes in leadership were once again com-
mitted even if superior power and especially the terrible effect of the
needle-gun brought about the decision. Meanwhile there prevails
in the Federal Army the most lamentable inactivity and confusion.
The Bavarians have now had a few skirmishes with the Prussians,
but on the whole no progress is made. It is the army of the Holy
Roman Empire over again. Prince William of Baden declared that,
in these circumstances, he wished to withdraw the Baden Corps
and only gave way because his troops then threatened to throw him
out of the window and to murder him. Oh shame and disgrace! . . .

Document 104   Goltz (Paris) to William I, 4 July 1866
(H. Oncken, *Die Rheinpolitik Kaiser Napoleons III 1863–70*,
1926, vol. i, p. 301)

. . . The Emperor [Napoleon III] answered me: Your urgent
wish, then, is that the existence of the Imperial Austrian state
should not be threatened. [He said] the destruction of Austria
would cause a gap in the European state system, which could not be
filled without a general conflagration. Russia would oppose her
destruction. Nor might France be able to remain quiet. The war

undertaken by Your Majesty was necessary to secure for Prussia a better position. It took courage that cannot be sufficiently admired for Your Majesty and Your Majesty's Minister President to undertake this war; for at first the country itself was against it and Europe no less so. Success must have exceeded Your Majesty's boldest hopes . . . He, therefore, advises Prussia not to go too far, to show moderation, and to be content with the consolidation of that position in the balance of power which she has justifiably won . . .

Document 105   Bismarck to Eulenburg,* 26 July 1866
(O. von Bismarck, *Gesammelte Werke*, vol. vi, p. 84)

If hostilities are not continued—their continuation is unlikely—we have the prospect of the following peace terms: exclusion of Austria; the closest North German Confederation under Prussia; its relations with south Germany reserved for free understanding; war costs; the annexation of the Duchies recognized, with a plebiscite in northern Schleswig; annexation of Hanover, Hesse-Cassel, Nassau, Upper Hesse,** and Frankfurt conceded by Austria and France; a treaty with Saxony containing the February terms with Holstein somewhat modified; no land from Austria. There is no more to be had. Work so that our newspapers demand no more, but come out strongly for the annexation of Hanover and Hesse.

Document 106   Preliminary Treaty of Peace between Austria and Prussia, signed at Nikolsburg, 26 July 1866***
(E. Hertslet, *Map of Europe by Treaty*, London, 1875, vol. iii, p. 1698)

Article I. With the exception of the Lombardo-Venetian Kingdom,**** the territory of the Austrian monarchy remains intact . . .
Article II. His Majesty the Emperor of Austria recognizes the dissolution of the Germanic Confederation as it has existed hitherto, and consents to a new organization of Germany without the participation of the Empire of Austria. His Majesty likewise promises to recognize the closer Union which will be founded by His Majesty the King of Prussia, to the north of the line of the Main, and he declares that he consents to the German states south of that line entering into a Union, the national relations of which, with the

* Count Fritz zu Eulenburg, Prussian Minister of the Interior, 1862–78. T.
** The part of Hesse-Darmstadt north of the Main. T.
*** The Peace of Prague, 23 August 1866, was the definitive Peace Treaty. T.
**** Ceded to the Kingdom of Italy. T.

North German Confederation, are to be the subject of an ulterior agreement between the two parties.

Article III. His Majesty the Emperor of Austria transfers to His Majesty the King of Prussia all the rights which the Treaty of Vienna of 30th October, 1864 recognized as belonging to him over the Duchies of Schleswig and Holstein, with the reservation, that the people of the northern districts of Schleswig shall be again united to Denmark if they express a desire to be so by a vote freely given.

Article IV. His Majesty the Emperor of Austria undertakes to pay His Majesty the King of Prussia the sum of 40,000,000 *thalers* to cover part of the expenses which Prussia has been put to by the war . . .

Article V. In conformity with the wish expressed by His Majesty the Emperor of Austria, His Majesty the King of Prussia declares his willingness to let the territorial state of the Kingdom of Saxony continue in its present extent, when the modifications are made which are to take place in Germany; reserving to himself, however, to regulate in detail, by a special Peace with His Majesty the King of Saxony, the questions as to Saxony's part in the expenses of the war, as well as the future position of the Kingdom of Saxony in the North German Confederation. [Articles VI-IX deal with Italian side, ratifications, arrangements for the conclusion of a definitive peace treaty, and armistice arrangements.]

Document 107 Extract from the diary of the Baroness Spitzemberg.

(R. Vierhaus, editor, *Das Tagebuch der Baronin Spitzemberg*, Göttingen, 1960, p. 72)

19 August [1866]. My dear husband looks splendid and is very pleased with the peace concluded in Berlin. They were very well received by Bismarck and came to an understanding at once. Württemberg is to pay 8 million *gelder* in war indemnity and, otherwise, is to remain with frontiers quite unaltered and unimpaired. There can be no question yet, on account of France, of entry into the North German Confederation. After peace had been concluded the King received our men and made them a very silly speech, that is, he scolded them soundly for standing by Austria. In addition Prussia has now annexed Hanover, Hesse-Cassel and Nassau. Baden is also to pay money. Bavaria seems likely to have to surrender both land and money. Austria has gained a favourable peace at our cost. Prussia has been recommended to turn to us

[the medium-sized states] for the damages she demanded in land and money and Austria esteems herself lucky to be rid of us. Since she gives up the cause, we too as a German state must give it up . . .

Document 108   Extract from a private letter
    (B. Beer, *Louis Schwarzkopff*, Leipzig, 1943, p. 87)

. . . On 25 July 1866* the cardinal question which must be put to the Members of Parliament in the present situation, and which I will then put to Herr von Unruh, is this: *Will you, now that war has broken out, and so long as war lasts, allow the Government money or not? If a candidate does not answer 'yes' to this question I will not give him my vote. I believe that many* Wahlmänner** *of this electoral college will agree with me in this* . . .

I must confess that the programmes which have recently been published by many former Members of Parliament have made me cautious. I have been elected *Wahlmann* of this district three times and have always voted for Schulze-Delitzsch. In such a time as the present I want to hear definitely from him whether he still maintains the attitude 'not a penny to this Ministry in any circumstances'. It is our incontestable duty as *Wahlmänner* in the present circumstances to inform ourselves afresh, before the election and before giving our vote, how our Members feel now . . .

Document 109   Speech of Bismarck in the Prussian Lower House, 1 September 1866
    (H. Kohl, *Bismarckreden*, 1847–95, 7th impression, Stuttgart, 1915, p. 68)

. . . The more sincerely the King's Government desires peace, the more Members of Parliament feel it their duty to refrain from retrospective criticism, whether to defend or to attack. During the last four years Members have spoken for their point of view repeatedly from both sides, some with hostility, some with goodwill. During the last four years nobody on one side has been able to convince anybody on the other. Each has believed he was acting right in acting as he did. The conclusion of peace in foreign relations, too, would be difficult to bring about if an acknowledgement were demanded from one of the two contracting parties; 'I perceive now, that I have acted wrong.' We wish for peace in this domestic conflict, but not because we are not equal to the struggle. On the

* The date of the second ballot in the elections to the Prussian Lower House. T.
** Electors of the actual M.P.s in the system of indirect election. Unruh and Schulze-Delitzsch were both candidates for re-election to the Lower House. T.

7

contrary, the tide is flowing more in our favour at this moment than it has done for years. Nor do we wish for peace in order to escape a possible accusation under a law to be enacted in the future about responsibility. I do not believe we shall be accused. I do not believe, that if we are accused, we shall be condemned. And even if that happened—well, many charges have been made against the Ministry, but never that of fear! (laughter). We wish for peace because in our view the Fatherland needs it at the present moment more than ever before. We wish for it and therefore seek it, because we believe that at the present moment we can find it. We would have sought it before could we have hoped to find it before. We believe we shall find it, because you will have recognized that the King's Government does not stand so far from the aims which the majority of you also strive after, as perhaps you have for years thought; nor so far as the silence of the Government over much that had to be kept quiet could have justified you in believing (Bravo!). For this reason we believe that we can find peace and seek it honourably. We have offered our hand to you and the commission's proposal indicates that you will clasp it. Thus we shall discharge the tasks, which remain to be discharged, with you jointly. I in no way exclude from them improvements of the domestic situation in fulfilment of the promises given in the constitution (lively cheers from all sides). But we can only discharge them in common in so far as each side serves the same Fatherland with the same goodwill without doubting the sincerity of the other. At this moment, however, the tasks of foreign policy are still undischarged. The brilliant successes of the armies have simply considerably increased the stake we have in the game; we have more to lose than before and the game itself is not yet won. The firmer we stand together in internal affairs, the more sure we are to win it.

It has often been said 'what the sword has won, the pen has spoiled', but I have complete confidence that we shall not hear 'what sword and pen have won have been destroyed' from this platform (lively applause).

Document 110 Extract from the speech of J. Miquel* in Osnabrück, December 1866
(W. Mommsen, *Deutsche Parteiprogramme*, Munich, 1960, p. 141)

... The simple task of the next Parliament consists in rallying the national elements, in overcoming the particularist reaction and in

* Miquel, leader of the National Liberal Party in the Prussian Parliament, was then Mayor of Osnabruck; cf. above, p. 114, note *. T.

supporting the Government, according to our strength, in its efforts to set up a united and strong north-German state.

What we have so far experienced of the course of negotiations justifies our confidence that the constitution, to be laid before Parliament for its enactment, truly expresses the nation's need for unity and power. Members of Parliament will, therefore, be in the fortunate position of fighting by the side of the Government for this aim for the first time since the awakening of German national feeling. The time for ideals has passed. German unity has climbed down from the world of dreams to the prosaic world of reality. Politicians today have to ask less what is desirable than what is attainable . . .

Document 111 Opening paragraph of the foundation programme of the National Liberal Party, June 1867
(Ibid., p. 147)

When the old Confederation broke up last year and the Prussian Government announced its serious determination to maintain the national bond and to set German unity on firmer foundations, we had no doubt that the Liberal forces of the nation would have to co-operate if the work of unification was both to succeed and to satisfy the people's need of freedom. For this purpose we were ready for co-operation, but it would only be possible if the Government abandoned its violation of constitutional rights, acknowledged the principles so vigorously defended by the Liberal Party, and asked for and obtained the indemnity. The groupings within the Parties, shaped by the constitutional conflict, could not suffice to secure this co-operation. The formation of the National Liberal Party, for the purpose of restoring the unity of Germany and of bringing her once again to power and freedom on the given principles, met the new need . . .

Document 112 Closing sentences of the election address of the Conservative *Reichstag* Party for elections to the Prussian *Landtag*, 24 October 1867
(Ibid., p. 52)

. . . The Conservative Party, without any change in its principles, seeks your firm support in loyal devotion to a King, who late in life went on to the battlefield for Germany's greatness and unity, and in devotion to a people which, with courage for sacrifice, followed him. It will hold sacred the maxim it has received from its kings, that what Prussia gains must be won for Germany, in trust in God who gave the beginning and will also confirm the completion [of the task] . . .

Document 113   Election programme of the Free Conservative Party, 27 October 1867
(Ibid., p. 54)

. . . We set the *Fatherland always above the Party;* we put the *national* interest above *everything.*

That has a deep meaning. The history of the Prussian state counts for us as the pre-history of the new Germany. The great task which was performed step by step in the creation of the Prussian state, the Zollverein, and the North German Confederation, goes now towards its fulfilment and completion: not only in the inevitable union with the German south, but also in the internal evolution of the new *German state* towards which, in this *Reichstag,* the first significant steps have been taken. In so far as we offer our support to the national policy of the Federal Chancellor, who pursues these aims in every way in which independent men, who are true to their convictions can do so, we realize, on our part, the thoroughly Conservative idea carefully to cherish the healthy elements of established institutions and those elements capable of development, and to carry them forward—not breaking with history nor seeking to alter the living reality according to doctrinaire standards. The North German Confederation, evolving into a German *Reich,* derived from the Zollverein, appears to us as the *German* development of the Prussian monarchy.

Even so, expressing the true Conservative spirit, we should candidly and duly acknowledge the entry of this monarchy into the ranks of the *constitutional states.* Absolutism has had its glorious past in Prussia. Nowhere in the world has it left a more imperishable memorial than this state, the work of complete royal power. But *the days of absolutism are over* . . .

We honour the state's constitution as a strengthening of the Kingdom, as a development of the nation, as a guarantee of the freedom of the Church, and of the parity of denominations, and a security that political rights shall be independent of religious confessions. We reject pseudo-constitutionalism as the degradation and debasement of public life. In the same way we contest the out-of-date, yet still propagated doctrine of the separation of powers, against which we hold with conviction the principle of the joint execution of the single power of the state . . .

We dedicate ourselves with complete devotion to the promotion of the economic interests of our people in the questions of taxation, of trade and communications, of agriculture, and of the important relationship between capital and labour. We dedicate ourselves no less to a serious care for the intellectual wellbeing of the nation, for its primary schools, grammar schools, universities, and academies.

We wish to support in manly independence the power of the Confederation and the government of the state, where its policy agrees with our principles and especially where it *puts national interest first*. In true loyalty to King and Fatherland we shall, however, maintain with decision our Free Conservative principles where it departs from them.

Document 114 The programme of the Saxon People's Party, Chemnitz, 1866
(Ibid., p. 307)

1. The unlimited right of self-determination for the people. Universal, equal and direct franchise with secret ballot in all fields of political life (Parliament, the Parliaments of the individual states, in the parishes etc.). Militias instead of the standing army. A Parliament endowed with more nearly complete power, able particularly to decide over peace and war.
2. The unification of Germany in a democratic form of state. No hereditary Central Power. No small Germany under Prussian leadership. Nor Prussia enlarged by annexations. Nor a great Germany under Austria's leadership. Nor a tripartite Germany. These and similar aspirations in a dynastic and particularist direction, which can only lead to slavery, fragmentation, and foreign domination, are to be fought by the Democratic Party in the most resolute way.
3. The annulment of all privileges of status, birth, and confession.
4. Encouragement of the physical, intellectual, and moral education of the people. The separation of school from Church, of the Church from the State, and of the State from the Church. The encouragement of institutions for training teachers and a better status for teachers. The raising of the primary school to a state institution, paid for out of the State Treasury and giving free instruction. The provision of the means for and the foundation of institutions of higher education for those who have grown beyond the primary schools.
5. Promotion of the general welfare and the liberation of work and the workers from all oppression and every fetter. The improvement of the position of the working classes. Freedom of movement,

freedom to engage in any calling, general German citizenship, promotion and support of co-operative enterprise, especially production co-operatives, so that the opposition between capital and labour may be smoothed away.

6. Parochial self-government.

7. Encouragement of a knowledge of the law among the people. Through the independence of judges and trial by jury, especially in political and Press cases; public and oral judicial procedure.

8. Promotion of the political and social education of the people by means of a free Press, free right of assembly and association, and the right to form any societies.

Documents 115a and 115b   Rothschild and the *Seehandlung*

115a   Rothschild to Camphausen, President of the Seehandlung, 24 August 1866
(Berlin, Hauptarchiv, Rep. 109, no. 363)

. . . I beg you to withdraw the notice* that has been given, so that out of my constant and sincere desire to be of service, I may continue to act in the interest of Prussian finances as heretofore. . . .

115b   Camphausen to Rothschild, 1 September 1866
(Ibid.)

. . . At present . . . it is not known when the definitive union of the town of Frankfurt with the Kingdom of Prussia will take place and what arrangements for the financial system there will be. In any event the *Seehandlung*** on its part will not be able to do anything about it, if the treaty is not renewed . . .

Document 116   Memorandum of Bismarck (Putbus), 30 October 1866
(O. von Bismarck, *Gesammelte Werke*, vol. vi, no. 615, p. 167)

Is Savigny*** acquainted with the current drafts of the North German Constitution? . . . He can gain a clear idea from them of the faults to be found in it. The drafts too much favour a centralized federal state for the future accession of the South Germans. In

---

* Notice of the expiry of the treaty which entitled Rothschild to dispose of Prussian loans in south Germany.

** The *Seehandlung* had become a state bank of Prussia with the special task of investing state loans.

*** Karl von Savigny, Prussian representative at the Federal Diet. T.

form, it will have to incline more to a league of states. It can be given the character, in practice, of a federal state by means of elastic turns of phrase apparently meaningless but in fact having wide implications. A Federal Diet,* not a Ministry, will act as the Central Executive, and there I believe we shall do well to rely chiefly on the system of voting used in the old Federation [of 1815].

We must make over to the central institutions the subjects on which they have power to legislate as soon as possible. We adhere to the programme, announced before the war, that federal laws shall be enacted by agreement of the majority of the Federal Diet* with that of the representative assembly.

The more one adheres to the old *forms*, the easier will matters be arranged. Any attempt. on the other hand, to cause a fully-armed Minerva to spring forth from the head of the Praesidium will bring us nowhere except to academic arguments ...

In my view, the essentials are: no assembly of Estates, no *Wahlmänner*, [i.e. no system of indirect voting] and no property qualification for the vote. The franchise may then be as wide as indicated above ...

Document 117 Memorandum of Bismarck (Putbus), 19 November 1866
(Ibid., no. 616, p. 168)

The composition of the Federal Diet* under the new German constitution will depend in fact upon whether a position as Head of the *Reich* or as *primus inter pares* among the other members of the Federation is to devolve upon the King of Prussia. If the first system is established, the King of Prussia could be made an independent factor in legislation, like the monarch of a constitutional state, and the prospective Federal Diet (Prussia having no, or little, share in it) could be given the position of an Upper House in a state Parliament. It will be more difficult to establish a monarchical federal state, or German imperial Reich, than to establish a system of *primus inter pares*, which is associated with recognized federal conceptions. The latter system will, therefore, gain easier acceptance by the participants, even if it assures Prussia the same dominant position. This would be roughly attained if we adopted the distribution of votes as it was, not in the small council, but in the *plenum* of the Federal Diet [of 1815]. According to the latter, Prussia would

---

* *Bundestag* in German, but what is being discussed is the institution which became the *Bundesrat* or Federal Council. T.

have 17 votes,* if the votes of the states recently annexed were added to hers, and the remaining states of the North German Confederation, if Darmstadt retained one of Upper Hesse's original three votes, would together carry 26 votes; the total number of votes would be 43, an absolute majority, 22. Prussia would thus have an absolute majority whenever five of the smaller states adhered to her. The danger that the Prussian government, in any questions that may be raised, should fall into a minority in both the *Reichstag* and the Federal Diet is unlikely to materialize owing to the numerical supremacy of Prussian representatives in the *Reichstag*. Even so the rule should be laid down that in all military questions the agreement of the federal commanders and a two-thirds majority (as for alterations of the constitution) is necessary. This two-thirds, according to the above reckoning, could not be brought into being without Prussia. On the eventual accession of the south Germans, the position would have to be safeguarded by increasing the number of Prussian votes to 20.

The advantages of this system consist in its dependence on established arrangements, so that the governments will more easily accommodate themselves to it because it seems customary and self-evident, than to any new scheme. Any arrangement must bear an arbitrary character, as arbitrary as the distribution of votes in the *plenum* originally was, except one in which the votes are distributed according to population. Such a distribution would allow the other governments, as compared with Prussia,** no votes at all.

If a *plenum* of 43 votes were established in this way, the governments could then nominate as many members of the assembly as they had votes, without the right to vote being made dependent upon the presence of all the delegates possessing votes. In this way Prussia could name 17 delegates, but, even if only one of them were present, still exercise 17 votes. The opportunity would thus be given to bring into the Federal Diet, besides the actual diplomatic representatives, the necessary experts for each of the special spheres of its legislative work. I intend as its Prussian members, beside the man who has been our envoy to the old Federal Diet, who would act as President and perhaps be made a member of the [Prussian] Ministry of State, people, for example, such as Voigts-Rhetz, Jachmann, Delbrück, Dechend, Günther, Camphausen, a high-ranking post and telegraph official, and a prominent member each

---

* This was the number of votes Prussia had in the *Bundesrat* or Federal Council under the North German Constitution and later the Imperial Constitution. The total number of votes in the *Bundesrat* after 1871 was 58. T.

** The population of Prussia was about five times that of Bavaria, the next largest state. T.

of the aristocratic, industrial, and merchant circles. Thus its members would stand over against the *Reichstag* as a bench of ministers with 43 places. I believe that the difficulties of putting a Ministry, in the nomination of which there might be competition from the governments bound to us, over against the *Reichstag*, could be avoided by using existing institutions and customary nomenclature. The Prussian delegates would naturally always agree among themselves how to vote and would jointly represent the views of the Government. It would, however, still be possible for the minority of the Federal Diet publicly to put their point of view before the *Reichstag*, if it diverged from the official proposals of the majority. Indeed, circumstances might arise in which Prussia would have to do this. Ministerial solidarity could, of course, not be binding upon the delegates of the various governments, each of which could recall its delegates whenever it chose . . .

Document 118 Wimpffen (Berlin) to Beust, 16 December 1866
(*Die Auswärtige Politik Preussens*, vol. viii, no. 136, p. 213)

Count Bismarck told me yesterday . . . that . . . he was enacting a constitution, from which, he hoped, a far better relationship to us and to the south than that in the Confederation [of 1815] would arise.

It would leave the individual states the greatest administrative freedom, but the entire military power [of Germany] would pass into the hands of Prussia* . . .

Document 119 Flemming (Karlsruhe) to Bismarck, 30 September 1866
(Ibid., no. 170, note i, p. 269)

. . . President von Freydorf assured Count Flemming 'that the Grand Duke, like his present ministry, was making resolute efforts to act with Prussia and, since the inclusion of Baden in the North German Confederation was not yet attainable, to make every possible preparation so that it could follow without difficulty in the near future.'

* The military alliances signed in 1866-7 (see above, pp. 14, 23, 140, 144) meant that in time of war the armies of the southern states would be under Prussia's command.

Document 120   Trauttmansdorf (Munich) to Beust, 24 January 1867
(Vienna, Haus- Hof- und Staatsarchiv, PA IV, no. 36)

The reception which Prince Hohenlohe* gave me, the readiness which he displayed to take the initiative in a searching and enlightening conversation about his position, his political views and his intentions, shows ... unmistakably his wish to cultivate good relations with the Austrian representative. I shall obviously take care to support this effort with my encouragement. Meanwhile, of course, I do not overlook the fact that his leaning towards Prussia is just as unmistakable and in many ways as visible as the circumstance that, if he followed his personal views and inclinations, he would recommend an even closer juncture with Prussia. He would recommend this if only the general position and his duties as the Minister of the Kingdom of Bavaria would allow it. But Bavaria, both in the person of its King and in the feeling of its population is very jealous of its undiminished sovereign rights ...

The main political ideas of the Prince are basically at present:

1. the idea of the unification of the German nation and the conviction of the need to take account of this strong prevailing tendency among all German people;
2. that Bavaria cannot permanently exist without a so-called constitutional alliance [with Prussia], which offers stronger guarantees than a political alliance; that
3. since this aim does not seem immediately attainable, a political friendship with Prussia must take its place; that
4. an imperious necessity demands immediate measures towards a comprehensive reorganization of the defence system of the south-German states ...

He was prevented from giving friendship with Prussia too firm and binding a form, in the first place by the well-founded jealousy of the King for his complete and free sovereignty ... and in the second place, by uncertainty whether there would be a parliamentary majority in favour of such a course.

... I do not expect any great decision or decisive action to follow immediately ...

* Minister President of Bavaria, 1867–70, Chancellor of the German Empire, 1894–1900. T.

Document 121   Bismarck to Goltz (Paris), 13 January 1867
(H. Oncken, *Die Rheinpolitik Kaiser Napoleons III 1863–70*,
vol. ii, no. 335, p. 180)

. . . However great the value that we attach to our relations with
France, we cannot afford to be beguiled into compromising ourselves by any initiative which would shake our whole position in
Germany to the deepest point. The French alliance, if bought by
a humiliating outrage upon German national feeling, is bought too
dear. Your Excellency will keep this, His Majesty's view, present
in your mind throughout these negotiations. Alliance with France
is in an eminent degree advantageous, but it is not the only aim of
Prussian policy nor an *overriding* one, to be striven for on *any* condition. If the conditions which France demands are unacceptable in
form or content, it will be Your Excellency's task, as my own, to
guard against French policy's being prematurely cast into an
anti-Prussian course by our immediate rejection. You should rather
hold back a decision by playing for time until events make it *easier*
or unnecessary. Your Excellency should not offer our hand to hasten
the alliance or, confusing ends and means, seek it even at the cost
of *damage* to our position in the balance of power . . .

Document 122   Economic report from the Austrian Ministry
of Trade
(Bonn, Auswärtiges Amt, IAAI, no. 54, vol. iv)

The present expansion in trade and industry

In contrast to the depressed condition of business in the Zollverein, France, and England, there has been lively activity in
Austrian trade and industry during the past year. Long-restrained
demand, hope for peaceful times after the end of the war, a plentiful
issue of paper money, the beginning of the construction of numerous
railway lines, and the excellent grain harvests constitute the
principal factors in this prosperity. The country people and the
owners of big estates again have money to spend; markets show a
quick and lively return; shops in the towns are more visited than
ever, so much so that in Vienna in the course of the season at least
twice as much was sold as in the previous year; warehouses are
emptied; factories obtain orders and are being enlarged; there have
not been such events for a long time.

In Hungary

Hungary, a rich producer, stands at the forefront of this expansion. The strong demand for grain which, on account of the bad

or insufficient yield of their own harvests, has developed in France, England, Spain, the Zollverein itself, and northern Russia has opened for Hungary a market, distinguished by a long-sustained, uninterrupted rise in prices. This unexpected, continuous rise in prices has injured countless speculators, especially in Pesth, who, without having made sure of the goods, had agreed to cheaper prices for delivery at some specified later date. Yet in business as a whole the favourable influence of the unusual grain market has been quickly felt. There is no doubt that the whole country is recovering because of the unusually high prices of the products of its soil.

In the western half of the Empire

As far as the German half of the Empire is concerned, an activity which has long been missed, though not indeed the same rapid expansion, may be recorded. Here it is especially the manufacture of sugar that is constantly expanding. Austrian unrefined sugar now reaches England and France ... The iron and machine industries are at last coming to life again. Iron foundries are fully employed with the production of lines for the new railways and the machine factories are not only also working for this domestic demand, but have obtained in addition big orders from Russia ... The textile industry in Brünn and Reichenberg is very busy for both the home and the foreign market. As far as the spinning of combed yarn is concerned, two establishments have been enlarged and in Bohemia new factories for cotton spinning have been set up. There has not been such expansion for a long time. Even the Vienna silk manufacture, which was thought to be dead, is stirring again and has realized a small export trade in plain stuffs to the Zollverein and to France ...

Document 123   Trauttmansdorff (Munich) to Beust, 19 February 1867
(Vienna, Haus- Hof- und Staatsarchiv, PA IV, no. 36)

... I spoke in the following sense: of course Bavaria must seek to maintain her independence; but she must also aim at winning for herself a leading role in south Germany. I remarked that alliance with Germany was the alliance which would always be desired by Austria. He must not, however, fail to understand how much it was in the interest of his monarch, of himself, and of his country to gain and develop a relationship with us which would justify us in having to negotiate such an alliance in Munich itself. I pointed out in decided terms that, if he intended to conclude conventions with Prussia in the economic field—a project which I could not deny his right to entertain—the relationship in which he then stood to Austria would necessarily be of great importance in deciding how far Prussia could consider such conventions as a step further along the road leading to the absorption of Bavaria. I believe I am not deceiving myself when I assert that the last observation made some impression upon the Minister . . .

Document 124 Bismarck to Bernstorff,* 14 January 1867
(H. Oncken, *Die Rheinpolitik Kaiser Napoleons III 1863–70*, 1926, vol. ii, no. 336, p. 186)

. . . We believe we should recognize—in the manner in which public opinion in England and the English Government have appraised the enlargement of Prussia and the extension of her power—the result of the attitude to the Continent which has now become habitual to England. We should also recognize in it a symptom of the conviction, which is beginning to count there, that a strong Prussia and a united Germany are of great importance for England's power in relation to France. We may hope for a further development in this direction . . .

Document 125 Bismarck to Bernstorff, 14 January 1967
(Ibid., p. 184, earlier paragraph of Doc. 124)

. . . We consider our immediate task to be the consolidation of the North German Confederation. We should be afraid to make the performance of this task more difficult for ourselves, and to disturb it by premature attempts to draw south Germany into our political sphere. Force of circumstances will be sufficient to guide the relations between the south-German states and Prussia along the right path towards the goal of German unification . . .

Document 126 Bismarck to Reuss,** 22 January 1867
(O. von Bismarck, *Gesammelte Werke*, vol. vi, no. 663, p. 240)

Confidential
I have already informed Your Excellency that we regard with satisfaction Prince Hohenlohe's efforts to bring about the reform of the armies of the south-German states in common, so that they

* Now again Prussian ambassador in London; see above, p. 54. T.
** See above, p. 104, note *; Reuss was now Prussian Envoy in Munich, but before the end of the year was appointed ambassador to St. Petersburg. T.

may approximate as much as possible in organization to that of Prussia and that we shall support this reform as far as we can ...

We are convinced of the present Bavarian Cabinet's sincerity in its efforts to bring about a relationship satisfactory to both sides and good for the national position of Germany. We, for our part, completely share these wishes. We regret that events have so fallen out as to tear apart the old bonds which bound us to Bavaria and the other south-German states and which, though incomplete, were organic. We would willingly lend a hand to create in their stead such new relations, as may answer to the interests of both sides ... We stand towards the south-German states in a different, one might say a more favourable, relationship than towards the north-German ones. Our own security demands that the bonds between us and the north-German states should be drawn as tight as possible within the federal situation, and that we should have the unconditional disposition of the domestic and foreign forces of the North German Confederation. Our need for security will, however, be satisfied by the compact organization of the North German Confederation and especially by the accession of Saxony to it. In regard to south Germany, we do not need the same strict form of union. We need only such an unambiguous expression of the national community of interests as will give us confidence that the south-German states will never be tempted into a hostile attitude towards north Germany or into reliance upon foreign Powers and that regard for the common economic interests of the German people will always be assured by common organic institutions. We shall, therefore, demand nothing in our relations with them, which would do more than give this confidence. These aims can be attained by a relationship to the south-German states, looser and less restrictive than that within the North German Confederation, and by one which would not need to limit the autonomy of the individual states so much as it is limited in the North German Confederation. We would go as far along the way to fusion as Bavaria herself wishes: but if her wishes should fall short of the sum of the demands made to us in north Germany, an understanding with us would not thereby be endangered ...

Document 127 Bismarck to the Crown Prince, 3 February 1867 (Ibid., no. 675, p. 255)

... Our policy must be to look to the future, and, putting aside the memory of past family quarrels, to seek and cherish national unity. Prussia has to bring about for all Germany what she once brought about for herself. As Prussia once, in land conquered from

Poland, France, and Saxony, made the conquered forget the conquest and raised them to a feeling of community and equality,
so now she must efface within *one* people the relationship—which
cannot permanently be maintained—between victorious and
defeated; she must fuse loyalty to particular sections of the German
people* or to particular states into a willing and proud attachment
to a *single German* commonwealth at whose head stands the King of
Prussia . . .

Document 128 Spitzemberg (Berlin) to Varnbühler,** 26
   January 1867
   (*Die Auswärtige Politik Preussens*, vol. viii, no. 207, p. 332)

. . . Besides working to found the North German Confederation,
the Government is striving for the association of this national
federation with the south, that is, for the establishment of a wider
league. For this reason it is encouraging the agitation in the south
for joining Prussia . . . Two kinds of circumstance will naturally
exercise an overwhelming influence in the question of the establishment of such a wider league: the economic and the military.
As is well known, views are now divided as to which part, the
north or the south, draws the greater advantage from the Zollverein.
The fact is that here the opinion prevails that the south gets more
out of it than the north and, therefore, the Zollverein should be
limited to the north. Moreover, the six months' notice hangs over
the heads of the south-German industrialists and traders like a
sword of Damocles. The continuation of the Zollverein and the
alteration of its precarious duration into a firm term of so many
years is, however, acknowledged to be in the interest of the south.
According to the views just advanced as those which now prevail
here, this will be looked upon as a concession, a favour, which on the
principle of *do ut des* must be answered with a counter-concession.
The south can provide this counter-concession in the military field.
Berlin has its attention firmly fixed on the possibility of attack
from France, allied with Austria. The alliance of south with north
Germany would be of priceless value for such an event. Its value
would rise with the south-German forces' power of performance.
Prussia would consider this all the greater, the more compact and
closely organized is the total body which the south-Germany army
corps constitute and the more these approximate, in their training

---

* The German word is *Stammesbewusstsein* and the reference is to the individual
German's sense of being, e.g., Swabian, Franconian, or Prussian. T.
** Minister President of Württemberg. T.

and arming, etc., to the Prussian army . . . The conclusion, then, to which the considerations just advanced lead me, is that Prussia will not let herself be disturbed in her work for the North German Confederation by the attitude of the south, but that it can cause her to promote the formation of a wider international league consisting of north Germany on one side and the southern states on the other. In this alliance the south will attain the more in the economic field, the more it is in a position to offer in the military field . . .

Document 129 Speech of Bismarck in the North German Parliament, 11 March 1867
(O. von Bismarck, *Gesammelte Werke*, vol. x, p. 327)

. . . In my opinion, our relations with south Germany will develop simply and safely out of the article on the subject which is to be found in the draft constitution.* We share with south Germany, first of all, a common concern in the Zollverein—a common concern which at the present moment, of course, is to a certain extent in the air, because the peace treaties have given the six months' notice of termination in order to allow us to come to an agreement over tariff relations with south Germany. This right to give notice before the termination of the old Zollverein was necessary in order to make agreement possible. I think, therefore, that as soon as we have completed the north-German constitution, we should make overtures to the south-German governments for conferences with us, to consider how we may attain a permanent, organic Zollverein instead of one that can be denounced every twelve years . . . Should the Zollverein continue with its present scope, the creation of organic institutions, by means of which south Germany can participate in legislating on tariff questions, is quite

* Article 79 provided that the relations between the Confederation and the south-German states should be settled by special treaties to be laid before the North German *Reichstag* for its approval. The war had broken the peace between the members of the Zollverein which came automatically to an end. Article 33 of the constitution of the North German Confederation provided that it should form a single area for tariff purposes. The south-German states were, thus, threatened with exclusion from the German tariff system. But the peace treaties which they had signed with Prussia in August 1866 provided that for six months the old Zollverein should continue. Prussia made new Tariff treaties with the four states (8 July 1867). This brought into being a new twelve-year Zollverein on 1 January 1868 with a Customs Parliament (composed of members of the North German *Reichstag* and elected representatives of the south-German states) and a Customs Council (composed of the *Bundesrat* and plenipotentiaries appointed by the governments of the south-German states). See above, pp. 149–50. T.

unavoidable. I refrain from indicating particulars, but I believe it is self-evident how such institutions should be created (Quite right!).

It is difficult to believe that such a common legislative institution for tariffs—I do not wish to underrate it by simply calling it disparagingly a Customs Parliament—What battles we have fought! Only a man who has stood at the heart of affairs can judge! How our tariff interests appeared to us in 1852 and 1864 as our highest interests—matters of political life and death! I do not wish to underrate the importance of its being possible to create an economic community for the whole of Germany. To resume, it is difficult to believe that such a common legislative institution, if once created, could avoid gradually appropriating to itself most of the remaining things that come under the heading of economic welfare and much formal legislation such as that on commercial procedure, or could avoid bringing into use regulations in these affairs common to the whole of Germany. As far as the question of power is concerned, I consider the unity of north and south Germany definitively assured* already against all attack whenever the security of German soil is at stake.

Document 130   Beust to Wimpffen (Berlin), 28 March 1867
(H. Oncken, *Die Rheinpolitik Kaiser Napoleons III 1863–70*, 1926, vol. ii, no. 433, note, p. 339)

... We shall formulate no protest and draw no conclusions from the state of affairs, but we cannot admit that any true harmony exists between the terms of our peace treaty with Prussia and the situation which the much discussed alliances have created.

Document 131   Bismarck to Goltz (Paris), 1 April 1867
(*Die Auswärtige Politik Preussens*, vol. viii, no. 375, p. 549)

An interpellation from the left in the *Reichstag* over Luxemburg stands for today. Its authors are alleged to have telegraphed their question direct to Moustier.** If you have an audience you should point out that I have often seriously warned Benedetti*** to avoid our being officially questioned about Luxemburg before [its sale] was executed. As soon as the King of Holland publishes his intention to sell, the negotiations at the Hague must be suspended and we must be consulted before they are resumed. At least as long as the *Reichstag* is in session, it must not come into the open ...

* i.e. by the secret military alliances, see above, p. 40 and the next document. T.
** Léonel, Marquis de Moustier, French Foreign Minister, 1867–9. T.
*** French ambassador in Berlin, 1864–71. T.

Documents 132a and 132b   Let us rather wage war

132a   Metternich (Paris) to Beust, 4 April 1867
  (H. Oncken, *Die Rheinpolitik Kaiser Napoleons III 1863–70*,
  1926, vol. ii, no. 400, p. 283)

  ... The Marquis de Moustier said to me: 'If the North German
Reichstag passes a hostile resolution, it is war.'

132b   Bismarck to Goltz (Paris), 9 April 1867
  (Ibid., no. 409, note, p. 302)

  ... I shall report to His Majesty, but I do not believe that, as the
situation stands in Germany, we shall be in a position to agree now
to the separation in any form of Luxemburg from Germany or to the
evacuation of the fortress. England must not hide from herself that
the European situation would be more thoroughly endangered by a
breach between the German governments and German national
feeling than by war between Germany and France. We at least, in
my opinion, must rather wage war than cut ourselves off from the
national mood of Germany or lose the esteem of the nation ...

Document 133   Note by Bismarck of a conversation with
  Wimpffen, 12 April 1867
  (Ibid., no. 418, p. 316)

  ... I have spoken to Count Wimpffen with complete frankness
about the present position and its significance for us and for Austria.
  I told him that Austria must now ask herself whether she wishes
to recover the friendship of Germany on the basis of mutual obligations in a defensive alliance.
  If she answers this question with 'yes', the present moment is
favourable for it, because German national feeling would joyfully
accept a *rapprochement* with Austria. Germany would accept it,
since it could preserve the peace that is now endangered. Public
opinion would also consent to such concessions as we could make
to Austria, in return for a *rapprochement*. An alliance of a firm and
durable nature could be established on that basis. This would
be of great importance for the maintenance of European peace and
for that tranquillity which is so necessary for all countries.
  Alternatively, if the Vienna Cabinet answers this question with
'no', we should then conclude that we must seek a closer understanding with Russia. If this came up against difficulties so far

unrecognized, the choice would then remain to us between waging war against France on our own—a war in which we saw the chances as not absolutely unfavourable to us—or entering a firm alliance with France, which we, as things now stand, consider it possible to do on conditions which could be acceptable to *us*.

Count Wimpffen explained to me that, as was to be expected, he had no instructions about this, but would report to Vienna.

Document 134 Circular despatch of Hohenlohe, 30 April 1867 (F. Curtius, editor, *Denkwürdigkeiten des Fürsten Chlodwig Hohenlohe-Schillingsfürst*, Leipzig, 1906, vol. i, p. 243)

... Württemberg, Baden, and Hesse are ready to negotiate with the North German Confederation. Bavaria has the choice between (a) taking up an influential position in these negotiations and of preventing, as far as possible, any infringement of the frontiers fixed by the treaties, and (b) foregoing any influence upon the reorganization [of Germany] without thereby counteracting the dangers which may possibly arise from it.

The economic interests of Bavaria are linked in such manifold ways with those of the rest of Germany that she could not let the links be cut except in a case of utmost necessity and, even then, only by endangering her own existence as a state. The King's Government cannot, therefore, exclude itself from negotiations with the North German Confederation about the reorganization of Germany; nor does it wish to do so ...

Document 135 Ladenberg (Vienna) to Bismarck, 2 September 1867 (Bonn, Auswärtiges Amt, IAA, no. 54, vol. iv)

... In the Press, as in the public at large, the question is actively and thoroughly discussed: what attitude would Austria have to take on the occurrence [of a conflict between Prussia and France]. Among the different views about it, which are put forward, I should like to draw special attention to three currents of opinion.

The first is one decidedly hostile to Prussia. The supporters of this opinion, though they form a numerical minority, mostly belong to the higher and privileged ranks of society and exercise, because of their rank and the wealth of which they can dispose, an influence that is not to be disparaged. This they seek to make effective less through their prominence in public life than through their hidden activity and systematic intrigue. This opinion finds its spokesmen among the Dukes, in the highest aristocracy, among the higher officials of Court and Army and among the higher Catholic clergy and in all regions dependent upon these elements. These circles cannot get over the idea of Prussia as the hated adversary which they will never be so deeply humiliated as to recognize as a fully sovereign state and Austria's equal. They breathe only detestation and revenge against Prussia and look with bitter dislike upon the successes of Prussian policy. Feeling their own powerlessness to stop these successes,[*] they speculate about French help in taking revenge on Prussia for the defeat Austria has suffered. They are afraid that the new order, founded in Germany by Prussia, will necessarily lead to a national German unitary state and that the reduction of the present transitional situation to the latter is only a question of time . . .

According to this line of thought, it is a duty to the self-subsistence of Austria that the opportunity, which is now once again and perhaps for the last time offered to foil this danger, should be used. The supporters of this policy perceive the means thereto in a league with France and they are, therefore, the most eager proponents and encouragers of a Franco-Austrian alliance . . .

A second and a third current of public opinion in Austria—I respectfully point out that I am speaking only of the opinion of the German population of Austria—have the common characteristic that they consider the maintenance of peace as a prerequisite for the success of Austria's constitutional reconstruction and both agree that an alliance with France, whatever the circumstances, would be very horrifying. The great majority of the German newspapers of the Austrian Press—and the most important among them—have spoken out in this sense in a very decided way . . .

However much the prevalent wish in Austria is to maintain peace, she is alive to the danger which the position in Europe as a whole might conjure up for her in the near future. She thinks first, in this connection, of the eventuality of a war between Prussia and France and considers what attitude she should take in that event to protect her interests as well as to improve her weakened position in the balance of power abroad. The wish of the German population of Austria to restore the loosened bond with Germany, in some form or other, stands in all this to the fore.

Views diverge on the question of how the bond is to be restored and about the scope within which it should operate. A large party in Austria cherished the hope after the war, and still may well yield to it, that a parliamentary life in the western half of the Austrian empire, developed on broad liberal principles, might exercise a strong attraction upon the south-German states and form a bridge to a closer league between them and German Austria . . .

The course of events, the existing organization of the relations of Prussia to the south-German states, and the recognition of the difficulties, which obstruct the development of constitutionalism in the direction hoped for in Austria, have since destroyed some of these illusions. The untiring efforts of a great number of Austrian newspapers bear witness, however, that they survive on many sides. These efforts are directed to throwing suspicion on Prussia's German policy, to drawing attention to the alleged reactionary tendencies of the constitution of the North German Confederation and to attacking the new situation in the states annexed to Prussia in the most spiteful and slanderous way.

This, party, indeed, does not presume so far as the bold thought of forcing Prussia, by means of a war, to revise the Treaty of Prague.* Nor does it wish to attempt to bring about such a revision with French help. None the less, it speculates about the political conjunctures which might force Prussia to make concessions in this connection to Austria. A warlike entanglement of Prussia with France is considered such a conjuncture. This party proclaims for itself a policy of acting on self-interest according to eventualities ...

If war should break out between Prussia and France, this party counts on Austria's being neutral at the beginning, but able to choose the right moment, whether called in or not, to intervene in the conflict with the utmost vigour ...

Public opinion in general inclines here to the assumption that this is the secret thought and aim after which Baron von Beust vaguely strives.

Finally, a third current of opinion openly declares that the formation of a south-German Confederation under Austria's leadership is, after the events of last year, no longer possible. I should designate this as the direction of opinion most widely supported and especially prevalent among the bourgeoisie. They acknowledge that after north Germany has been completed and south Germany, through its offensive and defensive alliances, has also been drawn into Prussia's sphere of power, a surrender of south Germany to Austria would be as good as requiring Prussia to give up something she has already won; and they are under no illusions that Prussia, despite all the dangers threatening from France, will ever willingly agree to that. In so far as the representatives of this direction of opinion further admit that the south-German states cannot be forced to unite themselves into a Confederation, they acknowledge that when the Peace of Prague speaks

* The Peace Treaty signed after the Austro-Prussian War, see above, p. 169, note ***. T.

of the establishment of a southern Confederation it does so only in a
permissive sense. They also acknowledge that the population of
south Germany might be reluctant to join Austria again, since she
has shown herself too weak a support for them.

This direction of opinion holds that the completion of the united
German state is compatible with the continued existence of the
Austrian monarchy. They wish, therefore, to avoid any intervention
by Austria and see no obstacle in the way of achieving an agreement
for closer relations between north and south Germany, as long as
it derives from a completely free decision.

The supporters of this policy wish for co-operation with Germany,
after it has been united under Prussia's leadership, and recommend
an understanding and settlement with Prussia on new principles.
They chiefly mean by these the restoration of closer links with
Germany. They aim here less at a constitutional alliance than
at an international league, a political alliance based on similar
economic interests. The advantages of such an alliance would have
to be sought by Austria less in Germany than in the Near East . . .

Document 136 Circular despatch of Bismarck, 7 September
1867
(*Die Auswärtige Politik Preussens*, vol. ix, no. 152, p. 216)

I have already informed Your Excellency of the declarations we
have received both from the Imperial Austrian and from the
Imperial French Government about the significance and character
of the meeting at Salzburg. We have been able to accept them with
satisfaction . . .

It is enough to satisfy us that we can draw from the Austrian and
French explanations the assurance that the visit of the Emperor
Napoleon arose solely from a feeling which we honour and with
which we sympathize, and that the meeting of the two rulers remained of the character which this motive provided. Thus the domestic affairs of Germany were not the subject of the discussions at
Salzburg in the way the first news allowed one to suppose . . .

We have made it our task, from the beginning, to guide the
stream of national development in Germany into a channel in which
it might work fruitfully and not destructively. We have avoided
everything which could have realized the national movement
precipitately. We have sought not to excite, but to tranquillize. We
shall succeed, we hope, in this effort, if equal care is taken by
foreign Powers to avoid anything that might alarm the German
people about foreign plans of which they might be the victims and
cause, as a result, a justifiable excitement of the feeling of national

dignity and independence. Therefore in the interest of the peaceful development of our own affairs, we greet, with lively satisfaction, the definite disclaimer of any intention to intervene in the internal affairs of Germany . . .

Document 137   Bismarck to Flemming (Karlsruhe), 3 December 1867
(O. von Bismarck, *Gesammelte Werke*, vol. via, no. 974, p. 154)

. . . I repeat that we keep the aim [of unification] steadily before us. For that very reason we have to watch each time we negotiate a new step forward that we do not endanger what has already been achieved and lies behind us, We must watch that the step forward which we take today does not lead us tomorrow into obstacles and dangers which we and our friends might not otherwise have incurred or might have met under more favourable conditions. In prescribing patience, difficult enough for individuals, I will not pursue the attempt to refer to the history of the German people who have to make amends for so many missed opportunities and so much over-hastiness . . .

The danger lies before us, that too quick an advance might drive Bavaria, with its strong Ultramontane and Particularist elements, into the enemy's camp in the event of a European complication. We must not run that risk so long as it can be avoided. I will not undertake responsibility for that . . .

The national affair has not, so far, made one retrograde step; one way, which I have already once permitted myself to indicate, lies open. By it great progress is possible with little danger. The Customs Parliament meets in a little while. Bavaria will be represented according to a suffrage law other than that which is valid for her own Lower House, and on the basis of elections taking place in a new situation. We consider ourselves bound to wait to see what temper this assembly shows. We find ourselves justified in hoping that it will be inclined to prepare the extension to the south-German states, according to the treaties, of the laws which have already been enacted for the North German Confederation, or are in process of being enacted, namely, those on citizenship, passports, and civil procedure. We are, finally, convinced that this development, once set moving, will draw out of itself the force to continue at an ever increasing speed . . .

Document 138   Bismarck to William I, 10 August 1867
(Merseburg, Deutsches Zentralarchiv, Rep. 89H II, Deutsches Reich, no. 5, vol. i)

According to the constitution of the North German Confederation, it rests with the Federal Chancellor, as the only responsible Minister, both to head the whole of the administration of the Confederation and to take the presidency of the Federal Council (*Bundesrat*). In order to head the administration, which embraces the whole Telegraph and Postal system within the Confederation, the supervision of the Consular system, and the collection and administration of the Customs and Excise duties, the Federal Chancellor needs a department in which the different branches of the administration converge and find their focus. He needs such a department too, as Your Majesty's Minister, in order to prepare with the co-operation of the interested ministries, according to their functions, such business as must be brought by Prussia both as head and member of the North German Confederation, before the *Bundesrat* and *Reichstag*. This department must be created by the establishment of a new Office which I respectfully propose shall be called the Federal Chancellor's Office.

The [Prussian] Ministry of State has declared itself agreed that this Office is necessary.

Over the details of its organization I reserve my proposals, until Your Majesty has been pleased to approve its establishment. I respectfully propose Ministerial-Director Delbrück for the position of President of the new Office.

I accordingly beg Your Royal Majesty to approve the establishment of the Federal Chancellor's Office through your gracious completion of the annexed decree and to be pleased to name ... Delbrück its President.

Document 139   Note by Hohenlohe, 6 November 1867
(*Die Auswärtige Politik Preussens*, vol. ix, no. 295, p. 361)

... Baron Beust came to me at 10 o'clock at night on his way from Paris to Vienna ... He said the notion now prevailed in France that Prussia wished to absorb south Germany. This notion disquieted public opinion and would lead to war unless it was removed. The French could only be quieted by the foundation of a south-German league, whether a confederation or union. The form was a matter of indifference ... Other observations of Baron Beust seemed to support the assumption that he regards a political union of the southern states with a common military and diplomatic organization, something like the Confederation of the Rhine [of 1806], but under Prussian protection, as the object of French and Austrian wishes. It is not quite clear whether in these overtures there lies a warning, a threat or something else . . .

Document 140   Rosenberg (Stuttgart) to Bismarck, 17 November 1867
(Ibid., no. 335, p. 409)

. . . I had learnt that Minister von Varnbühler addressed a despatch to Karlsruhe [Baden] at the beginning of this month in which he declared the Zollverein treaty and the alliance treaty to be the basis of the national approach to the North German Confederation and tried to influence the decision of the Karlsruhe Cabinet. He was especially moved by the fear here lest the Customs Parliament should overstep its limits . . .

Document 141   Bismarck to Flemming (Karlsruhe), 13 November 1867
(O. von Bismarck, *Gesammelte Werke*, vol. via, no. 934, p. 113)

. . . I can, therefore, only sum up my view in the assertion that for the interest of Germany as a whole that course seems to be most beneficial which will most quickly lead the south-German states voluntarily into the North German Confederation, but that that course is not yet so clearly recognizable and surely indicated that I can speak my mind out about it officially. Everything turns upon the direction in which public opinion in south Germany evolves and the speed with which it does so; and on that, any sort of confident judgement can only be made after the Customs Parliament has met. It follows from what I have said that the next task is to work for the speedy summoning of the Customs Parliament and to encourage, or to awaken, the demand for the extension of the scope of its jurisdiction and for drawing to it new subjects of discussion . . .

Document 142   Werthern (Munich) to Bismarck, 20 January 1868
(*Die Auswärtige Politik Preussesn*, vol. ix, no. 521, p. 626)

. . . The intrigue against Prince Hohenlohe creeps secretly to the steps of the throne. Richard Wagner, who has been back here now for some weeks, is bewitching the young King with the idea,

already sown in Pierrefonds, that he, as the true representative of
the German genius, and exalted by the music of the future and a
general German Church under Liszt's papacy, is destined to ascend
the German Imperial throne. He has recently, as a practical
result, let a bill of exchange for over 30,000 francs be again under-
written for him by his devoted pupil.

While the King's thoughts are thus more and more wafted
away from actuality and lose themselves in dreams, the Liberal
Party is developing all its strength in order to prepare for entry into
the North German Confederation through the elections to the Customs Parliament. The Government and the great mass of the population stand perplexed and discouraged between the two extremes.
This beautiful land drives rudderless towards an uncertain future
and whether her fate is hurried forward or delayed only depends on
whether or not a war with France lies ahead.

The approaching elections have recently offered me occasion,
often against my will, for political conversations with persons of
the most varied political colouring. Each, according to his Party
standpoint, sees in the Customs Parliament either the action which
shall save the unity of Germany, as a unitary state, or the bugbear
that shall devour Bavaria. The basic tone of both is discouragement:
they already give themselves up for lost ... Political artistry now
consists in preparing euthanasia for Bavaria and leading her
with a gentle hand to her death. She is lost either way.*

Documents 143a and 143b   The Elections in the south

143a   Extract from a contemporary article, 23 February 1868
  (*Württembergische Landeszeitung*, 4, no. 45, p. 1)

   ... The government *Party*, of which the Prussian Party talks so
much, is really no mere Party, but the whole Württemberg nation.
Over this attitude, of which the Government is spokesman, it is
wholly at one with its beloved King and his Government. The
nation will not let itself be excited into crossing the bounds agreed
upon for the unity which has now become necessary. It will remain
true to its old motto 'Hie gut Württemberg allewege', and stand
loyally and fearlessly by its dynasty and the independence and
freedom of its own Fatherland without evading the sacrifices
necessary for German unity. The Württemberg nation in this
attitude has more honourable intentions than the German Party
with its motto 'German unity' ...

   'The moment is serious,' the German Party says, 'it bids us
remain true to our national conscience.' Quite right! We say so

* Note by Bismarck: 'a somewhat overhasty prophecy?'

too. We make no mistake about the seriousness of the moment and beg our nation to do its duty loyally, but also to remain loyal to its Württemberg national conscience and not to let itself be misled by fine, hypocritical words. Let it show that in its heart, as in its deeds, it is a loyal, patriotic, and intelligent nation ...

143b   Election Address of the Deutsche Partei, 2 February 1868 (Schwäbische Volkszeitung 18, no. 27, p. 1)

Fellow Citizens: The elections to the German Customs Parliament are in front of us. It has long been the dearest wish of the German nation that its most important common affairs should be discussed and decided by freely elected representatives. By the side of representatives from all Germany, from the north and from the south, representatives of the Württemberg nation are to appear, in the same position as to numbers, and endowed with equal rights. Without privilege of birth or wealth, every citizen of full age is called to the voting urns. A most promising way for national development thus opens out ...

Fellow Citizens: The Parliament for which your votes are intended has the name Customs Parliament, but its significance is greater than its modest name implies ... We greet the Customs Parliament as a step towards the further political *rapprochement* of the south-German states to the North German Confederation. The fruits of economic unity cannot ripen until the federal constitution embraces all German states.

Guided by these views, we appeal to you, at the elections to the Customs Parliament, only to give your votes to those men
i. who in matters of trade and communications are resolved to further the principles of freedom and progress;
ii. who are of proved German loyalty and have the firm resolve to take the lead in realizing the right of the German nation to a single constitution for all.

Fellow Citizens: The events of the year 1866 have opened a way to that unification of the Fatherland for which we have yearned.

Thirty million Germans are united under the constitution of the North German Confederation: it still lacks the four south-German states. That the North German Confederation should become the German Confederation, that the Customs Parliament should become the German Parliament, is a demand whose fulfilment depends essentially upon us south Germans. Both our north-German brothers and foreigners watch the outcome of our elections with tense interest. Let us show that we are not allowing ourselves to be pushed and dragged into the future German federal state against our will, but rather that we wish actively to set to work to build it.

Let us avoid the sad reputation of always being the last or of standing peevishly aside.

A new base has been laid. Let us stand firmly on it, without faltering. Let us hold together with our German brothers in work and hope.

Vote, and vote German!

Document 144 Werthern (Munich) to Bismarck, 15 February 1868
(*Die Auswärtige Politik Preussens*, vol. ix, no. 596, p. 704)

Today the *Neuesten Nachrichten* gives the results of the elections as follows: Liberals: 14 sure, 6 expected; Centre: 9, including Prince Hohenlohe (in Upper Franconia), who has already accepted election; Ultramontanes: 20 . . .

The Ultramontanes have thus won a brilliant victory . . .

By and large, the result is very astonishing. It stands in direct contrast to the majority in the Lower House and affords proof that the great mass of the people are still quite incapable of thinking for themselves and are in the hands of a secret, powerful party, whose roots lie outside the country. This must now become widely known, and will not fail to have repercussions among the intelligent section of the people . . .

Document 145 Extract from a Swabian popular newspaper, 8 March 1868
(*Der Beobachter*, 38, no. 57, p. 1)

'The Protest of South Germany against Prussification'—we must certainly so characterize the outcome of the elections to the Customs Parliament in Baden and Bavaria, and the electoral campaign now going on in Württemburg. The latter deserves this description to an especially notable degree. It is well known that the *Volkspartei* has split over the question of the elections. Some wish to register a protest by abstaining from the elections and believe, just by that, to do so most sharply. Others vote as their essential duty so that no 'Prussian' shall represent the country. Both register the same protest only in different forms. The first mark it more sharply, the second state it more clearly. It is beyond a doubt that the protest, truly and unanimously took place. It is calculated that wretched Prussia has the chance of only one single electoral victory. It is a public chastisement for the great lies with which certain people have for years sinned against their Swabian homeland—and very wholesome for them it is, and must be a lesson to them. It is as well-deserved a censure, as ever any was, for the tasteless loud-mouthedness with which people who are nothing try to puff themselves out to be something ... With the establishment of the police division in the Prussian Legation in Stuttgart their little bit of courage has plainly risen and as their basis among the people diminishes, the more impudently, crying 'Bismarck, help!' do they stretch themselves out in the world, most wretched puppets that they are!

... Let the worms have their dust! There is something more important to consider. *What attitude will the Governments take towards the German protest of the population?* What impression has it made, what influence will it have upon them? In Baden the answer to the country has been the nomination of a Prussian Minister of War. Here in Württemberg something similar is said to be contemplated. In Bavaria one King has died and the other is ill: ill or dead it is the same thing.* There is no understanding anywhere for the spirit of the people, no advance to meet them anywhere, nor creative strength, nor guiding hand. There is only talk of a new Bavarian project, according to which she is to have the military headship of the whole south. A lesser Bavarian peak, with the great Prussian peak above it! It must be the good Hohenlohe's most recent device. Always the peak only, never the base, always the top, never building up from below. It is enough to make one despair.

If only south Germany had a statesman, just a single one who had confidence in himself, confidence in the people and the confidence of the people! ... The German saviour will not come from those states which have so far made the policy of south Germany. The German *Volkspartei* itself must be the saviour. It must turn the German protest of our people against Prussification into organization and action against Prussification. Such is the task which the sense, in which the nation has voted and is voting, makes it the Party's duty to adopt.

Document 146 Werner (Dresden) to Beust, 18 April 1868
(Vienna, Haus- Hof- und Staatsarchiv, PA V, no. 36)

... After I had read to the Minister [Baron von Friesen] the despatch to Berlin, he replied pretty much as follows:

---

* The reference is to Maximilian II, King of Bavaria, 1848–64 and Louis II, King of Bavaria, 1864–86. T.

'The standpoint of Saxony—as I well knew—over the possible inclusion of south Germany in the northern confederation was a different one from that of Austria. Whereas Austria, on good grounds, was horrified at its inclusion, whatever the circumstances, Saxony must wish that at least the prospect of this extension of the North German Confederation might never be definitively closed. As long as Prussia could still nurse the hope of at some time including the south-German states in her Confederation, she would consider herself obliged to treat those states already included with consideration, so as not to frighten off those left outside. Conversely, should she be obliged irrevocably to give up that hope, her present associates in the Confederation would be exposed to every kind of arbitrary action. There would be no lack of such action on the Prussian side' . . .

Document 147   Conversation of Bismarck with Suckow,* 11 May 1868
(O. von Bismarck, *Gesammelte Werke*, vol. vii, no. 201, p. 258)

I had a conversation with Bismarck on 11 May in the park of the Federal Chancellor's palace. He spoke as follows: 'The elections to the Customs Parliament, as they have now turned out, have shown that the south wishes to have no further connection with the north beyond customs treaties and the alliance treaties. The north has no reason to ask for more; for militarily the connection with the south, strategically considered, does not strengthen us; politically, we Prussians have no need to fuse ourselves with the heterogeneous elements of the south. I do not know whether the Particularists or the Democrats of the south are the more mischievous friends of Prussia. We all have national unity at heart, but for the calculating politician the necessary aim precedes the desirable one. First let us build our house and extend it afterwards. If Germany were to attain her national aim within the nineteenth century, that would appear to me something great enough. If it were to be within ten or perhaps five years that would be something miraculous, an uncovenanted blessing from God!

'First let the representatives sit together for a few years in the Customs Parliament. Then reconciliation will have begun and the south Germans will see that the use of force cannot come into the question. Nothing further is to be expected from this Customs Parliament and the question may even be asked whether it should

---

* Minister of War in Württemberg.

not be dissolved. But it is not the moment for that. Our whole sympathy belongs to our south-German brother to whom we are ready at any time to stretch out a hand, but we neither wish nor ought to force him to grasp it. Rather let us thirty million Germans build our house, then the other eight million will become reconciled in time, especially if we commit no act of force against them and so give the lie to their prejudices. I have always told the National Liberals that I consider the thing like a hunter, who has laid his bait. He does not shoot the first doe that comes, but waits until the herd has taken the food. . . .'

Document 148 Werther (Vienna) to Thile,* 6 January 1869
(Bonn, Auswärtiges Amt, IAA 1, no. 41, vol. 12)

. . . My official relations with Count [sic] Beust *par manque de communications* have sunk to nil and for nearly two months no 'political intercourse' [original English] has taken place between us. On meeting him yesterday . . . I found him receptive even to cool approaches. He makes bitter observations to the envoys of other small states (to those, for example, of Italy, Greece, and Bavaria) about the alleged calumnies against him, spread by Prussia and Russia. Yesterday he said to Count Bray, they try to stand in Berlin as well as possible with France and they raise hostile feelings against Austria in order 'not to let her grow stronger' . . .

Document 149 Münch (Berlin) to Beust, 1 July 1868
(Vienna, Haus- Hof- und Staatsarchiv, PA III, no. 99)

I use Herr von Bernath's departure today for Marienbad** as the means of allowing a few lines to reach Your Excellency through the Austrian Post Office.

Some days ago Herr Bleichröder expressed to other persons the view he had expressed to me, namely, that it seemed peace would probably be preserved for the next few months, but after that war would become inevitable. Thus one may clearly presume that he has followed a *mot d'ordre*, especially since another person, who is honoured with Count Bismarck's confidence, has, I hear, given utterance to exactly the same opinion.

The general need for peace is for Herr Bleichröder the guarantee of quiet during the next few months. After that, a situation of the

* Under Secretary in the Prussian Foreign Ministry. T.
** A spa, now called Marianske Lazny, in Czechoslovakia, but then in the Austrian Empire. T.

most widespread uneasiness is likely to arise owing to ever-increasing armaments. This will be impossible to sustain for any length of time and must necessarily lead to the outbreak of war. Both men seem in their conversation to have added each time that the danger of war came from France. Count Bismarck wished to avoid war because a conflict between Prussia and France was an endless conflict; for the beaten nation would always, after a short time, begin the struggle afresh.

One may clearly suppose then, that there prevails here, side by side with great mistrust, much uncertainty about the plans of France. Thus the last, much discussed, speech of the War Minister, von Roon, is by many considered neither a means of pressure upon the Members of Parliament, nor direct provocation to French national pride, but rather a feeler to see how strong is France's inclination to begin a war.

I permit myself to add that General von Roon will not accompany the King to Ems as has been widely asserted. Only the heads of the military and civil Cabinets* and the Secretary of Legation, Abeken, are in His Majesty's suite.

Document 150 Rosenberg (Stuttgart) to Bismarck, 9 March 1868
(Bonn, Auswärtiges Amt, IAA n, no. 26)

Despite the conciliatory tone of the programme of Ministerial candidates and the intention of the Minister, von Varnbühler, to put Ministerial candidates up against Democratic ones, a very spiteful current against Prussia has come to the surface in the local election campaign. Officials of the administration ask the electors whether they wish to remain Württembergers or to become Prussians. They add some criticism of Prussia's position, as, with similar turns of speech, has so far been peculiar to Radical newspapers. They say of the north-German constitution that it contains only three articles: 1. Pay, 2. Serve in the army, 3. Keep your mouth shut. Even officials are not ashamed to bring votes to the Ministerial candidates with such slogans ...

Document 151 Bismarck to Werthern (Munich), 26 February 1869
(O. von Bismarck, *Gesammelte Werke*, vol. vib, no. 1327, p. 2)

... I also think it probable that German unity will be forwarded through violent events. It is quite another matter, however, to bring

* i.e. the Emperor's personal secretaries for military and civil affairs.

about such a violent catastrophe and to bear responsibility for the choice of the time for it. Such arbitrary interventions in the development of history—interventions governed only by subjective reasons —have always had as their consequence only the striking down of unripe fruit. It is self-evident, in my opinion, that German unity at this moment is not a ripe fruit. If during the coming period of time, as much progress in the direction of unity is made as in the period since the accession of Frederick the Great or as in the period since 1840 (the year in which for the first time since the War of Liberation a national movement again made itself felt) we can face the future with tranquillity and leave it to our successors to go further. Behind the chattering and restlessness with which people outside public affairs seek for the 'philosopher's stone' able to establish German unity immediately, there hides as a rule a shallow and, anyhow, impotent ignorance of realities and their operation. I offer Your Excellency these general considerations as an antidote to the excusable influence of the situation in which you live which forms the subject of another despatch that goes to Your Excellency together with this. We can put our clocks forward, but time does not go any faster because we have. The capacity to wait while circumstances develop is one of the prerequisites of a practical policy . . .

Document 152   Bismarck to William I, 20 November 1869
(Ibid., p. 166)

In regard to the south-German situation, I think the line for Prussian policy is set by two diverse aims, the one distant, the other immediate. The distant and greater aim is the national unification of Germany. We can wait for this in security because the lapse of time and the natural development of the nation, which makes further progress every year,*(1) will have their effect. We cannot accelerate it unless out-of-the-way events in Europe, such as some

* *Marginal comments by King William I:*

(1) Agreed
(2) The same, that is agreed
(9) I shall not give up this attitude. But if Bavaria, through Württemberg's intrigues should be estranged from us *all the same*, Baden would then be by so much the more important to us; and for that reason we must *not* estrange Baden.
(10) If France saw that Prussia was not actively trying to attach Baden, peace would not be endangered.
(11) Not encourage, but still less hinder?
(12) On the contrary, our friends in Bavaria and Württemberg are only strengthened by Baden's conduct.

upheaval in France or a war of other Great Powers among themselves, offer us an unsought opportunity to do so. Apart from such events, every recognizable attempt of Prussia to determine the decision of the south-German princes, by pressure or agitation, will have as its consequence the opposite of the result sought, and will endanger our immediate aim, which though smaller is still necessary. I consider this aim to be to keep, first, the Bavarian Government and, secondly, the Württemberg Government in such a political direction that as long as the *status quo* lasts, neither Cabinet will co-operate[2] with Paris or Vienna nor find a pretext, on a favourable opportunity, to loosen or even to break the alliances that have been concluded . . .

It is certainly very desirable that the National Party in Baden should not lose hope. But if the only choice lies between this evil and the greater one of alienating Bavaria through the abandonment of the waiting attitude we have so far observed, I believe that we must accept the estrangement of Baden.[9] The driving restlessness of Baden's policy can seriously embarrass us and endanger the success which our policy of reserve and of maintaining peace with France is certain in the long run to achieve.[10]

If, feeling that we are superior to France in war, which I do not doubt, we were to encourage the impatient policy of the Grand Duke's Cabinet, both peace with France, and, which I think would be worse, our relationship with Bavaria and Württemberg would be destroyed;[11] since even our friends in these two countries will not tolerate being *forced* by Baden, their smaller neighbour, into a policy which sooner or later they would embark upon voluntarily . . .[12]

IV · THE FOUNDATION OF THE EMPIRE. THE DECISION FOR WAR

FROM the Prussian victory over Austria in 1866 onwards, Europe stood continuously on the edge of war. Prussia aimed at the unification of the German states. France sought to prevent it, and aspired to win for herself successes in foreign policy. The same applied to Austria. Russia collided with Austria in south-eastern Europe again. Britain's imperialist policy required, as a prerequisite for success, a European balance of weakness. In the tense atmosphere of the years 1868–70 a European conflagration could have arisen out of any incident whether such an incident sprang from Prussia's Germanizing policy in North Schleswig, from France's policy of compensations, or from Austria's aspirations in south-eastern Europe. The fact that war between France and Prussia-Germany finally broke out over differences of opinion in the Spanish Succession question may be considered almost an irony of history; for, when in the autumn of 1868 a revolution in Spain swept the Bourbons from the throne, Bismarck held that this event provided excellent means to keep Napoleon at peace. At the same time he gained an opportunity to meet the Franco-Austrian political offensive more vigorously.

Whereas the Bourbons in 1868 had been ready to enter an alliance with France, the new Spanish régime pursued an independent course (Doc. 153). It adopted Prince Leopold from the Hohenzollern Sigmaringen House (that is the Catholic line) on to the list of candidates for the vacant throne. This signified a development for the whole House of Hohenzollern of great historical importance (Docs. 154, 156a). Although ever since the summer of 1868 his envoy for confidential affairs, his banker, Gerson Bleichröder, had been in continuous communication with Spain, Bismarck, because of the domestic tension within Prussia and Germany, could not at once use the political capital, that lay to his credit (Doc. 155).

Only after the Spaniards had officially approached the Sigmaringen in February 1870 (Doc. 156), and Archduke Albert had gone at the same time to Paris for conversations about a military alliance between France and Austria, did Bismarck open his political counter-offensive. He had, for the time being, won a free hand. The building of the economic structure of the North German Confederation was over; the conflict with the Liberals over the question of taxation had been settled; things in Germany were in a bad way, were 'bogged down', yet—if Bismarck wanted to make any progress at all in his Germany policy, he would have to restrain French influence in the south. For this reason he now seized upon the Hohenzollern candidature and made it the focus of his political efforts (W. Bussmann) (Doc. 157).

Bismarck was ready to make the candidature the test case of the German question. He gained the support of Roon, Moltke, and Delbrück (Doc. 158). France, on her part, saw in the encirclement of her Empire by the House of Hohenzollern a direct threat to her position in Europe and was determined not to suffer a second Sadowa. So France too made the candidature into a test case—a test case for her power in Europe. Both states, though neither worked from the outset to bring war about, were resolved not to evade the issue, if the expected diplomatic crisis turned into a conflagration.

Bismarck was on the march. If he could succeed in taking the French by surprise and putting them in front of a *fait accompli*, Napoleon's prestige would drop still further. The victory of 1866 and a new success in 1870 would work together to breathe a little life again into German development. Lest the blow should miss the mark, the action must be so covered that Prussia could either appear to have had nothing to do with what was a dynastic family matter or else be seen to be defending German interests against the French, bent on aggression. A resort to arms, provided it was a national war—with all its repercussions—was, then, not an eventuality that she ought to avoid. In addition, Prussia felt herself militarily superior to the French. Things developed well.

Despite resistance by both the Sigmaringen Princes and King William, Bismarck succeeded in running the candidature into the channel of family business (Doc. 159). He saw things *couleur de rose*. But then events outran him.

The conditions—secrecy and isolation—under which Bismarck wished to conduct his diplomatic offensive were not realized. The candidature became known prematurely. The Spanish bombshell burst at the wrong moment (Doc. 160). France saw herself already looking foolish.

French public opinion was in the grip of great excitement. The Government was no less decided and it responded sharply to the Prussian offensive. War was not universally desired but Prussia must be put in her place. Counter-measures were initiated in the Press and the French Foreign Minister in a very aggressive speech in the French Chamber, with the general approval of its members, demanded that Prussia withdraw and abandon her intention of putting a Hohenzollern Prince on the Spanish throne (Doc. 161). Thus France had burnt her boats and passed back to Bismarck the Knave of Hearts in the pack of cards—that is, it was Germany's turn to face a loss of prestige (Doc. 162). It was now for Bismarck either to yield and to suffer a defeat or to push the matter further.

At Varzin, in the country, the North German Federal Chancellor was meanwhile contemplating the business in sceptical expectancy. He had sketched out to his subordinates the line of Prussia's conduct: officially they were to know nothing and to show themselves brusquely indignant (Doc. 163). This attitude, as Bismarck knew, would excite opinion in Paris still more. Next he received France's 'impudent' demands: but they came rather too quickly. If he were to fail now in linking the Prussian business with national enthusiasm, he would have to give up his plan of ruining the Napoleonic dynasty by diplomatic means. Yet Prussia still had an unassailable position in the eyes of Europe (as he had calculated in the spring she would have) because Europe and above all south Germany had learnt its lesson from him: that the candidature constituted 'a freely-willed act by the Spanish nation on one side, and on the other side, by the Hereditary Prince of Sigmaringen who was master . . . of his decisions and a private man'. To put the quarrel on the right ground was a delicate matter, so delicate that it has become a *cause célèbre* for European historians.

So long as Prussia remained true to her adopted attitude, that she had nothing to do with the whole thing, and so long as the Prussian King—who very reluctantly sanctioned this action that went against his soldierly conception of honour—supported the candidature, time was won in order 'to ask Germany' how much the affair mattered to the German people. For this reason it was necessary to have nothing officially to do with the candidature (Doc. 164). The original plan was indeed spoilt, but nothing was lost, precisely because Gramont's speech was so offensive to Prussia.

In this situation the independent activity of his ambassador in Paris, von Werther, robbed Bismarck of his sleep. Werther, alarmed by the French excitement, had already on 5 July gone off on a quasi-personal mission from Napoleon, to explain to his King, who was staying in Bad Ems, the possibility of a compromise with Paris (Doc. 165). Thus France sought to address herself directly to William I. Should the latter give up the position he had taken on the question of the Spanish succession, Prussia would be compromised and the fine-spun thread of Bismarck's policy be broken. Since King William was from the beginning disinclined to hold to the candidature at any price, Bismarck was angry at Werther's mission. If the King backed out, then his policy was a mere heap of broken china. Yet Werther would have to make his journey. If he stayed in Paris it would be proclaimed weakness. Everything turned on the King's acting as Bismarck intended. Once more Bismarck outlined his political course (Doc. 166), and begged his King 'to preserve the coolest possible view of the situation'.[1] Yet the King was indignant (Doc. 167). Nevertheless he decided in accordance with Bismarck's views. The question was how long would he continue to do so.

Meanwhile France had been active too. She had put herself into communication with the Great Powers, and, more important, with the south-German courts and now believed—since the reports were not unfavourable—that Prussia could expect no support in this affair (Doc. 168). Gramont and the President of the Council, Ollivier, took no care to read between the lines of the south-German utterances and believed they had already won their game.

Prussia, however, kept silent. No news came from Werther in Ems. It remained uncertain whether or not the Hohenzollern would give up the candidature. In Spain the meeting of the Cortes to choose a King drew ever nearer; what use would the diplomatic campaign be, if it was not certain from the outset that the Prussians would yield and would be publicly disowned? Gramont, therefore, decided to put a pistol to Prussia's head (Doc. 169). Count Benedetti, his ambassador in Berlin, was sent to the Prussian King in Bad Ems. By a personal mission he was to gain the renunciation of the candidature from the Hohenzollern House: either renunciation or war. Those were the alternatives (Doc. 170).

Although the King declined these alternatives (Doc. 171), he yet agreed that he and his First Minister had known of the candidature. Indeed, more, the King showed himself not disinclined to come out for its withdrawal (Doc. 172). This was a great success for Paris. Bismarck was in danger of having to back down. The King sought a compromise: he did not want to go to war for the sake of these obscure measures of his Minister. Did the French believe they could rest content themselves with the King's promise? If so, then Bismarck would have no further power to strengthen the reputation of Prussia and of the Hohenzollern House and the object of his policy, the attainment of an increase in Prussia's power through the unification of Germany, would be postponed to the distant future.

Yet France still did not yield. Gramont wanted more. He wanted, a public, definitive Hohenzollern renunciation of the Spanish throne (Doc. 173). In this he overplayed his hand and gave Bismarck the chance to stand forth as the attacked and injured party. Bismarck could now link together Prussian interests and the German national *élan*.

Bismarck seized his chance at once. He instructed the Press and announced his arrival in Ems (Doc. 174). Prussia was sure of Russia's friendship; Britain, in face of the French demands on Prussia, would remain neutral; even Austria would be silent. Finally he had the King told that he could no longer withdraw from the affair without suffering a serious loss of prestige (Doc. 175). The King remained firm in face of all French pressure. How would the south Germans now react? Their attitude was the matter next at stake.

In the south the attitude was for the time being reserved. Varnbühler and Bray-Steinburg did not wish to be drawn into the battle if it was for a Prussian dynastic ambition. The spark was wanting which would fire Germany's support to Prussia's position. Would France blindly rush on to 'the proffered sword' (G. Ritter)? Would King William not withdraw for the sake of his precious peace? These were certainly exciting hours and burdens which robbed the Prussian Minister of his sleep. He had miscalculated too often during this crisis and was juggling on the edge of a precipice. Meanwhile France did not step back. Gramont wanted the unmistakable diplomatic defeat of Berlin. France believed she had no choice but to act as she did (Doc. 176). And the King, too, could not yield any further without losing face.

Benedetti's mission—to gain from King William a declaration guaranteeing the Hohenzollern renunciation of the Spanish throne for all time—created for Bismarck the opportunity to win German public opinion for the Prussian cause (Doc. 178), by sharpening the point of the report from Ems in a despatch (Doc. 177), which has become famous, and the opportunity at the same time to isolate France. Bismarck urged Paris in a provocative way to make her policy plain (Doc. 179).

Bismarck, indeed, had not succeeded in causing the candidature to the Spanish throne to appear as a dynastic family measure. This game had failed. Instead of that he had the second possibility for solving the Spanish business safely in control. France appeared as the aggressor; Prussia, it seemed, had to defend Germany against the Caesar of the Seine. The candidature to the Spanish throne disappeared and the German question began (Doc. 180). The south now made haste to affirm its loyalty to the alliance with Prussia (Doc. 181); for national susceptibilities in Bavaria and Württemberg were injured (Doc. 182). After the origin of the war had thus been officially established, the French declaration of war— on 19 July 1870—arrived. War began under favourable conditions for Prussia. The south co-operated (Doc. 183) and there was great enthusiasm (Doc. 184). Austria, Italy, and Britain remained neutral as Russia did too (Doc. 185).

Arms decided the German question. Moltke saw a decision was to be gained, as in 1866, by attacking. On the model of the Bohemian campaign, he threw back the French with three encircling armies and succeeded in surrounding and defeating Napoleon in Sedan. Napoleon capitulated on 2 September; 100,000 Frenchmen entered captivity in Germany (Doc. 186); the Republic was proclaimed in Paris and France was summoned to further resistance. In Germany there was great rejoicing; the new Empire had its new national day: Sedan day: 'the day of divine judgement on the French, the victory of German loyalty over Latin knavery'.[2]

After the Prusso-German successes in arms, won by the *furor Teutonicus*, the diplomatic negotiations, which were to lead to the constitutional unity of Germany, could begin (Doc. 187). The Empire did not, after all, come into existence as the outcome of a popular movement, but as the result of individual diplomatic negotiations which respected prescriptive rights and were accommodated to the mentality of the existing sovereigns. That which years of revolution, wars of liberation, and almost a century of *Kabinettspolitik* had not achieved, because possible through success in war welcomed with the utmost emotion and celebrated with the liveliest joy.

The next step was to establish the Empire and make its constitution. The framework for the new constitution of the new, united, German structure of states had been made in advance in 1867. It was now only a question of how federal the planned Confederation should be and how much centralization Bismarck would consider necessary in order to guarantee Prussia's power to command the new ship of state.

Bismarck summoned Delbrück to military Headquarters (Doc. 188) for the negotiations with the southern states. After eight victorious battles the main lines of the German peace terms were marked out and Delbrück presented for the first time the idea of becoming Emperor to King William (Doc. 189). Then Delbrück set off to the southern states to find out 'their wishes'. The conditions for the institution of the new Empire, in accordance with Prussian interest and Bismarck's wishes, were favourable. Circumstances friendly to Prussia prevailed in the southern states. No wonder! The south was weak, Austria was weak, France was weak; Prussia was strong. She had only to exercise her will.

Bavaria, however, had no wish to make an unconditional entry into the North German Confederation. Bray hoped for the co-operation of the south against Prussia. But in these last negotiations, too, Bismarck and Delbrück were able to prevent the south from acting together (Doc. 190). Württemberg, Baden, and Hesse entered without reserve into negotiations with Prussia. Bavaria was thus isolated, and had to bury her plans for constructing anew the alliance and Zollverein treaties. Bismarck and Delbrück rejected the other Bavarian proposals too. These aimed at a wider and a narrower Confederation and a joint presidency of the Confederation by the King of Bavaria and the King of Prussia—that is to say, Louis II was to be co-Emperor. At the end of October the final negotiations with the southern states began in Versailles. They were conducted on parallel lines, but with each state individually. Bismarck thus prevented at the outset any joint action by the south. The basis of negotiations was the narrower Confederation only (Doc. 191). Bismarck and Delbrück did not force the pace. Rather they beguiled the south with the offer of special and honorific rights. Thus they won over Bavaria in the end by leaving her the command of her army in peacetime, sovereignty in railway, postal, and telegraph arrangements, and the taxing of beer and spirits. Württemberg was satisfied with fewer rights, retaining control only of her postal and telegraph administration. The Württemberg army corps henceforward belonged to the Prussian army (Doc. 192). By the end of November 1870 the German question was solved—solved in the style of a diplomatic compromise. While the siege of the 'fortress of Paris' went on, Bismarck had settled the question, had refused any proposal for direct 'mediatization'* of the south German dynasties, and circumvented the institution of an Imperial Ministry responsible to Parliament. The Empire was established by means of the voluntary agreement of the Princes and free cities. It was not established—as the imperial constitution of 1849 had been— by the nation. Its sovereignty was vested in the federated governments represented in the *Bundesrat*. Here, as in the

* See above, p. 87, note *. T.

North German Confederation, Prussia out-voted the rest: not so overwhelmingly as in 1867 (now by 17 out of 58 votes) but decisively enough. The army was put under the command of the Prussian King. The President, that is, the King of Prussia, nominated (as before) the Chancellor. The reserved rights of the southern states had thus little significance and almost no historical substance. Despite all the reserved rights, it was Prussia who commanded in the Empire. Bismarck needed the states of the Confederation as a counterweight to the parliamentary ambitions of the Liberals, but for nothing else. The new *Reichstag* was not called upon to govern any more than the *Reichstag* of the North German Confederation had been. It had, like the latter, a limited right to control. Political parties were only allowed, as before, to deliberate. The Empire was a federal, not a unitary state, and was a constitutional, not a parliamentary, monarchy. Thus Bismarck had, indeed, founded for the Liberals the unity they yearned for, but at the same time inflicted a fresh defeat upon them.

After 1862 and 1866 the Liberals had had in the same way to put up with the non-fulfilment of their military and unitary national programme. Thus the fundamental decisions of Bismarck's constitutional policy of 1862 and 1866–7 were underlined afresh. They were: that there should be no responsible Ministry and no direct influence by the representative assembly upon the way the money voted for the army was spent. The *Reich* Chancellor, nearly always also Prussian Minister President and Prussian Minister for Foreign Affairs, depended on the King or the Emperor, was not answerable to the *Reichstag*, was unchecked in foreign affairs and hardly checked in domestic affairs, and asserted his complete power in the new *Reich* as in the old North German Confederation. Bismarck had forcefully opposed tendencies towards a parliamentary system, and had, in the first instance, won. Liberalism was only to survive in economic matters, but even there was bound to the interests of the traditional ruling classes.

In a country that had had no successful revolution, this evolution was only consistent. Crown, nobility, army, and bureaucracy were here still the ruling forces, By their side the Liberal *bourgeoisie* and the rising proletariat might well claim an equal right to speak, but they never had the power to execute their will. Independent parliamentary organizations were alien to this Empire, and were a legacy of other developments; the Parliament created for the new Empire, the *Reichstag*, with only 'a kind of control', was sufficient for it.

Equally alien to this Empire (which although it came into being at this point in time through the energy of Otto von Bismarck, was yet the outcome of far older developments) was the resurrection of a German imperial title. Bismarck had solved this question, too, by diplomacy (Doc. 193). He had known how, with delicacy, to move the King of Bavaria to beg King William to accept the title of Emperor (Doc. 194). When the matter was settled and everything was decided with the Princes, the *Reichstag* was to pass a resolution begging King William to accept the imperial title (Doc. 195).

The representative assembly had, indeed, to say 'yes' to the adoption of the state treaties, or the new constitution. In the north a loud outcry was raised against the reserved rights of the south, but the treaties were accepted all the same (Doc. 196). In the south the Clericals, Democrats, and supporters of a *grossdeutsch* solution went once more to the barricades. In vain! The treaties, even if sometimes by narrow margins (in Bavaria only by 2 votes over the two-thirds majority) were accepted. Treaty-wise the German Empire existed from 1 January 1871—'not a breath of the spirit of the old stirred in the new' (Doc. 197).

When, on 18 January 1871, King William was proclaimed Emperor, unity was gained (Doc. 198). Prussian militarism, kingship, federal state, and universal suffrage had been forced by Bismarck into an amalgam. Contemporaries experienced the establishment of the Empire—like the victory over France and the annexation of Alsace Lorraine—as a division between epochs (Doc. 199). Their descendants have considered it so too. But to the critical eye of the historian, who has experienced two world wars, this caesura must become more and more questionable. The unification of the Empire will certainly remain a patriotic date. Yet whether it can be claimed that with Bismarck's achievement a new epoch began, and a historical turning-point occurred in which something new in the history of Europe and even of the world came to expression, must be very questionable (Doc. 200).

Document 153 Bismarck to Saurma (Madrid), 28 October 1868

(O. von Bismarck, *Gesammelte Werke*, vol. via, no. 1200, p. 426)

Your Excellency's recent reports, . . . written in the middle of events, reflect in many places the mood, which the sight of an old monarchy's fall is so apt to call forth. The more naturally, however, sympathy for the defeated side arises in the observer and, out of this sympathy, the more easily an antipathy against the institutions and persons, which replace it, develops, the more firmly must we bear ourselves so that the relations of the two Governments to each other are ruled solely* by the interests of the two states.

The fallen Government was ill disposed to us. Although there was no point in the political field of direct collision between us, we had to count it among our opponents in every political combination. Even the principles, which it followed in relation to economic matters, were unfavourable to the German Zollverein. Its removal is, therefore, an event that suits our policy. Taking the historical viewpoint, we shall regard this change calmly and accept the proceedings which must necessarily accompany it. We must bring the future organization [of Spain], without prejudice, to the touchstone of our interests.

On these grounds, I have implored Your Excellency to cultivate friendly relations with people and officials in Madrid. I beg you also in your reports to preserve a proper tone. They will then harmonize with the thought behind our policy. . . . Should you in the course of an impartial, objective report have information to give or verdicts to utter, you should on every occasion . . . use the cipher.

Document 154 Werthern to Princess Charles of Romania, 4 February 1867

(Ibid., vol. vib, no. 1389, p. 78, editorial note)

. . . 'Everything indicates . . . that the Bourbons are coming to an end. When, is uncertain. It can happen tomorrow or in ten years' time . . . If Queen Isabella is forced to leave Spain, a civil war will be inevitable. It will, however, be short, since economic interests are uppermost, and however great the antipathy of the Spaniards now is to a foreign sovereign, they will be obliged by force of circumstances to have recourse to one; for it is their only road to salvation.

* The word *nur*, is Bismarck's holograph addition.

They would then have the choice between an Austrian Archduke and a Prince of the Catholic line of the House of Hohenzollern. The army will decide and with the army the battle of Königgrätz weighs dreadfully! Any perceptive person will understand that the House of Hohenzollern is heir to the Habsburgs. If one pictures to oneself the world situation, which would result if it were possible for His Majesty the King and Emperor of Germany to touch with his left hand, through Prince Charles of Romania,* the near east and, with his right hand, through another Prince of his House, to touch Spain, one realizes that it is well worth the effort to put a man in Madrid, who is under an obligation to us, and to animate his innate sympathies. He will, for many years to come, however the die falls, exercise an immense influence on the army. This conjuncture of circumstances is far less chimerical than at first sight it may seem. It would only be a repetition of the position of Charles V. What was possible in the sixteenth century is still so today. The last war showed how quickly and wonderfully events proceed!'

Document 155   Bismarck to Solms (Paris), 11 May 1869
(Ibid., no. 1389, p. 82)

Confidential

Herr Benedetti visited me on the 8th inst., after his return from Paris, to communicate the impressions he had gained there. He expressed himself in an entirely peaceful and confident tone over the whole situation. The only thing that seemed to preoccupy him was the question whether Prussia would give a king of any sort to the Spaniards. I turned this question aside with a joke and told him that, of course, we had taken soundings recently in the princely House of Hohenzollern to see whether the Hereditary Prince had any wish to accept the crown, but that both he himself and his father had said they were for declining it and that His Majesty, the King, when he later learnt of it, said that he understood that very well . . .

---

* Younger son of Charles Antony of Hohenzollern-Sigmaringen. T.

Documents 156a and 156b   To accept or decline

*156a   Charles Antony of Hohenzollern-Sigmaringen to William I,
25 February 1870*
(R. Fester, *Briefe, Aktenstücke und Regesten zur Geschichte der
Hohenzollerschen Thronkandidatur in Spanien*, Leipzig, 1913,
vol. i, no. 103, p. 55)

I approach Your Majesty most respectfully and with deep
emotion, but with that unshakeable confidence which the importance of the situation demands.

It is again a question of the highest importance and a significant
one, heavy with consequences, which lies before us and presses for
decision.

It is the question of the candidature to the Spanish throne of my
son, the Hereditary Prince.

Had I to follow only my family feeling and the dictates of my
conscience, I should be able most positively to declare to Your
Majesty, in the name of my son and in my own, that we absolutely
declined.

I have considered it, however, my duty to appeal for Your
Majesty's judgement, since the present case and the decision
associated with it are of high significance and furthermore, the Royal
and Princely House of Hohenzollern is called upon to determine
herein an issue of great historical importance. May it please Your
Majesty, in your wisdom, to give the decision.

Over the context of the affair as a whole I have today given more
exact particulars to Count Bismarck, which he will doubtless put
before Your Majesty.

In my opinion, the time for temporizing is over, and it can now
only be a question of accepting or declining . . . If the interests of
Prussian power demand a solution of the question in the sense of
acceptance, Your Majesty will be pleased to let me be given to
understand so. If they do not demand this, our decision is already
taken: it is to decline. . . .

156b   Charles Antony to Bismarck, 25 February 1870
(Ibid., no. 104, p. 56)

. . . Heart and feeling tell me that acceptance of this throne would
be a hazardous venture.

Only a character steeled through many-sided experiences, great
self-control and a thoroughly trained political understanding would

be appropriate to the execution of such a task. My son has never yet had opportunity to afford proof of those characteristics.

The acceptance of this crown would represent, on one hand, an historical turning-point and show, on the other, a supreme consciousness of Prussia's political power.

In a dynasty which represents the centre of gravity of central Europe and whose branches might blossom on the Black Sea and beyond the Pyranees, the one governing a cultural community that belongs to the future, the other, one that belongs to the past— history has not seen such a dynasty since the time of Charles V— there rests a high mission, willed by Providence, and a call to be fit to govern the most heterogeneous elements.

These fleeting observations are only brief intimations of the view I entertain, namely that no one except His Majesty, the King, can speak the deciding word . . .

Document 157   Bismarck to William I, 9 March 1870*
   (O. von Bismarck, *Gesammelte Werke*, vol. vib, no. 1521, p. 271)

Your Majesty will, I trust, graciously permit me, with my humble duty to summarize in writing, the motives which, in my modest opinion, favour the acceptance of the Spanish crown by His Serene Highness the Hereditary Prince of Hohenzollern, now that I have already respectfully intimated them by word of mouth.

I am of the opinion that if the acceptance takes place it will bring both direct and indirect advantages for Prussian and German political interests and that, in the opposite case, disadvantages and dangers are to be feared.

Acceptance of the Spanish Royal Crown by a Prince of Your Majesty's illustrious House would strengthen existing sympathies between two nations which are, by way of exception, in the happy position of having no conflicting interests because they are not neighbours. Their friendly relations seem capable of considerable development. The Spaniards would feel a sense of gratitude towards Germany, if she were to rescue them from the state of anarchy into which they—a people predominantly monarchist in sentiment— threaten to sink for want of a King.

It is desirable for Germany to have on the far side of France a country on whose sympathy she can rely and with those suscepti- bilities France would be obliged to reckon . . .

---

* This is printed in G. Bonnin, *Bismarck and the Hohenzollern Candidature for the Throne of Spain* (London, 1957), p. 68, with William I's marginal notes. T.

French peaceableness towards Germany will always wax or wane in proportion to the dangers of war with her. We have in the long run to look for the preservation of peace not to the goodwill of France but to her impression of our power.

The prosperity of Spain and Germany's trade with her would receive a powerful impetus under Hohenzollern rule. If even in Romania the German dynasty has given a remarkable stimulus to trade relations between that landlocked country and Germany, it is to be assumed that in all probability the revival of friendly feelings towards Germany in Spain with her long coastline would provide new openings there for German trade, once so prosperous. ... The repute of the Hohenzollern dynasty, the justifiable pride with which not only Prussia regards its Royal House but Germany too—she tends more and more to glory in that name as a common national possession, a symbol of German fame and German prestige abroad; all this forms an important element in political self-confidence, the fostering and strengthening of which would be of benefit to national feeling in general and to monarchist sentiment in particular. It is therefore to Germany's political interest that the House of Hohenzollern should accept the standing and the exalted position in the world to which only its Habsburg antecedents in the time of Charles V offer an analogy. This element of pride in the dynasty is a factor of no little value working in favour of the contentment of our people and the consolidation of our position. Just as in Spain scant respect for the ruling House has paralysed the forces of the nation for centuries, so with us pride in an illustrious dynasty has been a powerful moral impetus to the development of Prussia's power in Germany. This impetus will grow mightily if the need of Germans for recognition abroad, hitherto so little satisfied, is met by the dynasty's assuming an incomparable position in the world.

To decline the proffered crown would have, it can be foreseen, undesirable consequences. ...

Document 158   Charles Antony to Prince Charles of Romania, 20 March 1870
(R. Fester, *Briefe, Aktenstücke und Regesten zur Geschichte der Hohenzollerschen Thronkandidatur in Spanien*, Leipzig, 1913, vol. i, no. 122, p. 65)

I have been here for the last fortnight on the most important family business. Nothing less is at stake than the acceptance or rejection of the Spanish throne for Leopold* which, of course

* Charles Antony's elder son. T.

under the seal of a European state secret, has been offered officially by the Spanish government.

This question is a great preoccupation here. Bismarck desires acceptance on dynastic and political grounds, but the King desires it only if Leopold answers the call willingly. On the 15th there was a very interesting and important council here presided over by the King, at which the Crown Prince, we two, Bismarck, Roon, Moltke, Schleinitz, Thile, and Delbrück were present. The unanimous conclusion of the deliberators was for acceptance as the fulfilment of a patriotic Prussian duty . . .

Document 159   Charles Antony to Leopold, 5 June 1870
(J. Dittrich, *Bismarck, Frankreich und die Spanische Thronkandidatur der Hohenzollern: Die 'Kriegsschuldfrage' von 1870*, Munich, 1962, no. 68, p. 394)

First, I should like to greet you on your arrival in Sigmaringen.

This may *perhaps* be the last time you salute your native town and homeland for some while. I have neither the will nor the power to think about it.

It breaks my heart. Transports of feeling are, however, of no use here. The present day demands realism. The days of ideal attitudes are associated for me with the categorical imperative of the present. I send you, enclosed, a copy of Bismarck's memorandum.

In addition, I have to inform you that yesterday I talked for half an hour in Giessen with the King and Bismarck who were there on their way through from Ems to Berlin. The King is *d'accord* with us, that is, he accommodates himself to the political constraint of Bismarck. The latter triumphs and is *couleur de rose*. Had we again refused, we should have had to pay for it; for the question of the Spanish throne is a prime factor in Bismarck's political calculations. I repeated our conditions to the King clearly and he agrees with our point of view. Perhaps some European event or other will yet come between to prevent it—if so, all the better.

Document 160   William I to Queen Augusta, 5 July 1870
(R. Fester, *Briefe, Aktenstücke und Regesten zur Geschichte der Hohenzollerschen Thronkandidatur in Spanien*, Leipzig, 1913, vol. i, no. 269, p. 125)

. . . The Spanish bombshell has, suddenly exploded, but in quite a different way from how we were told it would. We have not heard a syllable about it from our cousins. In Berlin the French *chargé d'affaires* has already spoken to Thile, who naturally said that the matter had been kept entirely from the Government and that what had been negotiated between Prim and the Hohenzollern family had not yet been communicated to the Foreign Office. In Paris the [Foreign] Minister questioned Werther in the same way. Werther could say with a very clear conscience that he knew nothing about it. Marie Hohenzollern writes to Antony that in Paris, too, men are putting their heads together over this question and saying it will be a second Sadowa, France should not let this happen to her, war is inevitable etc. . . .

Document 161   Speech of Gramont in the French Chamber, 6 July 1870
(*Les Origines diplomatiques de la Guerre de 1870–1871*, vol. 28, no. 8266, footnote)

. . . We have always shown our sympathy for the Spanish nation and have always avoided anything, which could appear like intervention in the internal affairs of a noble and great nation in the full exercise of its sovereign rights. In regard to the several claimants to the throne, we have not departed from the strictest neutrality and we have never shown for any one of them either preference or antipathy.

We shall persist in this conduct. But we do not believe that respect for the rights of a neighbouring people obliges us to suffer a foreign Power, by putting one of its Princes on the throne of Charles V, to alter the present balance of power in Europe to our disadvantage and to endanger the interests and honour of France.

This eventuality we firmly hope will not be realized.

To prevent it we count both on the wisdom of the German people and the friendship of the Spanish people.

If things fall out otherwise, strong in your support and in that of the nation, we shall know how to do our duty without hesitation and without weakness. . . .

Document 162   Report by Metternich of a conversation with the Empress Eugénie, 6 July 1870
(J. Dittrich, *Bismarck, Frankreich und die Spanische Thronkandidatur der Hohenzollern: Die 'Kriegsschuldfrage' von 1870*, Munich, 1962, p. 104)

. . . 'It will be very difficult for Bismarck to come out of the affair without either giving way to us completely or proving equal to taking the matter further. If he yields, he will do so under the threat of our attitude—a humiliation from which he will only recover with difficulty. . . .'

Document 163   Sourd (*chargé d'affaires* at Berlin) to Gramont, telegram, 4 July 1870
(*Les Origines diplomatiques de la Guerre de 1870–1871*, vol. 28, no. 246)

I have just seen Herr von Thile and I spoke to him of the news which has reached you relating to the acceptance of the Spanish crown by the Prince of Hohenzollern. The Secretary of State, at the outset of our conversation, asked me whether I was questioning him officially and declared that, in that case, he must, before he replied to me, take the orders of the King. I replied that I had come simply to draw his attention to a piece of news, which has caused a bad impression at Paris, and that I was not charged to elaborate to him, for the present, the reasons for this impression. I added that we were primarily interested in knowing whether the Prussian Government was a stranger to this negotiation. Visibly embarrassed, Herr von Thile told me that *the Prussian Government knew absolutely nothing of this affair* and that *it did not exist for it*. He concentrated on making it clear by his declaration that his Government had no responsibility, but Your Excellency will observe that he refrained from categorically affirming that the Berlin Cabinet did not know of the existence of the negotiation nor of its result. . . .

Document 164   Bucher* (Varzin) to Thile, 5 July 1870
(R. H. Lord, *The Origins of the War of 1870*, Cambridge, Mass., 1924, p. 128)

I have just telegraphed to Geheim Rath Abeken:
'If France should raise with us questions that only concern Spain, Baron von Werther is to refuse to discuss them and refer his questioners to Madrid and Reichenhall. With due regard to Spain's independence and with no call to intervene in Spanish constitutional questions, we leave them to the Spaniards and to those who wish to become Spaniards. If France wishes to influence them that is her affair and not ours. To accept discussion would be to spoil our otherwise impregnable position. Above all Baron von Werther should guard against giving the impression that he or we are to be intimidated. His journey to Ems will give this false impression.'

* Lothar Bucher, an official in the Prussian Foreign Ministry. T.

Document 165 Werther (Paris) to Bismarck, 4 July 1870
  (Ibid., p. 122)

I depart tomorrow evening for Ems to wait upon His Majesty,
the King, and shall bring with me a statement of the impressions
(which are of the most critical importance) of the Duke de Gramont
and Ollivier over the Hohenzollern project for the Spanish throne.
I consider it desirable that I should be able to speak to His Majesty
personally about it.

Document 166 Bismarck to Abeken (Ems), 5 July 1870
  (Ibid., p. 129)

I communicate for use in speaking to the King some views on the
handling of the Spanish question. In my opinion, Herr von Werther
should have repulsed any discussion of the matter as one foreign to
himself and to his Government. We must make his journey to Ems
pass for courteous readiness to inform himself about the matter and
to procure as speedily as possible all available enlightenment for a
friendly French government. We must chiefly take steps to see that
the journey of the King's ambassador does not seem to be caused by
the impressions, *'of the most critical importance'*, of Gramont and
Ollivier. The firm and fearless attitude, which we have so far
opposed to all the uneasiness of Paris, is our essential advantage
and one to which we owe the preservation of peace. France is more
afraid, in my opinion, of a serious breach than we are. If we let
the belief gain ground that we are the more afraid, French arrogance
will very soon leave us no other choice but war . . .
  Since the journey of Herr von Werther is not to be prevented,
permit me to make some suggestions for his instructions. . . .
  Everything which the King can legally and politically do in the
matter consists in exercising a dissuasive influence. This he has
already done. To intervene beyond that in the decisions of a subject
of such high rank [as Leopold of Hohenzollern] would not accord
with the self-respect of the King nor with the constitution of the
country. . . .
  When once we go beyond this line in our attitude to the matter;
when once we concede, even tacitly, that France has a right to call
us to account over this Spanish affair; when once we let it be thought
that we are showing ourselves the least little bit disturbed by the
impressions of Gramont and Ollivier (both Gascons in character
though only Gramont so by birth)—then, my Excellency, we
shall put ourselves in a false position and the affair will only end
in a reaction of public opinion to our disadvantage and in the

encouragement of France against us. It would much impair our capacity to live at peace with France. Above all, therefore, I advise you to provide Herr von Werther with the instruction to make plain in Paris his cool astonishment at the uneasiness which France is manifesting.

Document 167   William I in conversation with Waldersee, 8 July 1870
(A. Graf v. Waldersee, *Denkwürdigkeiten*, H. O. Meisner, editor, Stuttgart, 1922–3, vol. i, p. 73)

... 'We suddenly find ourselves in the middle of a very serious situation . . . This is Bismarck's fault. He has treated this matter lightly like so many others. First, I cannot mix myself in it at all. I hold firm to my original and correct standpoint. I do not deny that I am playing two parts, but I can keep them entirely separate. I have never directly or officially dealt with anyone about it, nor have I bound myself to anything. I can refer the French Government only to the Hohenzollern Princes and shall exercise no influence over them—so, let events find us prepared! (These words were spoken with great emphasis.) The world will readily believe that I, at my advanced age, have no wish to wage yet another great war and that I have not wantonly brought about this serious development. If, however, war is forced upon me, I shall wage it in firm confidence in my distinguished army. . . .'

Documents 168a and 168b   The south Germans aghast but reserved

168a   Saint Vallier (Stuttgart) to Gramont, 10 July 1870
(*Les Origines diplomatiques de la Guerre de 1870–1871*, vol. 28, no. 8392)

... Meanwhile, I think I should not conceal from Your Excellency the stupefaction and alarm which the serious news, that has so suddenly broken upon us, has created in public opinion. Württemberg knows that her independence, assured by the maintenance of the *status quo* and the preservation of peace, would be endangered by a rupture between France and Prussia. The population is animated by too strong an anti-Prussian sentiment not to tremble at the thought that the chances of war may put her at the mercy of the invader from the south. An immense disquiet reigns. With it is mixed a strong feeling of irritation against Herr von Bismarck, who is unanimously regarded as the author, or the inventor, of this

unexpected candidacy. Men agree in saying that Herr von Bismarck
has organized the whole intrigue with the sole purpose of creating
for France difficulties, serious enough to compel her to emerge from
her attitude of cold reserve and firm resolution. That attitude is a
safeguard for the existence of the German kingdoms of the south,
whose independence he will hasten to infringe as soon as he sees us
seriously preoccupied with our Spanish frontiers.

168b   d'Astorg (Darmstadt) to Gramont, 2 July 1870
   (Ibid., no. 8413)

'Prussia', the *Volksblätter* say, 'may have her own particular
reasons for setting the guns off; but Prussia cannot wish that the
German people should follow her. Herr von Bismarck is about to
make a war between Cabinets, there is no question of a war between
nations. . . .'

Document 169   Gramont to Benedetti (Berlin), 7 July 1870
   (Ibid., no. 8298)

. . . We are pressed for time, because we must strike first. In the
event of an unsatisfactory reply, and for the campaign to begin in a
fortnight, the troops must begin to move on Saturday. . . .
   If you obtain from the King the withdrawal of his consent to the
Prince of Hohenzollern's candidacy, that will be an immense success and a great service. The King will have assured the peace of
Europe. If not, it means war. . . .

Documents 170a and 170b   Gramont seeks clarification

170a   Gramont to Benedetti (Berlin) telegram, 10 July 1870
   (Ibid., no. 8368)

I have only this morning received your despatch of yesterday
evening and parts of it were mutilated. You should do all you can to
obtain a definitive reply; for we cannot wait without running the
risk that Prussia will get ahead of us in preparations. The day must
not end today without our making a beginning.
   I know from a sure source that at Madrid the Regent wishes for
the Hohenzollern withdrawal. As soon as you can, send me a telegram and write in cipher by the post.

170b   The same to the same, telegram, 10 July 1870
   (Ibid., no. 8369)

Write me a despatch, which I can read to the Chambers or publish, and show in it that the King knew of and authorized the acceptance of the throne by the Prince of Hohenzollern and, above
all, say that he asked you to agree with the Prince before he told
you what he had determined.

Document 171   Abeken (Ems) to Bismarck, 9 July 1870
   (R. H. Lord, *The Origins of the War of 1870*, Cambridge,
   Mass., 1924, p. 165)

His Majesty has just charged me with the following message for
Your Excellency:
   Count Benedetti did not mention a congresss at all; he said that
he had no commission except to appeal to the wisdom of the King
that he might speak the word which would restore tranquillity to
Europe. The King: It was not he who had disturbed Europe but the
Duke de Gramont; the latter only needed to acknowledge from the
tribune [in the Chamber] that Prussia had no share in the affair
and Europe would be tranquil. Count Benedetti: Nobody in
France would believe it; the Duke de Gramont was obliged to
speak as he had done, so as not to lose all support in the *corps
législatif* and to drive it to much worse declarations. The King:
Declarations in the *corps législatif* mean nothing: the Minister's
words were *très graves*. His Majesty then simply explained the
position of affairs: he had been asked for his assent, not as King of
Prussia, but as head of the family and, when the Prince after long
consideration had made up his own mind, he could not have
withheld his sanction; his consent, once given, he could not take
back; he did not know what the Hohenzollern Princes would do
and could not exercise any influence upon them. . . .

Document 172   William I to Charles Antony, 10 July 1870
   (R. Fester, *Briefe, Aktenstücke und Regesten zur Geschichte der
   Hohenzollerschen Thronkandidatur in Spanien*, Leipzig, 1913,
   vol. ii, no. 399, p. 64)

. . . Preparations for war on a large scale are in progress in
France, as you will see. The situation is, therefore, more than
serious. Just as I could not bid your son accept the crown, so I
cannot bid him withdraw his acceptance. Should he, however, so
decide, my 'adherence' will again not be wanting.

The French Ministry and especially Gramont wish for war (it is not clear to me whether the Emperor does) and have said, in so many words, that Spain is out of the picture and that their quarrel is with Prussia alone. It borders on madness. . . .

Document 173 Gramont to Benedetti, 10 July 1870
(*Les Origines diplomatiques de la Guerre de 1870–1871*, vol. 28, no. 8382)

. . . I urgently beg of you to write and telegraph something absolutely clear. If the King will not advise the Prince of Hohenzollern to withdraw, well then, it is war—and war at once. Within a few days we shall be on the Rhine. . . .

Documents 174a and 174b Bismarck begins to act

174a Bismarck to Thile, *10 July 1870*
(R. H. Lord, *The Origins of the War of 1870*, Cambridge, Mass., 1924, p. 172)

. . . It is now time for the semi-official Press to strike a blow* on the subject of the Duke de Gramont's presumptuous demand and threat.

174b Bismarck to Abeken, *10 July 1870*
(Ibid., p. 174)

Should His Majesty, the King, desire my presence in Ems, I am so placed that I can come.

Document 175 Bucher to Thile, 10 July 1870
(Ibid., p. 177)

I suggest that we communicate our information about armed preparations confidentially in London, St. Petersburg, and Madrid and publish the gist of it . . . in the Press without giving its source. Whether counter measures are necessary is a military question. To postpone on political grounds what is militarily necessary would be dangerous. Militarily, it seems to me useful that His Majesty should remain in Ems and perhaps summon Baron von Moltke. Count Solms is wrought up and I see nothing in his assertions except his

* The better text has the words 'to sound note of moral indignation', see G. Bonnin, *Bismarck and the Hohenzollern Candidature for the Throne of Spain* (London, 1957), p. 239. T.

own emotion. I hardly know Count Waldersee. The only positive thing he has to say is that the railways have been alerted;
that is cheap and we can do it too. Politically, our position would be
very favourable if France attacks. As to withdrawal, Prince Charles
Antony and especially the Hereditary Prince, Leopold, know themselves what they have to do. His Majesty cannot announce a change
of view just because of public opinion in Germany . . .

Document 176   From an account by Maurice Paléologue of a
   conversation with the Empress Eugénie, undated
   (M. Paléologue, *des entretiens de l'impératrice Eugénie*, Paris,
   1928, p. 145.

   . . . 'We could not retreat; we could not listen to reason; the whole
country would have risen up against us again if we had! . . . We
were already being accused of weakness. A dreadful saying had
come to our ears: "The Hohenzollern candidature is a Sadowa
prepared in advance! . . ." Oh, this word Sadowa! For four years our
bitterest enemies—Orleanists, Legitimists, Republicans—had not
wearied of throwing it at our heads. They began every day with their
disgusting refrain. Every day they inflamed our wounds as one might
turn the knife in an abscess. In order to be able to conjure up this
spectre they had brought the whole of France to believe that in 1866
we brought unforgiveable disgrace upon her—disgrace such as she
had not suffered since Rossbach. . . This you must remember
should you wish to judge our policy in July 1870. We could not have
exposed the Empire to a second Sadowa—it would not have survived
it. . . .'

Document 177   The Ems Despatch, 13 July 1870
   (*Quellen zur Geschichte*, edited by the Historischen Seminar
   der Universität Berne, Heft 27–9, pp. 24–5)

As sent by Abeken From Ems 3.10 p.m.	*As edited by Bismarck*
1. His Majesty the King writes to me:	After the news of the withdrawal of the Crown Prince of Hohen-zollern had been officially com-municated by the Kingdom of Spain to the Imperial French Government, the French Am-bassador put before His Majesty the King at Ems the demand that he should authorize him to
2. 'Count Benedetti caught me on the promenade to ask from me in an importunate way that I should authorize him to tele-graph at once that I pledged myself for the future never again	

to give my consent, if the Hohenzollern renewed their candidature.'

3. I repulsed him in a somewhat stern tone, since it is neither right nor possible to take such engagements *à tout jamais*.

4. Naturally, I told him, since I have as yet received no news and since he is earlier informed from Paris and Madrid than I am, he will readily perceive that my Government is no more involved in what is going on.

5. His Majesty has since received a letter from the Prince [Charles Antony].

6. Since His Majesty had told Count Benedetti that he was waiting for news from the Prince, His Majesty decided, in reference to the above demand, and on the suggestion of Count Eulenburg and myself, not to receive Count Benedetti again, but only to let him be told through an aide-de-camp: that His Majesty has now received from the Prince confirmation of the news which Benedetti had already received from Paris, and had nothing further to say to the Ambassador.

7. His Majesty leaves it to Your Excellency to decide whether Benedetti's fresh demand and its rejection should be communicated at once to our Representatives abroad and to the Press.

telegraph to Paris that His Majesty, the King, pledged himself for the future never again to give his consent, if the Hohenzollern should renew their candidature.

His Majesty, the King, thereupon declined to receive the French Ambassador again and let him be informed through the aide-de-camp on duty, that His Majesty had nothing further to communicate to the Ambassador.

Communicate this there.

Document 178   Extract from the diary of the Baroness Spitzemberg

(R. Vierhaus, editor, *Das Tagebuch der Baronin Spitzemberg*, Göttingen, 1960, p. 93)

13 July [1870]. We are all full of the greatest excitement the whole day long, as the result of two letters from Charles in which he considers the immediate outbreak of war between France and Germany extremely probable. A telegram came yesterday evening announcing that Count Bismarck was coming through Berlin, on his way to seek out the King and Benedetti in Ems. Charles writes: 'Today the matter, in a few sentences, stands thus: Prussia asserts that she has nothing to do with the choice of the Hohenzollerns. Spain can choose as her King whom she wishes. France demands that Prussia shall cause the Hohenzollerns to withdraw.' Had this been quietly agreed upon between the two Cabinets there would have been nothing to fear. Instead of this, the threatening speech of Gramont in the French Chamber, the outcry of the newspapers, and the armed preparations have brought everything to a head. Charles considers an understanding difficult, if not impossible. . . . After supper another telegram from Charles arrived. It ran: 'The Prince has renounced the candidature. Bismarck is not going to Ems, but will probably return to the country tomorrow.' The impression made by this news was very various: we women rejoiced over a hateful evil averted, whereas Niko (Below), that brave old soldier and lieutenant, almost wept for rage and would have sent King and Government to the devil, because they had yielded to the threats of France. We were also somewhat downcast at this yielding which, of course, has the appearance of weakness. But first one must hear how it actually happened.

14 July. We had scarcely risen from table when a new telegram announced that: 'After the renunciation of the Prince, Benedetti made further demands and was repulsed. Warlike events are in front of us. Charles.' So there we are. We telegraphed at once to Nicolai, who did not come back until half past ten at night. In Stolp the mobilization order is still being awaited tonight. We sat until one o'clock together, quite stiff from fear, anger, and astonishment.

Document 179   Bismarck to Abeken, 14 July 1870

(O. von Bismarck, *Gesammelte Werke*, vol. vib, no. 1615, p. 372)

It seems to me impossible that the King should accept such an offensive demand from the hand of his own ambassador, authorized only by an oral commission from the Minister of another country. Supposing now Gramont should say afterwards that he had not said this or that to Werther? We must have in such a serious case an authentic, written communication from the foreign government. I advise you to telegraph to Werther that the King considers his report *non avenu* and bids him declare to Gramont that on reflection he is not able to execute this somewhat presumptuous commission and must leave it to Gramont to bring his views and demands to the knowledge of the King by other means and through someone else. As soon as he has delivered this message, he must tell Gramont that he has asked for and obtained leave of absence. He must come at once to Berlin in order to give an explanation. He cannot, I believe, after such proceedings remain in Paris.

Document 180 Bismarck to Werthern (Munich), 13 July 1870
(Ibid., no. 1613, p. 371)

In communicating my open telegram about the demand of the French ambassador you should add:

His Majesty the King of Bavaria will sense that Benedetti spoke in a provocative way to the King on the promenade and forced himself upon the King in order to be able to make his demand.

Documents 181a and 181b The South will co-operate

181a Bismarck to William I, telegram, 13 July 1870
(Ibid., no. 1608, p. 365)

Your Majesty's *chargé d'affaires* in Stuttgart has reported: 'Minister von Varnbühler has just summoned me to him and told me that the last demands of Gramont, made despite the Hohenzollern renunciation, have deeply injured national feeling in Württemberg and must excite it against France.' He had authorized the French envoy to communicate this to Paris and had written to Count Bray* that he should speak to Count Cadore** in the same sense.
Marginal Comment by William I against the word 'demands'.
Which? Do they already know the fresh piece of insolence to Werther?

* Minister President in Bavaria. T.
** French Representative in Munich, see Doc. 188a. T.

181b   Werthern (Munich) to Bismarck, 12 July 1870
(R. H. Lord, *The Origins of the War of 1870*, Cambridge,
Mass., 1924, p. 213)

... Count Bray is too intelligent not to feel that I was right, but
also much too weak to undertake anything positive in one direction
or the other. Yet he assures me, as I informed you by telegraph,
that already yesterday he said to the French envoy: in the event of
an attack, France would find Germany united and Bavaria mindful
of her alliance with us ...

Documents 182a, 182b, and 182c   Full of calm decision

182a   Extract from a contemporary diary
(H. Count Lerchenfeld-Koefering, *Erinnerungen und Denkwürdigkeiten*, Berlin, 1935, p. 60)

... If we go with Prussia and she wins the war, she will be forced
to respect Bavaria's continued existence. If Prussia is defeated, we
may perhaps lose the Palatinate. But worse cannot happen to us;
for France must always favour the independence of the individual
German states. We could count on the same consideration if we
were to remain neutral and France were to win. But if Prussia were
to win, when we were neutral, then Hanover's fate would await us.
It would be *finis Bavariae*.

182b   Münch (Berlin) to Beust, 16 July 1870
(Vienna, Haus- Hof- und Staatsarchiv, PA III, no. 102)

From the beginning of the complication I have especially directed
my attention to two points. One of these seems to me of particularly
high importance for our policy. The two points are Prussia's relations with the south-German states and her alliance relationship
with Russia. In regard to the first, this Cabinet has completely
achieved its immediate purpose and without its having needed any
particular effort. The attitude of Bavaria and Baden from the
beginning was described here as completely correct. They were at
first displeased with Württemberg. Baron von Varnbühler hastened
in a very marked way, however, to allay all cause of discontent. The
Prussian Cabinet did not fail to evince its acknowledgement in the
most lively manner to the south-German Cabinets. It is now full of
attention to their Representatives. Count Bismarck has received
their envoys and military attachés in person and given to some of
them a full exposé of the situation—naturally extremely favourable
to Prussia and her chances. The military attachés—for Baden, a

Badenese officer summoned into the war ministry—have today received the necessary instructions about the mobilization and deployment of the army corps of the southern states, which will form the left wing of the army in the field. Baron Spitzemberg left yesterday for Stuttgart, at Count Bismarck's wish, in order to speed up preparations for war in Württemberg. Baron Perglas* will arrive here today.

As regards Prussia's relationship to Russia, I have, by observing it from the outside, reached the conviction that firm written agreements were concluded during Prince Gortchakow's visit. What I have so far been able to learn of their probable content may be summarized as follows: the agreements relate specifically to conditional entry into the war. For the immediate future Russia will remain neutral and will serve to hold Austria in check. For the time being, then, her action will be governed by ours. But Russia will enter the war as soon as France gains any extension of territory, whether in Germany or anywhere else as, for example, in Belgium. Today, as a means of pressure and to raise the confidence of the Representatives here of the south-German states, Count Bismarck made the following two assertions. They were naturally communicated to me only in the strictest confidence. He said: 'We know from a friendly Power and on the highest authority that Austria will preserve benevolent neutrality towards us'; and 'We are sure of Austria's neutrality because of the moral pressure Russia will exert on her.' The members of the Prussian legation in Munich appear calm and affect by their great calm an attitude as if the war was absolutely no concern of theirs. Prince Reuss is returning to Petersburg.

182c Extract from the diary of the Baroness Spitzemberg
(R. Vierhaus, editor, *Das Tagebuch der Baronin Spitzemberg*, Göttingen, 1960, p. 94)

16 July [1870]. In Berlin they are 'in great excitement but full of quiet resolution and firm reliance on their own strength'. They are equally carried away in south Germany, and Father** has declared to St. Vallier*** that these demands of France are offensive to national feeling in Württemberg and have a hostile ring. He has been thanked by telegram from Berlin for saying so. Sophie and I almost weep for joy about it. The French could not have arranged things more unintelligently. Instead of dividing us they have contrived to

* Bavarian envoy in St. Petersburg. T.
** von Varnbühler, Württemberg Minister President.
*** French envoy in Stuttgart. T.

complete Germany's unification. Nothing will cement her unity more firmly than this bloody war, waged in common, for her very existence. There would have been little inclination in south Germany to wage a dynastic war for the Hohenzollerns. The moderation, on the other hand, with which Prussia has acted in this question has stolen all our hearts. Her moderation was almost humiliating to her pride. Charles writes that 'countless telegrams express this idea.' One thing only I hope and long for, that we Württembergers should be true to our national duty to the last extreme and rather perish with honour than live by the grace of our hereditary enemy. I am happy, too, that Father should have an opportunity to show at the end of his life what a good German he is and to see his much abused name again respected. His conduct now sets the standard for the south . . .

24 July. On Sunday the christening of the Crown Prince's newly born daughter took place. Since the Kings of Bavaria and Württemberg were godfathers, we too had the pleasure of travelling by rail to the New Palace at Potsdam at 12 noon, I *décolletée* and with my hair waved, Charles in full dress—a show for the Berlin public. There were few people there, apart from the guests and the court. There was lunch after the christening. . . .

Document 183   Bismarck to Wentzel (Darmstadt), 15 July 1870
(O. von Bismarck, *Gesammelte Werke*, vol. vib. no. 1631, p. 381)

. . . Doubt about the *casus foederis** does not prevail in a single one of the south-German states. Without exception, they see a common German task in our defence against the threatened attack and are preparing themselves to act accordingly.

Document 184   The Crown Prince's account of his reception in Stuttgart, July 1870
(H. O. Meisner, editor, *Kaiser Friedrich III Das Kriegstagebuch von 1870–71*, Berlin, Leipzig, 1926, p. 342)

. . . In Stuttgart, on the platform at the railway station, I was received by the King surrounded by Princes, Generals, and a Guard of Honour. He received my communication with a stiff, official bearing, permitted me then to get into his carriage and drove with me through the vigorously cheering crowd to Queen Olga. My cousin was friendly and gentle, yet I found her pale and looking

---

* The treaties referred to are the military alliances of 1866–7, see above, p. 140. T.

ill. She permitted me to breakfast with her at once and afterwards the King, who is beginning to go grey, took me to my room. Here he spoke much of his 'kingly duties' and of having to know Württemberg well to judge it aright, since it was not so democratic as was commonly supposed; of course, the constitution, which had now existed for many years, had introduced many elements which had made bad blood and infected the Press; after the war one would, he hoped, be able to remedy these evils. He concluded with the remark that he must go to his work, for he knew from long experience what his office entailed; since he had come to the throne when he was twenty.

The War Minister, Lieutenant-General von Suckow, speaks like an honourable, brave soldier, is full of eagerness and longing for the great national rising, and in his office is a downright good fellow who lashes out with pertinent remarks at anyone whose conduct has not been clean and clear. The Minister, von Varnbühler, proved himself to be very patriotic—in which I encouraged him. He explained to me that not only had he himself always been convinced that Germany, in the event of a French attack, would stand as one man in the defence of the Fatherland, but that he had said this to the Emperor Napoleon in 1867 here at the railway station. . . . I received the rest of the Ministers, the Burgomaster and representatives of the National Party in my rooms and then made calls. . . .

A dinner *en campagne tenue*, as the saying goes, and a drive to the 'Villa Berg' with both their Majesties concluded my stay. At my departure, the crowds of people were even greater than in the morning and the cheers seemed as if they would never end, so that in truth the south Germans greeted me as warmly as we are accustomed to see the people do in our old provinces. I felt myself almost embarrassed towards the King, sitting beside me in the carriage, for this homage was unmistakably addressed, not to him, but to me as the representative of the Power who had taken the solution of the German question in hand, a task to which the Württemberg dynasty would hardly be equal.

Document 185   Eichmann (Vienna) to Bismarck, 12 July 1870 (Bonn, Auswärtiges AMT, IABC, Fiance, no. 68)

. . . The Austrian Imperial Chancellor describes the Parisian proceedings of the 9th as the beginning of the end. Prince Metternich* has warmly supported French alliance offers. Count Beust is

* Austrian ambassador in Paris.

9

happy to have got through the crisis without compromising himself, considers a republic in France to be possible, and asserts that Austria's armed preparations are calculated both for her defence now [and against a future French republic]. France has not concluded an alliance with Italy. In Vienna the idea is to play the same part in the peace negotiations as France played at Nikolsburg. . . .

Document 186   Extract from the diary of the Baroness Spitzemberg
(R. Vierhaus, editor, *Das Tagebuch der Baronin Spitzemberg*, Göttingen, 1960, p. 102)

3 September [1870]. The following telegram came very early: 'Before Sedan, 2 September, 1.30 p.m. A capitulation, whereby the whole army in Sedan has been taken prisoner, has just been concluded with General Wimpffen. . . .' What a turn of events! Any German would be proud to have lived through this day! God be praised! . . .

Document 187   Bismarck to Manteuffel,* 6 September 1870
(O. van Bismarck, *Gesammelte Werke*, vol. vib, no. 1787, p. 480)

. . . I have as little anxiety as Your Excellency over the future organization of Germany. The line of the Main, in my opinion, has, for all practical purposes in relation to the defence of Germany from outside, already been crossed because the alliance in the hour of danger was observed beyond expectation, and because of the existing brotherhood in arms. I have not the slightest doubt that the unification of the German states will, as Your Excellency says, 'in whatever form' proceed now to its full maturity. . . .

Documents 188a and 188b   Peace is being prepared

188a   Extract from the diary of the Baroness Spitzemberg
(R. Vierhaus, editor, *Das Tagebuch der Baronin Spitzemberg*, Göttingen, 1960, p. 105)

7 September [1870]. Delbrück left yesterday for Headquarters, where the German constitution is very probably now being made. In the Ministry here Father's resignation is now sincerely deplored. Delbrück said to Charles he considered it a downright misfortune; for he had especially counted on Father's decisive influence in

* Otto von Manteuffel, former Minister President of Prussia (1850–8).

Bavaria (on Bray as well as upon the King) in order to bring into being, at the peace negotiations, something permanent instead of another botched up peace. You may as well also know that it was Father's influence that alone prevented Bavaria from observing the strict neutrality she had once intended to maintain. When Bray came back from Stuttgart, things suddenly began to move! In order to convince Bray of France's unreliability as an ally, Father had advised him to ask Cadore whether it was decided, in the event of the neutrality of south Germany, to respect it unconditionally. The Frenchman assured him of this, but added that naturally small, temporary infractions, by marching through or crossing frontiers, were unavoidable! Bray had heard enough. But this was used to poor Father's disadvantage. It was so presented, when it was made public, as to make out that he himself had been unreliable in his loyalty! As long as I live, I shall think it the bitterest injustice of fate that Father should not have joined in the Triumph, entered Paris with the rest, and dictated peace there . . .

188b   Bismarck to Delbrück, 3 September 1870
(O. von Bismarck, *Gesammelte Werke*, vol. vib, no. 1777, p. 472)

The King wishes you to come to Headquarters for a little while, so that we may consider together how we may find a suitable business reason for the calling of the Customs Parliament and how turn to account the influence of this assembly and of the *Reichstag* as a factor in the German and European peace negotiations. Including your journey, your absence will have to last for eight or ten days. Arrange for your place to be taken during this time as best you can.

Document 189   Extract from Delbrück's memoirs
(R. von Delbrück, *Lebenserinnerungen*, Leipzig, 1905, vol. ii, p. 413)

. . . My conversations at the King's table and at Count Bismarck's table were such as to convince me that at Headquarters the establishment of a united Germany, with an Emperor at its head, was considered an easy task. Eight victorious battles, in which the sons of all the German states had fought and shed their blood side by side, had completed the unification of Germany in the consciousness of the army. The magic spell which the person of the King exercised over officers and men throughout the army seemed to gain its natural expression in the Emperor's Crown. In substance, all was done. In form, one needed 'only to will it' in order to get it done. Self-confidence, heightened by great deeds and great success, outweighed the army's feeling for the individual states whose contingents composed it. This self-confidence overshadows or overcomes every other feeling. He who did not consider feeling for Bavaria or for Württemberg as impermissible now and would not hear of ignoring or overcoming state particularism, ran the danger of passing for a dull or mean man, if not for something worse. This attitude, which I met again six weeks later in Versailles, sharpened in its expression by impatience and ambition, was satisfied for the time being when the calling of the Customs Parliament was settled. But two days after my arrival in Rheims, an important communication came in from Munich. The Bavarian Government voiced its conviction, more quickly than I had expected, that the development of the political situation in Germany, as it has been brought about by the events of the war, postulated a transference from the basis of international treaties, which so far had bound the south-German states to the North German Confederation, to the basis of a constitutional alliance. Bavaria added the wish that I might be sent to Munich to enter into discussion of the proposals she had prepared for the realization of this idea. I received, therefore, the mission to go to Munich.

I had first to complete the memorandum on the future organization of Germany. In Munich, indeed, I would only have to listen to prepared proposals and to comment on them out of my knowledge of the situation. I had, however, to make sure, if the conversations were to be successful, that Bismarck and the King agreed with the standpoint by which I should be guided in every question that might emerge. My work prospered in favourable external circumstances. I lived somewhat off the street in a well-kept garden, no noise reached my ears, and from my writing table I looked out upon the row of statues (as if they were enthroned in the treetops) with whose pointed niches the front of the Cathedral ends and above them upon the two uncompleted towers. I wrote out the plan for the reorganization of Germany looking out upon the Coronation Church of ancient France . . . It contained, taken as a whole, the idea of what has since come about as a result of the Versailles Treaty. I had learnt in contacts with the south-German plenipotentiaries to the Customs Federal Council and Customs Parliament what stipulations of the Federal Constitution were considered inacceptable in south Germany or in need of alteration. I paid attention to these views in as much as their justice was plain. Naturally, I could not have thought of things which arose out of the course of later negotiations (such as the still-born committee of

the Federal Council for Foreign Affairs), nor could I have undertaken to intimate in detail the position of the Bavarian and Württemberg army contingents. The conclusion of the memorandum gave
official expression, for the first time, to the thoughts filling all minds.
I offered reasons for the peremptory need for the King's bringing
himself to accept the imperial dignity. The reason for this decision,
that it was an unavoidable personal sacrifice in the interests of the
Fatherland, was the one which accorded with His Majesty's own
point of view. It went against the grain of his nature to appear
something that he was not. The imperial dignity seemed to him an
empty title. He was Commander-in-Chief of the North German
Confederation; the navy stood under his command; and for the
execution of the real power connected with these specific positions,
he had no need of the imperial dignity. The functions which,
according to the north-German constitution belonged to the
Presidency—their increase was not anticipated in the future
German constitution—involved no *imperium* and would gain through
the imperial dignity neither a wider basis nor greater significance.
The ideas associated with this dignity, reaching far beyond any
constitutional stipulations, were not at first discernible. It was
possible for it to seem a mere title. The King, on the other hand,
owed it to the nation to requite the patriotic devotion, which it had
shown since the outbreak of war, by satisfying its demand for an
Emperor.

Count Bismarck accepted my memorandum and laid it before the
King as I had written it. It suited him that the question of an
Emperor was raised at the outset by me. . . .

Document 190   Bismarck to Werthern (Munich), 24 September
1870
(O. von Bismarck, *Gesammelte Werke*, vol. vib, no. 1829, p.
516)

For Minister Delbrück

Bavaria proposes to exclude for herself a number of subjects—
which I need not specify—from the competence of federal legislation
in the new Confederation. This is, in my opinion, no reason in
itself to refuse Bavaria admission. Time must enable us to extend
its competence to them subsequently. The Rubicon has anyhow
been crossed. . . . Was the participation of Baden in your discussions
helpful? . . .

Document 191   Bismarck to Bray, 4 November 1870
(Ibid., no. 1905, p. 580)

. . . As the basis of these negotiations, I should prefer the establishment of a close Confederation to any other. This basis is, in my
view, the only one which meets the wishes of the German nation.
It is the only one, therefore, suitable for the foundation of permanent
institutions, while it is at the same time sufficient to assure such a
position to Bavaria in the German Confederation, to which on
account of her importance, she has a claim . . .

I can only consider the second alternative, mentioned by Your
Excellency, namely, the continued existence of the international
treaties, as multiplying the treaty relations which at present exist
between the North German Confederation and Bavaria. The short
time which has elapsed since the foundation of the Confederation
has already brought so many individual understandings between
north and south, and the foundation of a new Confederation,
comprising the remaining south-German states, will extend the
mutual relations on so many sides, that it will not be difficult to
regulate the many relationships in public law in a mutually satisfactory way.

Document 192   Berchem* to Radowitz,** 29 November 1870
(Merseburg, Deutsches Zentralarchiv II, Rep. 2, Nachlass
Radowitz d.J., vol. ii, 1)

How pleased I shall be to be able to write to you soon 'To the
Consul General of the German Confederation', and to be able to
confirm as an accomplished fact what today is still only in preparation and in process of being created, though, in my opinion, fully
assured. I refer to the existence of a German *Reich*, a German constitution under which all parts of the Fatherland live, without a *casus
foederis*, without Article 4 of the Peace of Prague*** and without
an Ultramontane majority in German questions. Joy in the military
victory has been absorbed and disappears before rejoicing in these
accomplishments. Who could have foreseen that the programme of

* Maximilian, Count von Berchem, served in the Bavarian Diplomatic Service,
1867–71, and after 1871 in the German Diplomatic Service; Under Secretary in
the Foreign Office, 1886.
** Joseph Maria, Baron von Radowitz, son of Frederick William IV's Minister,
Prussian Consul General at Bucharest, later Ambassador at Constantinople.
*** This article provided for a separate independent south German Confederation as well as for the North German Confederation and the exclusion of Austria
from Germany. For the Peace of Prague, see above, p. 169 note ***. T.

Marquard Barth (on the occasion of the debate on the Hohenlohe address) would have been found insufficient by Prauth, Bray, and Lutz within the year? Yet so it is. Yes, I must count it to the honour of those just named that the paper, which they brought, contained what a year ago would have been regarded as the death blow to Bavarian sovereignty. We enter the North German Confederation; leave to you the diplomatic and consular representation; generalize Article 4* of the constitution of the North German Confederation; transfer decisions over military service, the size of the army and the amount of military expenditure to the German Parliament; grant you an unlimited right of inspection in military matters; abrogate the alliance treaty and replace it by what up to now has been an article of the constitution of the North German Confederation, and so on. In return a diplomatic committee will be established in which Bavaria, Württemberg, and Saxony will have permanent seats and Bavaria preside. This is an institution of considerable importance for the period after the present Chancellor's death. We retain our system of indirect taxes, the administration of post, telegraphs, and railways, but legislation thereon devolves on the German Parliament. . . . I cannot trust more precise details to these sheets from considerations you know. . . . I am very pleased with the result. In Bismarckian circles the arrangement is found to answer. You yourself know best those who have other views, and there are such—there was even another little crisis. . . . The Liberals must be pleased. The patriots cannot let this Ministry fall, since it would only be replaced by a Liberal one. . . .

Document 193 Bismarck to the Foreign Office, 20 November 1870
(**O.** von Bismarck, *Gesammelte Werke*, vol. vib, no. 1921, p. 593)

For Minister Delbrück

I hope to come to the point of concluding with Bavaria. If I succeed, it seems certain that she will raise the question of the title of Emperor. Any agitation in the *Reichstag* would have a disturbing affect on this.

* Particularized, in separate items, the subjects of federal legislation and oversight. T.

Document 194 Bismarck to Werthen (Munich), 3 December 1870
(Ibid., no. 1942, p. 610)

Tell Count Bray that His Majesty, the King, has accepted with lively thanks, from the hand of His Royal Highness, Prince Luitpold, His Majesty King Louis's letter, dated 30th November, and, that he thanks King Louis for this fresh confirmation of His Majesty's patriotic attitude.

The difficulties which we feared would arise in the *Reichstag*, from the treaties, will I hope now be overcome. The German Princes, present here, will inform His Majesty King Louis by telegram of their consent. The order of business will, I think, be as follows: the Bavarian overture, as contained in the King's letter, has gone simultaneously to all the allied Princes and free cities; the Princes will publish their answer to it; then, according to the concluding passage of the King of Bavaria's letter, Bavaria will formally propose, at the final negotiations in Berlin for the establishment of the German Confederation, that the article of the Federal Constitution which mentions the Presidency and the command of the federal army, should be altered to provide for the title of Emperor. The readiness of His Majesty, the King, to accept is certain, but it can only be published officially after the King has sent his answer to the Bavarian invitation. The text of the King's letter will be telegraphed to you as soon as it is sent.

Documents 195a and 195b The *Reichstag* and the Imperial Title

195a Bismarck to Bismarck-Bohlen, * 12 December 1870*
(Ibid., no. 1970, p. 628)

The designation 'Emperor deputation' for the deputation to present the *Reichstag*'s address is to be carefully avoided. The expression is disagreeable to His Majesty, the King, and is improper; since the address does not relate only to the Emperor. Nor does the Empire derive its validity from the North German *Reichstag*. Nor is the Empire complete until the south-German Parliaments have approved the treaties and they have been ratified by the sovereigns. . . .

* Acting as Bismarck's adjutant.

195b   Report of the sitting of the Reichstag, 10 December 1870
K. L. Aegidi *et al.*, editors, *Das Staatsarchiv, Sammlung der offiziellen Aktenstücke der Gegenwart*, no. 20, 1871, Dok. no. 4197, p. 55)

... We cannot refrain from giving thanks for the joint action under arms of the whole of Germany. Its effects transcend the results won on the battlefield and foreshadow the peaceable completion of the work of unification. Supported by this knowledge as well as by the decisions we have taken, and not content with mere words and phrases, but using living words with real meaning, we address to His Majesty, the King of Prussia, the request that it may please him to accept the Imperial Crown and so consecrate the work of unification. We expect from this change alterations both of substance and form. The Confederation shall become a *Reich*, a united and closed state. We shall look to this state to afford us power, peace, prosperity, and that protection which alone can content its citizens in peacetime, the protection of freedom under the law. ...

The President: I open the discussion on the motion before us. I declare it closed, since no one offers to speak. The address will now be read and then voted. It reads: (The House stands) All highest and most powerful King! Your Majesty, King and Lord! At the summons of Your Majesty the nation rallied to its leaders and defended the Fatherland, on foreign soil with the strength of heroes—the Fatherland that had been wickedly provoked into war. The war demanded immeasurable sacrifices, but grief at the death in battle of her brave sons did not shake the nation's resolute will. It would not lay down its arms until peace had been guaranteed by secure frontiers against renewed attacks from its ambitious neighbour.

Thanks to the victories to which Your Majesty led the armies of Germany in loyal comradeship-in-arms, the nation now looks forward to permanent unity.

United with the Princes of Germany, the North German *Reichstag* approaches Your Majesty with the request that it may please Your Majesty by the acceptance of the Imperial Crown of Germany to consecrate the work of unification.

Your Majesty's acceptance of the German Crown will open for the reestablished *Reich* of the German nation an era of power, peace and prosperity, and freedom assured by the protection of the law.

The Fatherland thanks the leader and the glorious army at the head of which Your Majesty still stands on the field of victory, after

10

the battle has been won. The devotion and the deeds of her sons will never be forgotten by the nation. May the nation soon know that the Emperor, crowned with glory, restores peace to it. Germany, standing together in war, has born herself powerful and victorious under her highest commander. The united German *Reich* will be powerful and peaceful under its Emperor. . . .

Gentlemen, the result of the vote just taken is as follows: 197 members took part in it, of these 191 voted yes, and 6 voted no. The motion for the address to His Majesty the King of Prussia is therefore carried.

Document 196 Speech of Bennigsen in the *Reichstag*
(Ibid., Dok. no. 4193, p. 48)

Gentlemen. You will permit me, in the name of my political friends, who almost without exception are with me, to declare, and briefly to give my reasons for declaring, that, despite the serious doubts which we had about the Bavarian treaty, we shall not withhold our consent. (Bravo!) Some of our motions for alterations have been withdrawn, and some have been rejected on the second reading, after the declarations of the spokesmen of the Federal Government. We know very well that in a sense we endanger the further development of our north-German constitution by accepting into it elements, which have not been able so to grow together homogeneously with us over four years of internal struggle as the north-German and middle-German states and their representatives have been able to do. We do not deny that through the concessions, which have been made to the Bavarian Crown, dangers to future development are introduced into the north-German constitution, which is to be in future the German constitution. We accept this risk out of that national and patriotic feeling that must move a great assembly which, although it has so far only represented one part of Germany, has always felt the call to work so that representatives might, at some future date, be united in an assembly for all Germany. We accept this risk with full confidence in the national and patriotic attitude of our brothers in south Germany and in Bavaria, and with confidence in the insight and national-patriotic outlook of the Bavarian Government. . . . We are not accepting enemies into the German Confederation, but German comrades—German comrades, who have proved true in a struggle of fabulous glory for the position which is due to our Fatherland. This will now find its proper expression in a constitution for the whole of Germany, to be won from a mistrustful Europe and a hostile France. . . . The German nation will emerge victorious from this difficult, perhaps the most difficult and fateful, struggle that has ever been imposed upon it. This, we can assume, will be assured during the next few weeks. Why then should not a healthy and strong internal evolution also take place in the German nation, if victorious in this struggle, it labours together in shared work at home, under a single government, and in a free German Parliament? (Very true! Loud applause) Gentlemen, it *is* possible to have confidence in ourselves, and to have confidence in our south-German comrades. ... Gentlemen, serious and lasting opposition to what the nation, through the majority of its representatives in Parliament, demands, to what is necessary to the whole nation for a truly great internal political reorganization—such opposition will be impossible. ... So far we have had a single and monarchical government in substance, but not in name. In future, we shall have it in name too, and this name is more than a mere word. Because we have a monarchical government with so strong a foundation, and because it is a foundation laid on German soil alone, nothing in German history up to now is comparable to it in power. (Very true!) The monarchy of the Habsburg House in the time of Charles V may perhaps have been more brilliant, but that was a world of monarchy, which had other tasks beyond its German ones. These tasks came first with it, and its practical purposes lay outside Germany. It brought Germany into the greatest dangers, because it used German power for foreign purposes. In future, the German monarchy of the Hohenzollerns, sprung out of the needs of the German nation, and seeking its strength and force solely on German land and soil, will have the power and the will to act solely for German purposes. (Bravo!)...

Documents 197a and 197b 'At a great time'

197a   Address of the Prussian Upper House to William I, 21 December 1870
(Ibid., Dok no. 4209, p. 93)

All highest and most powerful King! Your Majesty, King and Lord! In this great time the first need of your most respectful Upper House, on being called together by Your Majesty, is to address Your Majesty. Loyal concern, but above all high enthusiasm, fills our hearts when we see our royal master, surrounded by German Princes, complete the new organization of Germany from the army camp before the gates of Paris. In a wonderful course of victories, our army, the flower of the nation, in a true comradeship of arms, with its allies, has defeated the enemy's armies, most accomplished in war though they were. German power alone has overthrown the arrogant and powerful enemy, who for centuries has sought to divide and to humble Germany and to steal her land, who wantonly provoked this present war. Germany is united as it has not been united for centuries. She shows herself in this unity, under Your Majesty's leadership, as powerful as she has scarcely ever been before. Your Royal Majesty, chosen to be Emperor by the Princes and free cities of Germany, will afford the protection of the law to the German *Reich* and will cherish the free unfolding of the German spirit in its manifold and rich variety and in its varied racial individuality, as the motto of your All Highest House guarantees. Yet the Kingdom of Prussia will not lose thereby the King's name, which through an unparalleled history and a succession of great Princes, has become dear to it. Thankfulness towards God for this His guidance moves our hearts as it does Your Majesty's . . .

All highest King and Lord! A great, just and national war has allowed Germany unity to grow out of the red heat of battle. The new German *Reich* arises as Prussia arose and grew through the deeds of her Princes. The forces of a genuine German, Prussian, and monarchical spirit, effectual for its creation, will also support and govern its further evolution. Your Royal Majesty, in association with the German Princes and free cities, will know, in your wisdom, how to found those institutions, which will assure and guarantee to the new *Reich*, evolution in accordance with that spirit.

197b   Address of the Württemberg Lower House to William I, 30 December 1870
   (Ibid., Dok. no. 4206, p. 74)

Your Majesty has summoned us at a great time and for great work. Never has Germany fought a more just fight. Never have Germany's armies been so gloriously led. Never have they achieved such success as in this war, wickedly forced upon her. The troops of Württemberg had their share in the glorious combats and victories of the German army; they showed themselves worthy of the renown of their fathers. . . . The German nation, the nation in arms, like the nation in peaceful work, wishes, as the reward of the fight and the victory, for the unity, which it has so long striven for and so often been disappointed of, unity as the surest guarantee of a lasting peace. These are the thoughts and emotions of Württemberg. In exultation it heard of Your Majesty's noble decision to prepare the way for the restoration of a German federal state. The state gratefully welcomes the treaties Your Majesty's Government has concluded and it has announced, in an unambiguous way, its consent. It attaches the most joyous hopes to the revival of the ancient and venerable names 'Emperor' and '*Reich*' . . . Together with our noble Prince we pray to heaven that God may bestow upon a united and powerful Germany and the states bound together within her a time of peace, prosperity, freedom and order. God bless and sustain Your Majesty! . . .

Document 198   Extract from the Crown Prince's diary recording a meeting of the Prussian State Council at Versailles, 17 January 1871
(J. Hohlfeld, *Deutsche Reichsgeschichte in Dokumenten*, 1927, vol. i, p. 69)

In the afternoon a meeting of the Council took place, in the presence of the King, at which Count Bismarck, Minister of the Household, von Schleinitz, and I were present. When Count Bismarck met the Minister of the Household, von Schleinitz, in the anteroom, he said to him somewhat roughly that he did not understand what business the Federal Chancellor and the Minister of the Household could have jointly to transact with the King. For three hours, in an over-heated room, we deliberated on the title of the Emperor, the name for the Crown Prince, the position of the Royal family, the Court and the army in relation to the *Reich* and so on.

As to the title of the Emperor, Count Bismarck acknowledged that, in the discussions on the constitution, the Bavarian representatives and plenipotentiaries had not wished to permit the designation 'Emperor of Germany', and that he [Bismarck] had finally given way but, of course, without asking His Majesty first, and conceded the title, 'German Emperor'. This designation, with which no real idea is associated, displeased the King as well as myself. We did our utmost to gain in its stead that of 'Emperor of Germany'. Count Bismarck remained firm. Further, he tried to show that the expression, 'Emperor of Germany', signified a territorial power such as we did not in any way possess over the *Reich*, whereas, on the other hand, 'German Emperor' was the natural sequel to *imperator Romanus*. So, alas, we had to submit. This was the occasion for a most painful debate about the relation of Emperor to King. It arose because His Majesty, contrary to the old Prussian traditions, placed an Emperor higher in dignity than a King. The two Ministers and I, with them, opposed this view extremely clearly, by reference to historical documents in our archives, in which King Frederick I, in recognizing the Russian Tsar as Emperor, explicitly mentioned that he should never take precedence over the Prussian King. It was further adduced that King Frederick William I had once demanded, even in a meeting with the Holy Roman Emperor, that he should enter a pavilion, which had two entrances, at the same time as the Emperor did, so that the latter should not claim precedence over him. Finally, Count Bismarck pointed out that King Frederick William IV had introduced the principle of subordination to the archducal House of an Imperial state on grounds of humility before Austria, well known and personal to himself. The King was not, however, at all convinced by this evidence. He grew angry and declared that King Frederick William III, on the occasions of his meetings with the Tsar Alexander, had laid down that the latter as Emperor had precedence, that the will of his royal father was for him the standard to be observed and was the deciding factor in the present case. Nor could we make good our claims to superiority in relation to the English royal family to which, admittedly, precedence over all other princely European Houses belongs. When, then, in the course of the proceedings, it was decided that our family should retain its present position, the King, on his side, demanded that we should formulate the equality of its position with that of Imperial Houses. It was finally decided that on this nothing definitive should be done. . . .

The question of the national colours raised little discussion, since the King made no essential objection to the black-white-red cockade, the less so, because, as he himself put it, this, unlike the black-red-yellow one, had not climbed out of the street-dirt. Even so, he would only suffer the above three colours to be flown *side by side* with the Prussian ones.

The coat of arms proposed by Count Bismarck and myself met with no opposition, but was also not expressly accepted.

The more clearly, however, in the course of the proceedings the consequences of adopting the titles of 'Emperor' and '*Reich*' became evident, the more enraged the King became. Finally, he broke out in words to the effect that he was taking on only a shadow empire, nothing more than another designation for 'President'; he was just like a major who was promoted 'acting lieutenant-colonel'. Now that things had gone so far, he must bear this cross, but he wished to be the only one to suffer; he could not, therefore, permit that he should be expected to make the same demand from the army as from his own person. Therefore, he would not hear of calling it the 'Imperial Army'; he wished to protect, at least, the Prussian army from such things. He could not tolerate it that Prussian troops should be asked to accept German names and designations. The navy might be called the 'Imperial Navy'. Further, he said in the utmost excitement that he could not describe to us at all how desperate he felt at having to take leave tomorrow of the old Prussia to which he alone held steadfast, and wished to hold steadfast in the future. Sobs and tears interrupted his words. . . .

With things thus unsettled, and one man asking the other, 'now what would happen', we left the Prefecture. . . .

Under such impressions we ushered in the wonderful German festival, fixed for the following day. . . .

Documents 199a and 199b United in one *Reich*

199a Extract from the diary of the Baroness Spitzemberg
(R. Vierhaus, editor, *Das Tagebuch der Baronin Spitzemberg*, Göttingen, 1960, p. 116)

31 December [1870]. What events this one short year has brought! Immortal glory for our nation a spirit inconceivably magnificent and majestic, the resurrection of the German Empire—and withal such endless grief, misery, tears, and horror!

199b Extract from the diary of the Baroness Spitzemberg
(Ibid., p. 121)

3 March [1871]. . . . What a peace treaty for us Germans! More magnificent and glorious than ever! United into one *Reich*, the greatest, the most powerful, the most feared in Europe; great by reason of its physical power, greater still by reason of its education and the intelligence which permeates it! Every German heart hoped for it, none suspected that its dreams would be fulfilled, in this way, so soon and so magnificently. We are fortunate in that we not only saw the star of Germany's greatness and magnificence rise, but are still young enough to warm ourselves under its rays, to enjoy, if God will, the fruits, rich and full of blessings, which grow out of this seed, sown in blood and tears. . . .

Document 200 Extract from a private diary
(Hamburg, Staatsarchiv, Family Papers of the Benecke family)

22 January 1871. Extra sitting of the Senate in Burgomaster Gossler's House, Georgsplatz. Concerning King William the Conqueror's letter to the Senate, that he should accept the title of Emperor (he says dignity of Emperor) offered to him, etc. On this point, decisions were to be taken of a purely external character.

Discussion; unconstructive. Petersen, a great admirer of the Prussian successes, and so of this Emperor of successes, put it through that the Hammonia should fire 101 guns as a salute. It was amusing that *faute de mieux* Hammonia will fire these 101 shots from her rear quarters (into a blind alley) and indeed from old ship's cannon which are served by night-watchmen and the police. Hammonia no longer possesses any other cannon or artillerymen with which to inaugurate the 'new *Reich*' the 'German Emperor', this King of the Wends and their allies. Without lunch, home towards 2. A ruined Sunday.

NOTES

PREFACE

1. Discussion among scholars about the origins of the war of 1870–1 has recently sprung to life again owing to the publication of several new works. Older arguments have a strongly chauvinist colouring. Recent research has been guided, by contrast, by a calm, objective interpretation with a real attempt to set the subject in perspective. This especially applies to that done on the material, hitherto little known, in the family archives of the Hohenzollern-Sigmaringen. Attention is particularly called, therefore, to the critical review article by B. Schot, 'Die Geschichte der Hohenzoller-ischen Thronkandidatur im Lichte neuer Veröffentlichungen', *Hohenzollerische Jahreshefte*, xxiii (1963), 173 and to G. Bonnin, *Bismarck and the Hohenzollern Candidature for the Throne of Spain* (London, 1957; documents from the German diplomatic archives translated into English by I. M. Massey). The last book was reviewed by R. Morsey in *Historische Zeitschrift*, clxxxvi (1958). See also, R. Morsey, 'Geschichtsschreibung und amtliche Zensur', *Historische Zeitschrift*, clxxxiv (1956); J. Dittrich, *Bismarck, Frankreich und die spanische Thronkandidatur der Hohenzollern* (Munich, 1962); J. Dittrich, 'Bismarck, Frankreich und die Hohenzollernkandidatur', *Welt als Geschichte*, xiii (1953) 42; L. D. Steefel, *Bismarck, the Hohenzollern Candidacy and the Origins of the Franco-German War of 1870* (Cambridge, Mass., 1962); L. von Muralt, 'Der Ausbruch des Krieges von 1870–71', *Der Historiker und die Geschichte* (Zürich, 1960) p. 295; J. Droz, *L'Époque contemporaine, I Restuarations et Révolutions*, Clio ix (Paris, 1953); W. A. Fletcher, *The Mission of Vincent Benedetti to Berlin, 1864–70* (The Hague, 1965). The following are representative of earlier publications on this special problem: K. Th. Zingeler, *Karl Anton, Fürst von Hohenzollern* (Stuttgart, 1911); R. Fester, *Neue Beiträge zur Geschichte der Hohenzollerischen Thronkandidatur in Spanien* (Leipzig, 1913); R. Fester, *Briefe Aktenstücke und Regesten zur Geschichte der Hohenzollerischen Thronkandidatur in Spanien*, 2 vols. (Leipzig, 1931); H. Hesselbarth, *Drei psychologische Fragen zur spanischen Thronkandidatur Leopolds v. Hohenzollern* (Leipzig, 1913); F. Frahm, 'Frankreich und die Hohenzollern Kandidatur bis zum Frühjahr 1869', *Historische Vierteljahresschrift*, xxix, 342.

2. H. Böhme, *Deutchlands Weg zur Grossmacht. Studien zum Verhältnis von Wirtschaft und Staat während der Reichsgründungszeit 1848–81* (Cologne, Berlin, 1966).

CHAPTER I

1. For the problem of nationalist political journalism, see the distinguished critical bibliography of K. G. Faber, *Die national-politische Publizistik Deutschlands von 1866 bis 1871* (Düsseldorf, 1963). This is the first comprehensive compilation of the essential publications on the German question in these years in newspapers, periodicals, and in specially or privately printed articles. It is arranged under key-phrases. It is a continuation of H. Rosenberg's bibliography which went from 'the beginning of the New Era in Prussia up to the outbreak of the German War'. There are in addition many important scholarly studies which throw light on public opinion before 1870. See especially, A. Rapp, *Die Württemberger und die nationale Frage 1863 bis 1871* (Stuttgart, 1910); Th. Schieder, *Die kleindeutsche Partei in Bayern in den Kämpfen um die nationale Einheit, 1863–1871* (Munich, 1936); G. Körner, *Die norddeutsche Publizisitk und die Reichsgründung im Jahre 1870* (Hanover, 1908); G. Ritter, *Die preussischen Konservativen und Bismarcks deutsche Politik 1858–1876* (Heidelberg, 1913); G. Reinhardt, *Preussen im Spiegel der öffentlichen Meinung Schleswig-Holsteins 1866–1870* (Neumünster, 1954).

2. On the problem discussed here, in addition to the works by Rapp, Schieder, and Ritter, the following studies among the large number of investigations, should be mentioned: M. Doeberl, *Bayern und die Bismarck'sche Reichsgründung* (Munich, 1925); M. Doeberl, *Entwicklungs-Geschichte Bayerns*, vol. iii (Munich, 1931); W. Seefried, *Mittnacht und die deutsche Frage bis zur Reichsgründung* (Stuttgart, 1928); K. Hofmann, *Badens Anteil an der Reichsgründung* (Karlsruhe, 1927); F. Hartung, 'Die Entstehung und Gründung des Deutschen Reiches', *Volk und Reich der Deutschen*, i (Berlin, 1929).

3. Staatsarchiv Hamburg, Familienarchiv Benecke II/B6, vii.

4. J. Burckhardt, *Briefe* edited Max Burckhardt (Basel and Stuttgart, 1963), pp. 103 ff.

5. O. von Bismarck, *Gesammelte Werke* (Berlin, 1924–35), vol. vx, p. 329.

6. See for the discussion immediately before the year 1870, C. Franz, 'Die Naturlehre des Staates als Grundlage der Staatswissenschaft', *Deutsche Vierteljahreshefte* (1868) iii, 70; iv, 149; (1869) i, 19; ii, 72; iii, 72; K. Th. v. Inama-Sternegg, *Die Tendenz der Gross-Staatenbildung in der Gegenwart. Eine politische Studie* (Innsbruck, 1869); O. Klopp, *Wer ist der wahre Erbfeind von Deutschland* (Munich, 1868); Arkolay (W. Streubel), *Das Germanenthum und Österreich* (Darmstadt, 1870); for the standpoint of South Germany and Austria, see especially the position taken up by J. Jörg in the *Historisch-politischen Blättern für das katholische Deutschland*, lx 253,637; lxii, 1,560; lxiii, 1,479, lxv. 1 and that taken by E. Trautwein von Belle in the *Deutschen Vierteljahresschrift*, published in Stuttgart, xxxii. (126) 1, (127), 142; xxxiii. (129), 50. Among the nationalist writers, both Liberal and Prussian Conservative, see the following: J. L. Bluntschli, *Die nationale Staatenbildung und der moderne deutsche Staat*; A. Wagner, 'Die Entwicklung der europäischen Staatsterritorien und das Nationalitätsprinzip', *Preussische Jahrbücher* (1867)

xix, 540; xx, 1; xxi, 290; W. Hoffmann, *Deutschland Einst und Jetzt im Lichte des Reiches Gottes* (Berlin, 1868); H. A. Oppermann, *Der Weg zum Jahre 1866 und seine Nothwendigkeit für das Heil Deutschlands* (Berlin, 1869); H. von Treitschke, 'Das constitutionelle Königthum in Deutschland', *Historische und Politische Aufsätze*, new series, 2 (Leipzig, 1870), 745. For the Prussian and National Liberal viewpoints, see especially the *Preussische Jahrbücher* and the *Grenzboten* among periodicals. In the *Jahrbücher* articles by Treitschke, Duncker, Wagner, and Wehrenpfennig are particularly important (xix. 469, 602; xxii. 742; xxiii. 98, 242, 483; xxvi. 240). G. Freytag, J. von Eckhardt, and A. Springer dominated the *Grenzboten* (1867) ii. 276, 396; (1868) i. 66; ii. 241; (1870) iii. 395, 399, 424).

7. C. G. Bruns, *Deutschlands Sieg über Frankreich* (Berlin, 1870); D. F. Strauss, *Krieg und Friede. Zwei Briefe an Ernst Renan* (Leipzig, 1870); H. von Treitschke, 'Was fordern wir von Frankreich?', *Preussische Jahrbücher* (1870) xxvi, 367, 491; 'Luxemburg und das deutsche Reich', ibid., 605; 'Die Verträge mit den Südstaaten', ibid., 648; 'Parteien und Fractionen', ibid. (1871) xxvii, 175, 347; *Zehn Jahre Deutsche Kämpfe* (Berlin, 1874); F. Thudichum, *Klar und Wahr. Zuruf an die Wähler Württembergs* (Tübingen, 1870); H. Baumgarten, *Wie wir wieder ein Volk geworden sind* (Leipzig, 1870); W. Hoffmann, 'Das Jahr 1870 und die von ihm begründete Zukunft Deutschlands', in *Deutschland*, 1871, pp. 1–69; for the same problem cp. further suggestions in Faber, *Publizistik*, ii. 640.

8. Cp. W. Mommsen, *Stein, Ranke und Bismarck* (Munich, 1958), pp. 160 ff.

9. Ibid., pp. 114 f.

10. 7 vols. (Munich, 1889–94) but written in the seventies.

11. 5 vols. (Leipzig, 1879–94); see also H. von Treitschke, *Zehn Jahre deutsche Kämpfe, 1865 bis 1874* (Berlin, 1874).

12. *Das Briefwerk Rankes*, ed. W. P. Fuchs (Hamburg, 1949), p. 363.

13. See, for example, H. Oncken, *Bismarck und die Zukunft Mitteleuropas* (Heidelberg, 1915); D. Schäfer, *Bismarck*, 2 vols. (Berlin, 1915); J. Haller, *Bismarcks Friedensschlüsse* (Munich, 1916; 2nd impression, Stuttgart, 1917).

14. A select list of such works: K. Biedermann, *Dreissig Jahre deutsche Geschichte 1840–70*, 2 vols. (Breslau, 1881–2); D. Schäfer, *Das neue Deutschland und sein Kaiser* (Breslau, 1888); K. Binding, *Die Gründung des Norddeutschen Bundes* (Leipzig, 1889); *Die politischen Reden des Fürsten Bismarck*, ed. H. Kohl, 14 vols. (Stuttgart, 1892–1905); *Bismarckjahrbuch*, edited by the same, 6 vols. (1894–9); *Bismarcks Ansprachen 1848–97*, ed. H. von Poschinger, 2 vols. (Stuttgart, 1895–1900); H. von Poschinger, *Fürst Bismarck und der Bundesrat*, 5 vols. (Stuttgart, 1896–1901); W. Oncken, *Unser Heldenkaiser* (Berlin, 1897; 16th impression 1898); E. Marcks, *Kaiser Wilhelm I* (Leipzig, 1897; 8th impression 1918); H. Friedjung, *Der Kampf um die Vorherrschaft in Deutschland 1859–66* (Stuttgart, 1897; 10th impression 1916); G. Anschütz, *Bismarck und die Reichsverfassung* (Berlin, 1899); G. Schmoller, M. Lenz, and

E. Marcks, *Zu Bismarcks Gedächtnis* (Leipzig, 1899); E. Berner, *Der Regierungs-anfang des Prinzregenten von Preussen und seiner Gemahlin* (Berlin, 1902); O. Lorenz, *Kaiser Wilhelm und die Begründung des Reiches 1866–71* (Jena, 1902); G. von Eppstein and P. von Roell, *Bismarcks Staatsrecht* (Berlin, 1903); W. Busch, *Die Kämpfe um Reichsverfassung und Kaiserstaat 1870–71* (Tübingen, 1906); E. Brandenburg, *Briefe und Aktenstücke zur Geschichte der Gründung des Deutschen Reiches 1870–71*, 2 parts (1911); E. Brandenburg, 'Der Eintritt der süddeutschen Staaten in den Norddeutschen Bund' in *Festschrift für M. Lenz* (Berlin, 1910); E. Brandenburg, *Bismarck, 1863–66. Untersuchungen und Aktenstücke zur Geschichte der Reichsgründung* (Leipzig, 1916); G. Egelhaaf, *Bismarck* (Stuttgart, 1911); M. Lenz, *Kleine historische Schriften* (Munich, 1910); W. Stolze, *Die Gründung des Deutschen Reiches im Jahre 1870* (Munich, 1912); H. Welschinger, *Bismarck* (Paris, 1912); G. Ritter, *Die preussischen Konservativen und Bismarcks deutsche Politik 1856–76* (Heidelberg, 1913); F. Löwenthal, *Der preussische Verfassungsstreit 1862–66* (Munich and Leipzig, 1914); O. Baumgarten, *Bismarcks Glaube* (Tübingen, 1915); R. Seeberg, 'Der Christtag Bismarcks', *Bibliographische Zeit- und Streitfragen*, new series, no. 6 (Berlin, 1915); M. Lenz and E. Marcks, editors, *Das Bismarckjahrbuch* (Hamburg, 1915); E. Marcks, *Otto von Bismarck* (Stuttgart, 1915; 20th impression, 1919); D. Schäfer, *Bismarck*, 2 vols. (Berlin, 1915); M. Spahn, *Bismarck* (München-Gladbach; 3rd impression, 1915); E. Marcks and K. A. von Müller, editors, *Erinnerungen an Bismarck* (Stuttgart, 1915; 6th impression, 1924); A. Gasparian, *Der Begriff der Nation in der deutschen Geschichtsschreibung des 19. Jahrhunderts* (Leipzig, 1916); F. Meinecke, *Preussen und Deutschland im 19. und 20. Jahrhundert* (Munich, 1918).

15. W. Bussmann, 'Das Zeitalter Bismarcks' in *Handbuch der deutschen Geschichte*, ed. L. Just, ii, 2 (Constance, 1965), 247.

16. For continuity in outlook and historical style see the writings of K. A. von Müller: *Bayern im Jahre 1866 und die Berufung des Fürsten Hohenlohe* (Munich and Leipzig, 1909); 'Bismarck und Ludwig II im September 1870; *Historische Zeitschrift*, cxi (1913), 89; 'Die Tauffkirchensche Mission nach Berlin und Wien.' in *Festschrift für S. Riezler* (Gotha, 1913) *Deutsche Geschichte und deutscher Character* (Stuttgart, 1926).

17. *Die auswärtige Politik Preussens 1858–71* (Berlin, 1932–39)—diplomatic documents edited by the Historischen Reichskommission, vol. vii covering April to July 1866 is still not published; O. von Bismarck, *Gesammelte Werke* (1924–35): vols. i–vic; political writings; vols. vii–ix, conversation; vols. x–xiii, speeches; vol. xiv, letters; vol. xv, *Gedanken und Erinnerungen*.

18. H. Ritter von Srbik, *Quellen zur deutschen Politik Österreichs 1859–1866* (Oldenburg, 1934–8).

19. F. Meinecke, *Weltbürgertum und Nationalstaat. Studien zur Genesis des deutschen Nationalstaates* (Munich and Berlin; 5th impression 1919); K. Scheffler, *Bismarck, eine Studie* (Leipzig, 1919); A. Stern, *Geschichte Europas seit den Wiener Verträgen von 1815 bis zum Frankfurter Frieden von 1871* (Berlin,

1919) vols. vii–x; L. Bergsträsser, 'Kritische Studien zur Konfliktzeit' in *Historische Vierteljahreshefte*, xix (1920); E. Zechlin, *Bismarcks Stellung zum Parlamentarismus bis zur Gründung des Norddeutschen Bundes*, Dissertation (Heidelberg, 1922); E. Zechlin, *Bismarck und die Grundlegung der deutschen Grossmacht* (Stuttgart, 1930); R. Stadelmann, 'Das Jahr 1865 und das Problem von Bismarcks deutscher Politik' supplement no. 29 to *Historische Zeitschrift* (Munich, 1923); W. Windelband, *Bismarck und der Partikularismus 1870–71* (Darmstadt, 1923); H. Hertzfeld, *Deutschland und das geschlagene Frankreich 1871–1873* (Berlin, 1924); A. O. Meyer, *Bismarcks Orientpolitik* (Göttingen, 1925); A. O. Meyer, *Bismarcks Kampf mit Österreich am Bundestag zu Frankfurt 1851–1859* (Berlin and Leipzig, 1927); K. von Raumer, 'Das Jahr 1859 und die deutsche Einheitsbewegung in Bayern', in *Quellen un Darstellungen zur Geschichte der Burschenschaften*, vol. viii (1925); M. Doerberl, *Bayern und die Bismarcksche Reichsgründung* (vol. ii of *Bayern und Deutschland*) (Munich, 1925); G. Franz, *Bismarcks Nationalgefühl* (Leipzig, 1926); H. Oncken, *Die Rheinpolitik des Kaisers Napoleon III von 1863 bis 1870*, 3 vols. (Leipzig, 1926); H. Oncken, *Grossherzog Friedrich I von Baden und die deutsche Politik von 1854–1871*, 2 vols. (Stuttgart, 1927); L. Dehio, 'Die Pläne der Militärpartei und der Konflikt,' *Deutsche Rundschau* xiii (1927); F. Engel-Jánosi, *Graf Rechberg. 4 Kapitel zu seiner und Österreichs Geschichte* (Munich, 1927); G. Roloff, 'Brünn und Nikolsburg', *Historische Zeitschrift*, cxxxvi (1927); G. Roloff, 'Bismarcks Friedensschlüsse mit den Süddeutschen 1866,' ibid., cxlvi (1932); K. Hofmann, *Badens Anteil an der Reichsgründung* (Karlsruhe, 1927); W. Seefried, *Mittnacht und die deutsche Frage bis zur Reichsgründung* (Stuttgart, 1928); H. O. Meisner, 'England, Frankreich und die deutsche Einigung', *Preussische Jahrbücher*, ccxi (1928); F. Hartung, 'Die Entstehung und Gründung des Deutschen Reiches', *Volk und Reich der Deutschen*, i (Berlin, 1929); G. Bayerhaus, *Probleme der Reichsgründung im Jahre 1870* (Bonn, 1929); W. Michael, *Bismarck, England und Europa. Eine Studie zur Geschichte der deutschen Reichsgründung* (Munich, 1930); H. Goldschmidt, *Das Reich und Preussen im Kampf um die Führung. Von Bismarck bis 1918* (Berlin, 1931).

20. J. Ziekursch, *Politische Geschichte des neuen deutschen Kaiserreiches*, 3 vols. (Frankfurt, 1925).

21. F. Hartung, *Deutsche Geschichte 1871–1919* (Stuttgart, 1920; 6th impression, 1952).

22. O. Scheel, *Bismarcks Wille zu Deutschland in den Friedensschlüssen 1866* (Breslau, 1934); W. P. Fuchs, *Die deutschen Mittelstaaten und die Bundesreform 1853–60* (Berlin, 1934); E. Marcks, *Der Aufstieg des Reiches. Deutsche Geschichte von 1807 bis 1871–78*, 2 vols. (Stuttgart, 1936–43); A. Ritthaler, 'Reichsgründer und Reichsgründung im Licht neuer Quellen', *Historisches Jahrbuch*, lvi (1923), 351; W. Ebel, *Bismarck und Russland vom Prager Frieden bis zum Ausbruch des Krieges von 1870*, Dissertation (Frankfurt, 1936); A. Wahl, *Bismarck* (Cologne, 1937).

23. E. Brandenburg 'Deutsche Einheit', *Historische Vierteljahresschrift*, xxx (1936), 757.

24. F. Hartung, 'Preussen und die deutsche Einheit' in *Forschungen zur brandenburgischen und preussischen Geschichte*, xlix (1937), 1.

25. H. Ritter von Srbik, 'Zur gesamtdeutschen Geschichtsauffassung. Ein Versuch und sein Schicksal', *Historische Zeitschrift*, clvi (1937), 227.

26. H. Ritter von Srbik, *Deutsche Einheit, Idee und Wirklichkeit vom Heiligen Reich bis Königgrätz*, 4 vols. (Munich, 1935–42).

27. A. Richter, *Bismarck und die Arbeiterfrage im preussischen Verfassungskonflikt* (Stuttgart, 1935); H. Rothfels, *Bismarck und der deutsche Osten* (Leipzig, 1934); H. Rothfels, *Ostraum, Preussentum und Reichsgedanke* (Leipzig, 1935); H. Rothfels, 'Zur Geschichte der Bismarckschen Innenpolitik', *Archiv für Politik und Geschichte*, lxvii (1926), 284; Otto Vossler, 'Bismarcks Sozialpolitik', *Historische Zeitschrift*, clxvii (1943), 336.

28. E. Franz, *Der Entscheidungskampf um die wirtschaftspolitische Führung Deutschlands 1856–1867* (Munich, 1933); E. Franz, *Ludwig Freiherr v.d. Pfordten* (Munich, 1938) (cp. W. Mommsen in *Historische Zeitschrift*, clx (1939), 582); E. Franz, 'Ludwig Frieherr v.d. Pfordten—ein "Grossdeutscher"', *Historische Zeitschrift*, clxi (1940), 326; L. Dehio, 'Beiträge zur Bismarckschen Politik im Sommer 1866, unter Benutzung der Papiere Keudells', *Forschungen zur brandenburgischen und preussischen Geschichte*, xlvi, (1934); A. O. Meyer, *Bismarcks Glaube* (4th impression, Munich, 1936); A. O. Meyer, *Bismarck der Mensch und der Staatsmann* (Leipzig, 1944); Th. Schieder, 'Die Bismarcksche Reichsgründung vor 1870–71 als gesamtdeutsches Ereignis', *Festschrift für K.A. v. Müller* (Stuttgart, 1943); E. Marcks, *Der Aufstieg des Reiches* (Stuttgart and Berlin, 1936); H. Mombauer, *Bismarcks Realpolitik als Ausdruck seiner Weltanschauung* (Berlin, 1936); A. Scharff, *Im Kampf um Deutschlands Einheit und Mitteleuropa. Preussisch-deutsche Politik 1850–51*, Dissertation (Kiel, 1937); W. Schüssler, *Deutsche Einheit und gesamtdeutsche Geschichtsbetrachtung* (Stuttgart, 1937); O. Vossler, *Der Nationalgedanke von Rousseau bis Ranke* (Munich, 1937); F. Greve, *Die Politik der deutschen Mittelstaaten und die österreichischen Bundesreformbestrebungen 1861–63*, Dissertation (Rostock, 1938); M. van Hagen, 'Das Bismarckbild der Gegenwart', *Zeitschrift für Politik*, xxviii, 196–202, 241–52, 404–12; K. Kaminski, *Verfassung und Verfassungskonflikt in Preussen 1862–66* (Königsberg and Berlin, 1938); H. M. Elster, *Bismarcks Grösse und Tragik, Macht und Mass* (Hamburg, 1939); W. Menzel, *Das Volkstum in der deutschen Geschichtsschreibung seit den Befreiungskriegen* (Halle, 1939); G. A. von Metnitz, *Die deutsche Nationalbewegung 1871–1933* (Berlin, 1939); K. Borries, 'Deutschland und das Problem des Zweifrontendrucks in der europäischen Krise des italienischen Freiheitskampfes', *Festschrift Haller* (Stuttgart, 1940); W. Frauendienst, 'Bismarck und Napoleon III', *Berliner Monatshefte*, xviii (1940); E. Görlich, 'Grossmitteleuropa und Kleinmitteleuropa', *Welt als Geschichte* (1941); W. Frauendienst, *Bismarck als Ordner Europas* (Halle, 1941); W. Frauendienst, 'Bismarck und die deutsche Reichsgründung', *Berliner Monatshefte*, xix (1941); B. Schwerdtfeger, *Im Kampf um den Lebensraum, 1870–1940* (Potsdam, 1940); F. Stieve, *Das aussenpolitische Lage Deutschlands von Bismarck bis Hilter* (Langensalza, 1940); O. Becker, 'Bis-

marcks kleindeutsche und gesamtdeutsche Politik', *Kieler Blätter* (1942), pp. 45 ff.; E. Ebersbach, *Studien zur deutschen Politik Österreichs Preussens und der deutschen Mittelstaaten von Villafranca bis Oktober, 1861*, Dissertation (Leipzig, 1942); E. Michels, *Hannover und die deutsche Politik Österreichs 1859–66*, Dissertation (Bonn, 1942); S. von Kardorff, *Bismarck im Kampf um sein Werk* (Berlin, 1943).

29. E. Eyck, *Bismarck. Leben und Werk*, 3 vols. (Zurich, 1941–4); F. Meinecke, *Die Deutsche Katastrophe* (Wiesbaden, 1946); F. Schnabel, 'Das Problem Bismarck', *Hochland*, xlii (1949–50); F. Schnabel, 'Bismarck und die Nationen', *Europa und der Nationalismus* (Baden-Baden, 1950), p. 91; F. Darmstaedter, *Bismarck and the Creation of the Second Reich* (London, 1948); C. de Grunwald, *Bismarck* (Paris, 1949); B. Kautsky, 'Bismarck und die deutsche Gegenwart', *Monat*, xix, 49; R. Riemeck, 'Bismarck und sein Werk', *Laterne*, ii (1949); A. Dorpalen, 'The German Historians and Bismarck', *Review of Politics*, xv, 53; J. Streisand, 'Bismarck und die deutsche Einigungsbewegung in der westdeutschen Geschichtsschreibung', *Zeitschrift für Geschichte*, ii, 349; H. Heffter, *Die deutsche Selbstverwaltung* (Stuttgart, 1950); P. Renouvin, *L'empire allemand au temps de Bismarck* (Paris, 1950); G. Mann, 'Fragment über 1870', *Monat*, lxxxviii, 85; G. Mann, 'Bismarck,' *Beilage Parlament*, B 44 (1961); H. Wagner, 'Bismarck heute', *Radius* (December 1959).

30. G. Ritter, *Europa und die deutsche Frage* (Munich, 1948); G. Ritter, 'Bismarck und die Rheinpolitik Napoleons III', *Rheinische Vierteljahres-blätter*, xv–xvi, 339; G. Ritter, 'Grossdeutsch oder kleindeutsch', *Festschrift für S. A. Kaehler* (Düsseldorf, 1950); G. Ritter, 'Das Bismarckproblem', *Merkur*, iv (1950), 657; M. Lehmann, *Bismarck* (Berlin, 1948); A. O. Meyer, *Bismarck der Mensch und der Staatsmann* (1944; new edition, Stuttgart, 1949)—reviewed by O. Pflanze, *American Historical Review*, lvi (1951), 565, and by W. Conze, *Aussenpolitik*, i, 70; A. O. Meyer, 'Bismarcks Werden und sein Weg zur Macht', *Milit. wiss. Rundschau*, v. 1; H. Herzfeld, Review of E. Eyck, *Bismarck*, in *Deutsche Literaturzeitung*, lxix (1948); S. A. Kaehler, 'Zur Deutung von Bismarcks "Bekehrung" ', *Glauben und Geschichte. Festschrift für F. Gogarten* (1948); S. A. Kaehler, *Vorurteile und Tatsachen* (Hameln, 1949); H. Rothfels, 'Probleme einer Bismarck-Biographie', *Deutsche Beiträge* (1948), pp. 162–83 (cp. the same in *Review of Politics*, ix (1947)); H. Rothfels, 'Bismarck und das 19. Jahrhundert', *Festschrift für S. A. Kaehler* (Düsseldorf, 1950); H. Rothfels, 'Zur Krise des Nationalstaates', *Viertel-jahreshefte für Zeitgeschichte*, i (1953), 138; H. Rothfels, 'Bismarcks Staatsan-schauungen', *Geschichte in Wissenschaft und Unterricht*, iv (1953), 676; H. Rothfels, *Bismarck und der Staat* (Darmstadt, 1953); H. Rothfels, 'Zum 150 Geburtstag Bismarcks', *Vierteljahreshefte für Zeitgeschichte* (1965), 225; O. Becker, 'Der Sinn der dualistischen Verständigungsversuche Bismarcks vor dem Kriege 1866', *Historische Zeitschrift* clxix (1949), 264; O. Becker, 'Wie Bismarck Kanzler wurde', *Festschrift für O. Scheel* (Cologne, 1952); W. Gembruch, *Bismarck und der nationale Gedanke*, Dissertation (Frankfurt, 1950); W. Richter, 'Das Bild Bismarcks', *Neue Rundschau*, lxiii (1950), 43; W. Schüssler, 'Noch einmal: Bismarck und die Nationen',

Nouveue Clio, 1–2 (1950); H. Hölzle, 'Die Reichsgründung und der Aufstieg der Weltmächte', *Geschichte im Wissenschaft und Unterricht*, ii (1951), 132; Th Schieder, 'Bismarck und Europa', *Festschrift für H. Rothfels* (Düsseldorf, 1951); Th. Schieder, *Das Deutsche Kaiserreich von 1871 als Nationalstaat* (Cologne, 1961); O. Vossler, 'Bismarcks Ethos', *Historische Zeitschrift* clxxi (1951), 263; E. Marcks, *Bismarck. Eine Biographie 1815–48* (Stuttgart and Berlin, 1909; reprinted 1951); E. Kessel, 'Gastein', *Historische Zeitschrift* clxxvi (1953), 521; R. Koop, *Das Problem des Präventivkrieges in der Politik Bismarcks*, Dissertation (Freiburg, 1953); L. von Muralt, *Bismarcks Politik der europäischen Mitte* (Wiesbaden, 1954); L. von Muralt, *Bismarcks Verantwortlichkeit* (Göttingen, 1955); L. von Muralt, 'Die Voraussetzungen des geschichtlichen Verständnisses Bismarcks', *Archivalia et historica* (1958), pp. 337–53; G. A. Rein, 'Bismarcks Royalismus', *Geschichte in Wissenschaft und Unterricht*, v (1954), 331; H. Valloton, *Bismarck et Hitler* (Paris, 1954); H. Valloton, *Bismarck* (Paris, 1962); G. Franz, *Liberalismus, die deutsche liberale Bewegung in der habsburgischen Monarchie* (Munich, 1955); A. Meyer, *Der Zollverein und die deutsche Politik Bismarcks*, Dissertation (Freiburg, 1958); H. Geuss, *Bismarck und Napoleon III 1851–71* (Cologne, 1959); G. Hinrichs and W. Berges, *Die deutsche Einheit als Problem der europäischen Geschichte* (Stuttgart, 1960); E. R. Huber, *Deutsche Verfassungsgeschichte seit 1789*, vol. iii (Stuttgart, 1957).

31. As in vol. iii, part 2 of the *Handbuch der deutschen Geschichte* ed. L. Just (Constance, 1956) where W. Bussmann writes under the title, 'The Age of Bismarck'; or in part 3 of vol. i of *Westermanns Studienhefte* (Brunswick, 1950) where H. Herzfeld writes 'Liberalism and Nationalism in the Age of Bismarck'; P. Kluke in Rassow, *Deutsche Geschichte im Überblick*, adopts an older form in arranging his ideas under the titles 'The Battle between the two German Great Powers over the shape of Germany, 1851–66' and 'The Foundation of the Empire, 1867–71'; Th. Schieder in *Gebhardts Handbuch*, vol. iii, 8th edn. (Stuttgart, 1960), focuses his view firmly on the year 1871, calling his section 'From the Germanic Confederation to the German Empire'. In this *Handbuch* economic problems are consigned to a kind of appendix: W. Treue, *Wirtschafts- und Sozialgeschichte Deutschlands im 19 Jahrhundert*. Economic historians are forced to fit into traditional *schemata* as in E. Engelberg, *Lehrbuch der deutschen Geschichte* vol. vii. *Deutschland 1849–71* (Berlin, 1959) and R. Kiau and H. Gemkow, *Kämpfe um die deutsche Einheit. Von den Befreiungskriegen bis zur Reichsgründung* (Leipzig, 1955). The volume, however, in *Propyläen-Weltgeschichte* edited in the old series by W. Goetz and in the new by G. Mann, attempts to separate the different sections of historical knowledge from one another. But even here the old divisions (politics, society, economics, ideas) still persist.

32. W. Lotz, *Die Ideen der deutschen Handelspolitik von 1860 bis 1891* (Leipzig, 1892); J. H. Clapham, *The Economic Development of France and Germany 1815–1914* (Cambridge, 1921); W. Sombart, *Die deutsche Volkswirtschaft im 19. Jahrhundert und im Anfang des 20. Jahrhunderts* (7th impression, Berlin, 1927); W. Bussmann, 'Gustav Freytag. Massstäbe seiner Zeitkritik', *Archiv für Kulturgeschichte*, xxxiv (1952), 262; W. Bussmann, 'Zur Geschichte

des deutschen Liberalismus im 19. Jahrhundert', *Historische Zeitschrift* clxxxvi (1958); F. C. Sell, *Die Tragödie des deutschen Liberalismus* (Stuttgart, 1953); W. P. Fuchs, *Franz v. Roggenbach, Karlsruhe Academische Reden*, new series (Karlsruhe, 1954); L. Bergsträsser, *Geschichte der politischen Parteien in Deutschland* (11th edn., Munich, 1962); Th. Schieder, 'Die Theorie der Partei im älteren deutschen Literalismus', *Festschrift für A. Bergsträsser* (Düsseldorf, 1954); Th. Schieder, 'Das Verhältnis von politischer und gesellschaftlicher Verfassung und die Krise des bürgerlichen Liberalismus', *Historische Zeitschrift*, clxxvii (1954), 49; Th. Schieder, 'Der Literalismus und die Strukturverwandlungen der modernen Gesellschaft', *Relazioni* of the International Congress of Historical Sciences, v (Rome, 1955); F. Hartung, *Deutsche Verfassungsgeschichte* (6th edn., Stuttgart, 1954); H. Bechtel, *Wirtschaftsgeschichte Deutschlands im 19. und 20. Jahrhundert* (Munich, 1956); H. Seier, 'Sybels Vorlesung über Politik und die Kontinuität des staatsbildenden Liberalismus', *Historische Zeitschrift*, clxxxvii (1959), 90; F. Lütge, *Deutsche Sozial- und Wirtschaftsgeschichte* (2nd edn., Heidelberg, 1960); H. A. Winkler, *Preussischer Liberalisms und deutscher Nationalstaat* (Tübingen, 1964); P. Joachimsen, *Vom deutschen Volk zum deutschen Staat* (1920, 2nd edn. revised by J. Leuschner, Göttingen, 1965).

33. O. Brunner, *Neue Wege der Sozialgeschichte* (Göttingen, 1956); K. E. Born, 'Sozialpolitische Probleme und Bestrebungen in Deutschland von 1848 bis zur Bismarckschen Sozialgesetzgebung', *Vierteljahresschrift für Sozial- und Wirtschaftsgeschichte* xlvi (1959), 29; W. Conze, *Die Strukturgeschichte des technischindustriellen Zeitalters als Aufgabe für Forschung und Unterricht* (Cologne, 1957); W. Conze, *Staat und Gesellschaft im deutschen Vormärz* (Stuttgart, 1962); O. Hintze, 'Wirtschaft und Politik im Zeitalter des modernen Kapitalismus', *Zeitschrift für Staatswissenschaft*, lxxxvii (1929); W. Treue, 'Industrialisierung als ein Faktor des wirtschaftlichen Wachstums', *Communications* to the International Congress of Historical Sciences (Stockholm, 1960); W. Zorn, 'Wirtschafts- und sozialgeschichtliche Zusammenhänge der deutschen Reichsgründungszeit', *Historische Zeitschrift*, cxcvii, (1963) 318; F. Zunkel, *Der rheinischwestfalische Unternehmer, 1834–79* (Cologne, 1962).

34. L. Halphen and P. Sagnac, ed., *Peuples et Civilisations*, xvi–xviii (Paris, 1937); P. Renouvin, *Histoire des rélations internationales* (Paris, 1953); volumes by J. Droz and P. Renouvin in the Clio series (Paris, 1954); E. M. Carroll, *Germany and the Great Powers, 1866–1914* (New York, 1938); *The New Cambridge Modern History* vol. x (Cambridge, 1960); F. Valsecchi, 'Considerazioni sulla politica europea di Napoleone III', *Rivista storica italiana*, lxii (1950). The following are important: O. Pflanze, 'Bismarck and German Nationalism', *American Historical Review* (1960), p. 548; O. Pflanze, *Bismarck and the Development of Germany*, vol. i (Princeton, N. J., 1963); E. N. Anderson, *The Social and Political Conflict in Prussia, 1858–64* (Lincoln, Neb., 1954); A. J. P. Taylor, *The Struggle for Mastery in Europe, 1848–1918* (London, 1954); A. J. P. Taylor, *Bismarck. The Man and the Statesman* (London, 1955); W. E. Mosse, *The European Powers and the German Question* (Cambridge, 1958); W. Näf, *Die Epochen der neueren Geschichte*, vol.

ii (Aarau, 1947); Z. R. Dittrich, *De opkomst van het moderne Duitsland* (Groningen, 1955–6).

35. E. Zechlin, 'Zur Kritik und Wertung des Bismarckreiches', *Neue Jahrbücher für Wissenschaft und Jugendbildung*, x (1934), 538; E. Zechlin, 'Bismarck und der ständische Gedanke' *Nationalsozialistische Monatshefte*, v, 560; O. Hintze, *Gesammelte Abhandlungen* (3 vols., 1941–3); W. Mommsen, 'Der Kampf um das Bismarck-Bild', *Universitas*, v (1950); W. Mommsen, *Stein, Ranke, Bismarck* (Munich, 1954); W. Mommsen, 'Der Kampf um das Bismarck-Bild', *Neue politische Literatur*, iv (1959); M. von Hagen, 'Das Bismarckbild der Gegenwart', *Zeitschrift für Politik*, xxviii; H. Rothfels, 'Bismarcks Staatsanschauungen', *Geschichte in Wissenschaft und Unterricht*, iv (1953), 676; H. Rothfels, *Zeitgeschichtliche Betrachtungen* (Göttingen, 1959); K. Mielcke, *Bismarck in der neueren Forschung* (Brunswick, 1954); W. Bussmann, 'Wandel und Kontinuität der Bismarck-Wertung', *Welt als Geschichte*, xv (1955), 126–36; W. Bussmann, 'Zur Geschichte des deutschen Liberalismus im 19. Jahrhundert', *Historische Zeitschrift*, clxxxvi (1958), 527; H. Gollwitzer, 'Die Reichsgründung', *Kontinuität und Tradition* (Bonn, 1956), p. 37; L. von Muralt, 'Bismarck-Forschung und Bismarck-Problem', *Schweizerische Monatshefte*, xxxiv, 148, 243; R. Morsey, 'Geschichtsschreibung und amtliche Zensur', *Historische Zeitschrift*, clxxxiv (1956); W. Schmidt, *Bismarck in der englischen Geschichtsschreibung von den Zeitgenossen bis zur Gegenwart*, Dissertation (Berlin Free University, 1956); B. Knauss, 'Neue Beiträge zum Bismarckbild', *Politische Studien*, x (1959); S. A. Kaehler, *Studien zur deutschen Geschichte des 19. und 20. Jahrhunderts* (Göttingen, 1961); F. Schnabel, 'Das neunzehnte Jahrhundert. Ein Literaturbericht', *Geschichte in Wissenschaft und Unterricht*, vi–vii, x (1955–56, 1959).

CHAPTER 2

1. Prokesch Osten (Berlin) to the Austrian Foreign Office, 12 September 1851, Haus- Hof- und Staatsarchiv (Vienna), PA II, no. 76.

2. Károlyi (Berlin) to Rechberg, 13 July 1860, ibid., PA III, no. 70.

3. Württembergische Staatsarchiv (Ludwigsburg), E 222, Fach 182, no. 885.

4. G. Mann, *Deutsche Geschichte des 19. und 20. Jahrhundert* (Frankfurt, 1959), p. 303; English edition, *The History of Germany since 1789* (London, 1968), p. 152.

5. Memorandum by Bismarck, July–October 1861, Otto von Bismarck, *Gesammelte Werke*, vol. iii, no. 234, pp. 268 ff.

CHAPTER 3

1. H. von Srbik (editor), *Quellen zur deutschen Politik Österreichs 1859–1866* (Berlin, Oldenburg, 1934–8), vol. iv, no. 1818.

2. *Vierteljahreshefte*, iii (1863), 186.

3. *Nationalzeitung*, 28 May 1865.

4. O. von Bismarck, *Gesammelte Werke*, vol. vi, no. 460.

5. Ibid., no. 498.

6. Ibid., no. 675.

7. *Die auswärtige Politik Preussens*, vol. viii, no. 217.

8. O. von Bismarck, *Gesammelte Werke*, vol. via, no. 854.

9. Ibid., no. 841.

10. Vienna, Haus- Hof- und Staatsarchiv, PA VI, no. 30.

11. Bonn, Auswärtiges Amt, IA Ar, no. 41, vol. xi, 4 February 1868.

CHAPTER 4

1. R. Fester, *Briefe, Aktenstücke und Regesten zur Geschichte der Hohenzollerschen Thronkandidatur in Spanien* (Leipzig, 1913), i (269), 125.

2. Golo Mann, *Deutsche Geschichte des 19. und 20. Jahrhundert* (Frankfurt, 1959) p. 374; English edition, *The History of Germany since 1789* (London, 1968) p. 191.

SUGGESTIONS FOR FURTHER READING

COLLECTIONS OF DOCUMENTS for reference

AEGIDI, K. L., etc. (editors), *Das Staatsarchiv. Sammlung der offiziellen Akten-stücke der Gegenwart* (20 vols., 1860–80).

BISMARCK, OTTO VON, *Gesammelte Werke* (Friedrichsruhe Ausgabe, 15 vols., Berlin, 1924–35).

—— *Gedanken und Erinnerungen*, is vol. xv of above.

BONNIN, G., *Bismarck and the Hohenzollern Candidature for the Throne of Spain* (London, 1957). The documents are translated into English.

BRANDENBURG, E., etc. (editors), *Die Auswärtige Politik Preussens 1858–71* (Berlin, 1932–4). Vol. vii, April–July 1866; the volumes for 1869–71 are still not published.

British and Foreign State Papers (London, 1812 onwards). Volumes for the relevant years.

Documenti diplomatici italiani, 1 serie, 1861–70 (1 vol., Rome, 1952).

HUBER, E. R., *Dokumente zur deutschen Verfassungs Geschichte 1803–1933* (Stuttgart, 1961–6). Vols. 1 and 2 are relevant. Contains the treaties of the south-German states with Prussia of 1870 and has election statistics.

Les Origines diplomatiques de la Guerre de 1870–1871, published by *Ministère des affaires étrangères* (29 vols. Paris, 1910–32).

LORD. R. H., *The Origins of the War of 1870* (Cambridge, Mass., 1924). The documents are in German, commentary in English.

ONCKEN, H., *Die Rheinpolitik Kaiser Napoleons III von 1863 bis 1870* (Stuttgart, 1926).

SRBIK, H, VON (editor), *Quellen zur deutschen Politik Österreichs, 1859–66* (5 vols., Berlin, Oldenburg, 1934–8).

GENERAL HISTORIES in english

CARR, W., *A History of Germany, 1815–1945* (London, 1969). The biblio-graphy names a few other general histories not listed here.

CLAPHAM, J. H., *The Economic Development of France and Germany, 1815–1914* (Cambridge, 1921). But compare the relevant chapters of *The Cambridge Economic History of Europe*, vol. vi, edited by H. J. Habakkuk and M. Postan (Cambridge, 1965) which partly supersedes it.

HOLBORN, H., *A History of Modern Germany 1840–1945* (London, 1970).

MANN, G., *The History of Germany since 1789* (London, 1968). Translated from the German.

PFLANZE, O., *Bismarck and the Development of Germany, 1815–71* (Princeton, N.J., 1963).

PINSON, K. S., *Modern Germany: Its History and Civilization* (New York, 1955).
RAMM, A., *Germany, 1789–1919* (London, 1967).

MEMOIRS FOR REFERENCE AND BIOGRAPHIES INCLUDING BIO-GRAPHIES OF BISMARCK

ANDREAS, W., *Franz Freiherr von Roggenbach* (Heidelberg, 1933).
BERNSTORFF, A. VON, *Im Kampfe für Preussens Ehre* (Berlin, 1906).
BEUST, F. F. VON, *Aus drei Vierteljahrhunderten* (Stuttgart, 1887).
BRAY-STEINBURG, O. VON, *Denkwürdigkeiten aus meinem Leben* (Leipzig, 1901).
BUSSMANN, W., *Treitschke, Sein Welt- und Geschichtsbild* (Göttingen, 1952).
CHARMATZ, R., *Minister Freiherr von Bruck, der Vorkämpfer Mittel-Europas* (Leipzig, 1916).
DELBRÜCK, R., *Lebenserinnerungen* (Leipzig, 1905).
EYCK, E., *Bismarck. Leben und Werk* (Berlin, 1941–4).
——— *Bismarck and the German Empire* (London, 1950). A much abridged English version of the above. E. Eyck was a Liberal and critical of Bismarck.
FRANZ, E., *Freiherr Ludwig von der Pfordten* (Munich, 1938).
HASSEL, P., *Joseph Maria von Radowitz* (Berlin, 1905–13).
HOLBORN, H. (editor), *Aufzeichnungen und Erinnerungen aus dem Leben* ... *J. M. von Radowitz* (Stuttgart, 1925).
MEDLICOTT, W. N., *Bismarck and Modern Germany* (London, 1965). A brief analysis.
MEINECKE, F., *Radowitz und die deutsche Revolution* (Berlin, 1913). A continuation and completion of Hassel's work named above.
MEYER, A. O., *Bismarck. Der Mensch und der Staatsmann* (Stuttgart, 1949).
MOMMSEN, W., *Bismarck, ein politisches Lebensbild* (Munich, 1959). A scholarly and balanced biography.
ONCKEN, H., *Rudolph von Bennigsen: ein deutscher liberaler Politiker* (Stuttgart, 1910).
——— *Lassalle, eine politische Biographie* (Stuttgart, 1923).
——— (editor), *Grossherzog Friedrich von Baden und die deutsche Politik von 1854–1871* (Berlin, 1927).
RICHTER, W., *Bismarck* (London, 1964). A translation from the German which makes absorbing reading.
SCHÜSSLER, W. (editor), *Die Tagebücher des Freiherrn von Dalwigk-Lichtenfels aus den Jahren 1860–71* (Stuttgart, etc., 1920).
SCHWARZENBERG, A., *Prince Felix zu Schwarzenberg. Prime Minister of Austria, 1848–1852* (New York, 1946).
TAYLOR, A. J. P., *Bismarck. The Man and the Statesman* (London, 1955).

BOOKS AND ARTICLES ON SEPARATE TOPICS MOSTLY IN ENGLISH, BUT INCLUDING A FEW GERMAN WORKS OF BASIC RESEARCH FOR REFERENCE

ANDERSON, E. N., *The Social and Political Conflict in Prussia, 1858–64* (Lincoln, Neb., 1954)

BECKER, O., *Bismarcks Ringen um Deutschlands Gestaltung* (Heidelberg 1958)· A discussion of the constitution.

BENAERTS, P., *Les Origines de la grande industrie allemande* (Paris, 1933).

BERGSTRÄSSER, L., *Geschichte der politischen Parteien in Deutschland* (7th edition, Munich, 1952). A revised edition (1955) continues until 1954 but compresses earlier sections. Compare *Die bürgerlichen Parteien in Deutschland, 1830–1945*. An encyclopaedia of political associations published in the East German Republic, Vol. i A–F (Leipzig, 1968). Wonderfully comprehensive in facts and bibliography.

BÖHME, H., *Deutschlands Weg zur Grossmacht* (Cologne and Berlin, 1966). This is the subject of an important review article: O. Pflanze, 'Another Crisis among German Historians?', *Journal of Modern History* (1968).

BONDI, G., 'Zur Vorgeschichte der "Kleindeutschen Lösung", 1866–71', *Jahrbuch für Wirtschaftsgeschichte* (1966).

BORRIES, K., *Preussen im Krimkrieg* (Stuttgart, 1950).

CARR, W., *Schleswig-Holstein, 1815–48* (Manchester, 1963).

CLARK, C. W., *Franz Joseph and Bismarck* (Cambridge, Mass., 1934).

CRAIG, G., *The Politics of the Prussian Army* (Oxford, 1955).

—— 'Portrait of a Political General, E. von Manteuffel and the Constitutional Conflict in Prussia', *Political Science Quarterly* (1951).

DORPALEN, A., 'The Unification of Germany in East German Perspective', *American Historical Review* (no. 4, 1968). A bibliographical article.

ENGELS, F., *The German Revolutions: The Present War in Germany and Germany: Revolution and Counter Revolution*, edited by L. Krieger (Chicago and London, 1967).

—— *The Role of Force in History. A Study of Bismarck's Policy of Blood and Iron*, translated by J. Cohen and edited with an introduction by E. Wangermann (London, 1968).

EYCK, F., *The Frankfurt Parliament* (London, 1968).

FISCHER, F., 'Der deutsche Protestantismus und die Politik im neunzehnten Jahrhundert', *Historische Zeitschrift* (1951).

FISCHER, W., 'Ansätze zur Industrialisierung in Baden, 1770–1870', *Vierteljahrschrift für Sozial- und Wirtschaftsgeschichte* (1960).

FLETCHER, W. A., *The Mission of Vincent Benedetti to Berlin* (The Hague, 1965).

FRIEDJUNG, H., *The Struggle for Supremacy in Germany* (London, 1935) is a translation of a much abridged version of the author's *Der Kampf um die Vorherrschaft in Deutschland* (Stuttgart, 1897).

FRIESE, C., *Russland und Preussen vom Krimkriege bis zum Polnischen Aufstand* (Berlin, 1931).

HALBERG, C. W., *Franz Joseph and Napoleon III, 1852–1864* (New York, 1955).

HAMEROW, T. S., *Restoration, Revolution and Reaction: Economics and Politics in Germany, 1815–71* (Princeton, N.J., 1958).

—— 'The Elections to the Frankfurt Parliament', *Journal of Modern History* (1961)

—— 'The German Artisan Movement', *Journal of Central European Affairs* (1961).

HANTSCH, H., *Die Geschichte Österreichs* (Vienna, 1951).

HENDERSON, W. O., *The Zollverein* (2nd edition, London, 1959).

HESS, A., *Das Parlament, das Bismarck widerstrebte, 1862–66* (Cologne, 1964).

KANN, A., *The Multinational Empire. Nationalism and National Reform in the Habsburg Monarchy, 1848–1918* (New York, 1950).

KOHN-BRAMSTEDT, H., *Aristocracy and the Middle Classes in Germany. Social Types in German Literature* (London, revised edition 1964).

KRIEGER, L., see ENGELS, F.

LAMBI, N. I., *Free Trade and Protection in Germany, 1868–79* (Wiesbaden, 1963). A Beiheft to the *Vierteljahrschrift für Sozial- und Wirtschaftsgeschichte*.

MORGAN, R. P., *The German Social Democrats and the First International* (Cambridge, 1965).

MOSSE, W. E., *The Rise and Fall of the Crimean System, 1855–71* (London, 1963).

—— *The European Powers and the German Question, 1848–71* (Cambridge, 1958)

NAMIER, L. B., *1848: The Revolution of the Intellectuals* (Oxford, 1944).

NOYES, P. H., *Organisation and Revolution: Working Class Associations in the German Revolutions of 1848–49* (Princeton, N.J., 1966).

O'BOYLE, L., 'The Democratic Left in Germany, 1848', *Journal of Modern History* (1961).

PRICE, A. H., *The Evolution of the Zollverein* (Ann Arbor, Mich., 1949)

REAL, W., *Der deutsche Reformverein. Grossdeutsche Stimmen und Kräfte* (Lübeck, 1966).

REIN, G. A., *Die Revolution in der Politik Bismarcks* (Göttingen, 1957).

SHANAHAN, W., *German Protestants face the Social Question* (Notre Dame, Ind., 1954).

STADELMANN, R., *Das Jahr 1865 und das Problem von Bismarcks deutscher Politik* (Munich, 1933). A Beiheft to the *Historische Zeitschrift*.

—— *Sozial und politische Geschichte der Revolution von 1848* (Munich, 1948).

STEEFEL, L. D., *The Schleswig-Holstein Question* (Cambridge, Mass., 1932).

—— *Bismarck, the Hohenzollern Candidacy and the Origins of the Franco-German War of 1870* (Cambridge, Mass., 1962).

VALENTIN, V., *1848. Chapters of Germany History* (London, 1940) is a translation of a much abridged version of the author's *Geschichte der deutschen Revolution von 1848–49* (Berlin, 1930–1).

WINDELL, G. G., *The Catholics and German Unity, 1866–1871* (Minneapolis, 1954).

WINKLER, K. A., *Preussischer Liberalismus und deutsche Nationalstaat* (Tübingen, 1964).

ZORN, W., 'Wirtschafts- und Sozialgeschichtliche Zusammenhänge der deutschen Reichsgründungszeit 1850–79', *Historische Zeitschrift* (1963).

INDEX OF PERSONS

DATE DUE